Ensuring Corporate Misconduct

Ensuring Corporate Misconduct

How Liability Insurance
Undermines Shareholder Litigation

TOM BAKER AND SEAN J. GRIFFITH

THE UNIVERSITY OF CHICAGO PRESS   CHICAGO AND LONDON

TOM BAKER is professor of law at the University of Pennsylvania and the author of *The Medical Malpractice Myth*, also published by the University of Chicago Press, among several other books.

SEAN J. GRIFFITH is the T. J. Maloney Professor of Business Law at Fordham University.

The University of Chicago Press, Chicago 60637
The University of Chicago Press, Ltd., London

ISBN-13: 978-0-226-03515-4 (cloth)
ISBN-10: 0-226-03515-8 (cloth)

Library of Congress Cataloging-in-Publication Data
Baker, Tom, 1959–
    Ensuring corporate misconduct : how liability insurance undermines shareholder litigation / Tom Baker and Sean J. Griffith.
        p. cm.
    Includes bibliographical references and index.
    ISBN-13: 978-0-226-03515-4 (cloth : alk. paper)
    ISBN-10: 0-226-03515-8 (cloth : alk. paper) 1. Executives' liability insurance—United States. 2. Executives' liability insurance—Law and legislation—United States. 3. Stockholders' derivative actions—United States. 4. Liability insurance—United States. I. Griffith, Sean J. II. Title.
    HG8053.8.B35 2010
    368.5'6—dc22

                                                              2010026804

Contents

Acknowledgments

This book has been a long time in the making, and there are, accordingly, more people to thank than we could hope to name in a short list. Still, we would be remiss in failing to acknowledge the critical assistance of a handful of individuals and institutions.

First, this project obviously would never have come to be without the generous cooperation of our participants, whose observations and insights contributed greatly to our understanding of the subject and in fact make up the bulk of this research. We are also indebted to the Insurance Law Center at the University of Connecticut School of Law, which provided us an institutional framework for pursuing the project when it was first conceived and with financial support in conducting the research. Subsequently, we received important institutional and financial support from Fordham Law School and the University of Pennsylvania School of Law. Specifically, Baker would like to thank the Measey Foundation for funding his chair at Penn, and Griffith would like to thank the Maloney family for funding his chair at Fordham. Thanks also to the Fordham Corporate Law Center for organizing a roundtable discussion devoted to the project and to the many universities that have invited us to speak on the subject in recent years. The comments we received in those presentations and workshops were invaluable in refining our thinking on the subject.

We received much research and editorial help, but we are particularly indebted to Yan Hong for superb research assistance and to Paul Fattaruso for help with the manuscript. We also owe much to the editors at the University of Chicago Press, especially John Tryneski, who immediately recognized the importance of what might have seemed to be an esoteric topic in the interstices of corporate and insurance law. We are similarly indebted to Ed Rock, who pushed each of us to see the bigger picture and think in terms of a larger book-length project when we were still toiling away on discrete law review articles.

Some of the analysis in this book has appeared in prior law review articles, including Griffith, Uncovering a Gatekeeper: Why the SEC Should Mandate Disclosure of Details Concerning Directors' and Officers' Liability Insurance Policies, 154 *University of Pennsylvania Law Review* 1147 (2006); Baker and Griffith, The Missing Monitor in Corporate Governance: The Directors' and Officers' Liability Insurer, 95 *Georgetown Law Journal* 1795 (2007); Baker and Griffith, Predicting Corporate Governance Risk: Evidence from the Directors' and Officers' Liability Insurance Market, 74 *University of Chicago Law Review* 487 (2007); Baker and Griffith, *How the Merits Matter: D&O Insurance and Securities Settlements*, 157 *University of Pennsylvania Law Review* 755 (2009). Thank you to Charles Fincher for allowing us to reprint his insightful D&O insurance cartoon in chapter 5.

Finally, we owe our greatest debt to our wives, Sharon Baker and Negin Griffith, who encouraged our work, tolerated our travel, and supported us in countless ways throughout the research and writing process.

CHAPTER ONE

Introduction

Financial crises present opportunities for introspection. Beyond the initial concern over what happened and why, they present an opportunity to reflect on the regulatory framework as a whole and to consider the effectiveness of each element of the law affecting business, to ask what aspects of the regulatory structure work well and what aspects may benefit from some correction. In this book, we take the opportunity afforded by the recent financial crisis to reflect on the effectiveness of shareholder litigation in regulating corporate conduct.

Shareholder litigation forms an important part of the structure of law and regulation affecting American business. Because public regulators cannot oversee every company at every moment and cannot anticipate or even respond to every report of a potential wrong, a variety of remedies are left in the hands of shareholders themselves. Shareholders who have suffered at the hands of a corporation in which they have invested can sue—either as a class or on behalf of the company itself—to right these wrongs. They thus assume, with their counsel, the role of "private attorneys general," with strong personal incentives to detect and prosecute corporate wrongdoing. The lawsuits they bring fill an important gap in the regulatory framework affecting American business.

Shareholder litigation exerts its regulatory effect through the mechanism of deterrence. That is, prospective wrongdoers realize, through the threat of litigation, that they will be made to account for whatever harms they cause and, thus internalizing the cost of their conduct, forswear bad acts. This basic mechanism of deterrence explains much civil litigation. Corporate officers and directors, understanding that they may be held liable to their investors for the harms they cause, refrain from engaging in conduct that will harm investors and induce them to sue. In this way, shareholder litigation regulates corporate conduct.

The problem with this story in the corporate context is that officers and directors are typically covered under a form of insurance, known as "Directors' and Officers' Liability Insurance" or "D&O insurance," that insulates them from personal liability in the event of shareholder litigation. D&O insurance also protects the corporation itself from liabilities it may have in connection with shareholder litigation. This insurance disrupts the deterrence mechanism by transferring the obligations of the prospective bad actor (the officer, director, or the corporation itself) to a third-party payer (the insurer). An actor that is no longer forced to internalize the costs of its actions is no longer deterred from engaging in harmful conduct—managers who are no longer personally at risk for investor losses are less likely to take care in avoiding them, and corporations that are no longer at risk from shareholder litigation are less likely to monitor the conduct of their managers—and the regulatory effect of shareholder litigation is diminished, distorted, or destroyed.

Unless, that is, the insurer does something to prevent this outcome. The introduction of D&O insurance essentially establishes the D&O insurer as a third-party intermediary in the regulatory dynamic. If shareholder litigation is to deter bad corporate acts, it must be through the intermediary agency of D&O insurers who will have an opportunity to influence corporate conduct through the insurance relationship. Because they are the ones ultimately paying for the harms caused by their corporate insureds, insurers have ample incentive to exert this sort of constraining influence, and they have the means to do so. We identify three ways in which the insurance relationship may influence corporate conduct—through underwriting, monitoring, and the settlement of claims. The question thus becomes what influence D&O insurers do in fact exert through this relationship and whether this influence is sufficient to reintroduce the deterrence mechanism, thus preserving the effectiveness of shareholder litigation as a regulatory device.

There is a lot riding on this question. Indeed, if D&O insurers fail to preserve the deterrence mechanism, then shareholder litigation would seem to have little chance of regulating corporate conduct and thus would appear to be, as critics have long contended, mere waste, a tax on business that supports an unnecessary plaintiffs' bar. In order to answer this question then, we must examine corporate and securities law through the lens of liability insurance.

That is precisely what this book seeks to do. In the pages that follow, we examine shareholder litigation through the lens of liability insurance in order to evaluate whether shareholder litigation accomplishes its regulatory objective. Through extensive interviews with professionals working in this area, we analyze each of these three ways in which insurers may preserve the deterrence function of shareholder litigation and we evaluate how well each works in achieving that end. The short answer, unfortunately, is not very well. As it is currently structured, D&O insurance significantly erodes the deterrent effect of shareholder litigation, thereby undermining its effectiveness as a form of regulation. The situation is not without hope, however, and we end by offering three narrowly tailored corrections that a rule maker such as the Securities and Exchange Commission (SEC) might enact to rehabilitate the deterrent effect of shareholder litigation, notwithstanding the presence of liability insurance.

But this brief preview of the analysis to come has taken much for granted. From this point onward we will be more careful. In the remainder of this chapter, we explain our assumptions and define some of the terms that we will use throughout the book. We also describe our empirical methodology and lay out, in some detail, the questions that we will confront in each chapter. Finally, we preview our policy prescriptions, recommending relatively simple reforms of SEC rules in order to prevent D&O insurance from subverting the deterrence function of securities litigation.

Shareholder Litigation

Throughout this book, we use the term "shareholder litigation" to encompass all civil actions brought by current or former shareholders of a corporation against the corporation or its managers for losses the shareholders have suffered as a result of actions taken by the corporation or its managers. This definition excludes criminal actions brought by prosecutors or other public authorities as well as enforcement actions brought by regulatory agencies, such as the SEC. It includes, principally, claims brought by shareholders under either federal securities law or state corporate law.

Among these claims, securities class actions represent, by far, the largest potential source of liability. Shareholders filed 210 federal securities class actions in 2008, thirty-three more than they had filed in 2007 and eighteen more than the average number of class actions filed per year from 1997 through 2007.[1] Allegations in 94 percent of these claims were centered on misrepresentations in financial statements. In 2008, 2.23 percent of all companies listed on the NYSE, Nasdaq, and Amex at the beginning of the year became defendants in securities class actions filed later that year, down from 2.32 percent the year before and in line with the 2.24 percent average going back to 1997.[2] These numbers are somewhat higher for Standard and Poor's 500 companies, 9.2 percent of which were sued in a securities class action in 2008, up from 5.2 percent in 2007 and the highest since 12.0 percent were sued in 2002.[3]

In securities class actions, current or former shareholders are given the right to sue the corporation collectively for misrepresentations that allegedly induced the shareholders to trade. The allegations underlying such claims typically revolve around misrepresentations in financial documents or in the company's projections concerning future results. Shareholders who trade on the basis of this false information suffer losses when the market price of the security reverts to its "true" underlying value—that is, the price at which a trade might have occurred had it not been for the false information released by the defendants. Securities law thus gives investors the right to sue for this difference in price, which can grow to extremely large amounts once aggregated over the total number of shares transacted during the period of the misrepresentation.

In addition to federal securities class actions, shareholder claims can be brought against corporate defendants under state corporate law. These actions may be representative in form, as when a class of shareholders is deprived of a right, such as voting, that the shareholders possess in common, or they may take the form of shareholder derivative suits when the underlying harm is suffered primarily by the corporation itself and only derivatively by the shareholders, such as when a manager is vastly overcompensated or otherwise wastes corporate funds. Individual or representative claims brought under state corporate law often seek injunctive relief—for example, an order enjoining an unfair reorganization or requiring the board of directors to solicit additional bids in a merger transaction. Derivative suits, by contrast, are most often brought seeking damages. The damages in derivative suits, however, are limited to losses caused by the underlying misconduct—the amount of loss suffered by the corporation, for example, in overpaying its managers or in wasting assets in a particular transaction—not to losses measured by share price fluctuations. Therefore, damages in derivative suits typically do not grow to the size of losses alleged in securities litigation. Additionally, a number of substantive rules and procedural requirements operate as barriers to recovery in derivative suits. As a result, state corporate law litigation is often viewed as secondary to securities law claims. Indeed the phenomenon of the "tagalong derivative suit," discussed in chapter 2, illustrates the way in which state corporate law claims often follow in the wake of more significant federal claims.

Regardless of how state corporate law and federal securities law claims compare in terms of relative importance, for purposes of this research we treat the two basic types of claims together under the rubric of shareholder litigation. Both types of claims feature shareholders seeking relief from the corporation or its managers for investment loss. Both types of claims principally involve monetary damages, not administrative sanctions or criminal penalties. And both types of claims focus on misconduct by the corporation or its managers leading to losses suffered by shareholders. Not all aspects of these claims are identical, and going forward we will be careful to make the distinction when an argument or line of analysis applies to one but not the other. Nevertheless, the claims seem to share the same basic functions, of both compensating shareholders for losses suffered at the hands of the corporation's managers and deterring conduct that might cause such losses in the first place.

This leads us to consider the regulatory function of shareholder litigation. What, in the larger picture, is shareholder litigation meant to accomplish? Two possibilities present themselves. The basic goal of shareholder litigation may be to compensate shareholders, to make them whole for losses suffered at the hands of the corporation and its managers. Alternately, the purpose of shareholder litigation may be to deter bad acts in the first place, to create incentives for corporations and managers to avoid claims. The perspective we choose on this question will have important implications for our policy analysis. So, which is it, compensation or deterrence?

Compensation or Deterrence?

Like other forms of civil litigation, shareholder litigation may be supported by either of two public policy justifications: compensation or deterrence.[4] According to the compensation rationale, shareholder litigation is meant to make shareholders whole for losses they suffer at the hands of the corporation and its managers. Alternately, according to the deterrence rationale, shareholder litigation is meant to create incentives for the corporation and its managers to prevent conduct leading to certain kinds of loss. These two rationales are independent—the success or failure of one does not depend upon the other—so one or both or neither may in fact apply to justify shareholder litigation. Let us take a moment to examine each, starting with the compensation rationale.

Although the compensation rationale makes a great deal of intuitive sense, an emerging consensus among most corporate and securities law scholars rejects compensation as a justification for shareholder litigation.[5] Three forceful critiques of the compensation rationale compel this conclusion. First, shareholder litigation often involves mere "pocket shifting" since many plaintiffs are also shareholders of the corporate defendant and the corporate defendant, directly or indirectly, funds most settlements. Second and related, over time, diversified shareholders generally will not benefit from the most common form of shareholder litigation—the prototypical 10b-5 class action involving a nontrading corporation and alleging fraud on the market—because the plaintiffs' losses will be offset by gains to other groups of investors, which may, in the long run, include the plaintiffs themselves. Third, most shareholder litigation recovers only a small fraction of total shareholder loss and does so at very high transaction costs, suggesting that it is at best a very inefficient means of providing compensation for investors who have been harmed.

The first critique—that settlements and damages paid in shareholder litigation typically amount to pocket shifting and are therefore of no economic value—focuses on the fact that many plaintiffs are also shareholders. This is so in the context of many securities law claims, especially those for which the plaintiff class consists of those who purchased shares at a price allegedly inflated by fraud and who remain shareholders through the bringing of the suit. But it also applies to those 10b-5 claims for which the plaintiff class consists of those who sold shares at an allegedly deflated price as long as the plaintiffs do not sell all of their shares and thus remain invested in the corporate defendant, as will often be the case for fund holders and other long-term diversified shareholders. In these cases, the plaintiffs are essentially suing themselves and, if they "win," merely moving dollars from one pocket to another, minus very substantial litigation costs.

The pocket-shifting critique applies not only to many securities claims but also to many state corporate law claims, especially derivative suits for damages. In fact, as we shall describe in greater detail in chapter 2, state law forbids indemnification of derivative suit settlements precisely because of pocket-shifting concerns (since the indemnification would essentially amount to a payment from the corporation to make whole a manager defendant who had just paid a settlement to the corporation). Nevertheless, as we shall see, state law permits such settlements to be insured, and, as a result, corporations now fund the settlements indirectly (through the insurance premium), even if they cannot fund them directly (through indemnification). This kind of circular wealth transfer is pocket shifting in the extreme. It is the type of transaction from which no one benefits, at least in compensation terms, except perhaps attorneys, who, on the plaintiff's side, receive a portion of the settlement and, on the defendant's side, receive hourly fees. From the actual plaintiff's perspective, however, this is not a good deal. Plaintiffs clearly do not benefit from compensation when they effectively pay it themselves minus whatever portion they pay out in attorneys' fees and other costs.

The second critique—that there is no real economic gain to diversified shareholders from being compensated for their losses in a typical 10b-5 claim—turns on the law of large numbers and the likelihood that, over time, a diversified shareholder will gain as often as he or she loses from mispricing in the market. All market transactions, obviously, involve buyers and sellers. Sometimes buyers will gain from mispricing due to faulty corporate disclosure—specifically, when the disclosure has the effect of unjustifiably deflating securities prices at the time of their purchase—and sometimes sellers will gain—that is, when the disclosure has the effect of unjustifiably inflating securities prices at the time of their sale. Over time, however, diversified investors are as likely to be on one side of the transaction as on the other, and their losses from some mispricing are likely to be offset by their gains in others. Systematically, therefore, they lose nothing at all under the facts of a typical 10b-5 claim. And, of course, if nothing at all is lost, then there is nothing at all to compensate. A diversified shareholder thus would not favor a rule that, in the words of two eminent commentators, "force[d] his winning half to compensate his losing half over and over."[6] Moreover, when the compensation system is as costly as the system of shareholder litigation in fact is—involving large payments to attorneys and other professionals on both sides, costs that from the perspective of a diversified shareholder are pure waste (unless there is a deterrent benefit, which we address separately)—rational investors would clearly prefer to forgo such compensation altogether.

Finally, the third critique—that the compensation offered by shareholder litigation is inefficient and wasteful because it returns a very small portion of shareholder losses at very high transaction costs—focuses directly on the costs and benefits of the current system from a compensation perspective. Settlement values in 10b-5 claims are a tiny fraction of investor loss. In 2008, the median settlement was only 2.7 percent of total investor loss, a percentage that has been fairly consistent for a number of years—2.3 percent in 2007, 2.2 percent in 2006, and 3.2 percent in 2005.[7] The obvious implication of these statistics is that investors are not well compensated for their losses. If we imagine that shareholder litigation makes investors whole for market losses surrounding a corporate misrepresentation, then that is just what we are doing—imagining it. Shareholder litigation, in fact, compensates only pennies on the dollar of total investment loss (although, as we describe in chapter 8, investor loss is at best a crude proxy for losses from securities fraud). Moreover, the transaction costs associated with this compensation scheme—the plaintiffs' attorneys' commission and the defense lawyers' hourly rates—further reduce the benefit ultimately received by shareholders. Simply stated, the system is so costly and inefficient that it is difficult to believe that it provides meaningful compensation to investors.

As forceful as each of these critiques is on its own, taking all three of them together effectively destroys the compensation rationale as a justification for most shareholder litigation. We say "most" here because each of these critiques applies most clearly to the most common form of shareholder litigation—the prototypical 10b-5 claim. They do not apply as well to securities claims involving market manipulation or insider trading, but, as we describe in chapter 2, the vast majority of class actions under the federal securities laws do indeed center on what we are calling the prototypical 10b-5 claim—involving, essentially, a nontrading corporate defendant and allegations of fraud on the market. These critiques thus speak to the vast majority of securities claims. Moreover, they apply with equal force to much state corporate law litigation, especially the typical shareholder derivative suit. However, direct shareholder actions under state law, especially those challenging the fairness of corporate acquisitions and seeking additional compensation in the transaction, are not affected by these critiques and therefore may offer the best case for the applicability of the compensation rationale. We will therefore treat this type of claim as an exception to the rule that the compensation rationale does not supply a credible justification for shareholder claims. Nevertheless, having effectively dispensed with compensation as a possible justification for the bulk of shareholder litigation, we are left with the deterrence rationale, for which there is considerably more support, both within the academic literature and in the courts.

Deterrence works when a prospective wrongdoer, recognizing that he or she will be forced to pay the full cost of any harm he or she causes (and more, perhaps, to account for a less than perfect likelihood of detection), therefore forswears the harmful conduct.[8] Widely recognized as a basic purpose of much civil litigation, deterrence essentially makes plaintiffs—or more accurately, plaintiffs' lawyers—into private attorneys general who serve a public purpose in bringing private claims. Each acts on the basis of his or her private incentives by bringing claims but in doing so creates a public good— namely, the *in terrorem* effect, basically inducing potential defendants to be good in order to avoid the liabilities associated with being bad. The deterrence justification for shareholder litigation thus focuses on the value it creates by preventing corporate managers from engaging in conduct leading to investor loss. The deterrence rationale is not without controversy, with much of the academic debate focusing on the incentives of the plaintiffs' attorneys and the related question of whether the deterrence effect of shareholder litigation is set at the optimal level or whether there is too much deterrence or not enough.[9] Deterrence is nevertheless widely accepted as the fundamental purpose of shareholder litigation by courts and commentators alike. The U.S. Supreme Court, for example, has long viewed the deterrence effect of private shareholder litigation as "a necessary supplement to [Securities and Exchange] Commission action."[10]

The deterrence function of shareholder litigation connects it to corporate governance. "Corporate governance" is a broad concept that much of the legal literature has given a narrow definition. Scholars discuss it most often in the context of specific regulatory reforms or in terms of charter provisions and other structural characteristics of firms. But corporate governance may refer more broadly to any system of incentives and constraints operating within a firm. Corporate governance is designed to constrain bad acts on the part of corporations and their managers. Insofar as these are the same acts that will lead to liability in shareholder litigation, corporate governance and shareholder litigation pursue similar ends—both seek to make managers better serve the interests of their shareholders. Good corporate governance ought to lead to less shareholder litigation, and the risk of shareholder litigation ought to lead prospective defendants to improve their corporate governance.

If we are thus to take deterrence as the basic rationale behind shareholder litigation, supplying it with its underlying purpose and justifying its existence, we are left primarily with questions about how well shareholder litigation in fact accomplishes the end of deterrence. If shareholder litigation systematically fails to deter, it would fail to accomplish its underlying purpose and would have no reason to exist. Indeed, if shareholder litigation fails to deter, radical reform would seem to be appropriate, either to correct the defects of shareholder litigation or to abolish it altogether. These possibilities are presented most starkly when the underlying risks are covered by insurance.

Introducing Insurance

D&O insurance funds shareholder litigation. Almost every publicly traded corporation in the United States purchases D&O insurance to cover the risk of shareholder litigation.[11] And most shareholder litigation settles within the limits of these policies. D&O insurance transfers shareholder litigation risk away from individual directors and officers and the corporations they manage to third-party insurers.

This risk transfer is not complete. There have been approximately twenty so-called mega settlements over the past ten years that have significantly exceeded the value of existing D&O insurance policies, and there have been more cases in which corporate defendants paid a significant amount of corporate funds on top of the available insurance. It is difficult to know precisely how often or how much corporate defendants contribute to settlement because corporations are required to disclose neither D&O insurance limits nor how settlements are funded. Nevertheless, using the information on class action settlements available at the Stanford Class Action Clearinghouse Web site, we estimate that approximately 15 percent of class action settlements include a payment by the defendant in addition to the available insurance. In most of these cases, the amount of the corporation's contribution was substantially less than the amount paid by the corporation's D&O insurers, and, in some cases, the payment may have been part of satisfying an insurance deductible.[12] Michael Klausner and Jason Hegland, who run the Clearinghouse, recently looked carefully at a sample of cases in their database and concluded that corporations paid more frequently in their sample than we estimate, but they concluded, nevertheless, that "corporations' payments into settlements, on average, constitute relatively small portions of total settlements."[13] Thus, as far as we can tell on the basis of publicly available information, the risk transfer from the insured to the insurer is not quite complete, but it is very nearly so.

This creates a problem for deterrence. With liability risk transferred to a third-party insurer, prospective defendants are no longer forced to internalize the full cost of their actions. With little or nothing at risk, in other words, they are unlikely to be deterred from the sorts of actions that may lead to shareholder litigation. Worse, once the reins of deterrence are loosened, prospective defendants may be more likely to engage in conduct leading to losses, thus creating a moral hazard problem in which the effect of insurance, paradoxically, is to increase loss. This is the insurance-deterrence trade-off analyzed so elegantly in economists' formal models, explored empirically in connection with personal injury litigation, and largely ignored in corporate and securities law scholarship.[14]

Even from the perspective of compensation, D&O insurance is problematic. D&O insurance serves to guarantee investors that they will be compensated for losses stemming from shareholder litigation. But if D&O insurance merely performs this compensatory function, then it is not a good investment from the shareholders' perspective, because the price of an insurance contract is always greater than the expected payout under the contract—insurance companies, after all, do not sell their products for free. And the same protection against loss could be obtained by shareholders for free (or very nearly so) simply by holding a diversified portfolio of investments, since the effect of diversification is essentially to cancel the risk of unexpected events (like shareholder litigation) that is associated with any one holding. Because diversification provides shareholders with essentially the same protection against loss as insurance and does so at a lower cost, rationalizing D&O insurance from the compensation perspective turns out to be as problematic as justifying shareholder litigation on the basis of the compensation rationale.

Insurance thus poses a challenge to the aims and ends of shareholder litigation. Indeed, to the extent that insurance weakens deterrence, it undermines the basic justification for shareholder litigation. Nevertheless, it would be leaping to conclusions to assume, without more, either that insurance necessarily destroys the basic rationale of shareholder litigation or that the purchase of D&O insurance cannot be justified. Insurers, after all, have both the incentive and the influence to design mechanisms to control the risk of loss, and in seeking to control their own losses under the policy, insurers may reintroduce the deterrence function of shareholder litigation. Our basic question then is, Do they? What do insurers do to

control losses and thereby reintroduce the deterrence function of shareholder litigation?

Corporate and Securities Law through the Lens of Liability Insurance

Insurance has recently been revealed as a shadowy force shaping many
aspects of public policy. Who can think about health care reform without
thinking almost immediately about health insurance or about the current
rash of bank failures without thinking of the Federal Deposit Insurance
that dampens their effect? Similarly, public policy debates link automobile
accidents with automobile insurance, hurricanes with property insurance,
death with life insurance, aging with social security and long-term care insurance, medical malpractice with medical malpractice insurance, and tort
litigation more generally with liability insurance. Insurance, to paraphrase
sociologist Richard Ericson, is a form of governance.

Yet, to a large extent, this understanding of insurance as governance
has extended only to insurance that addresses (or fails to address) the
needs and problems of individuals and families. Within law and policy, the
attention to insurance similarly extends primarily to fields that address
these same problems, such as health, tort, and elder law and policy. With
few exceptions, the focus is on insurance for individuals and the only large
organizations that come into this picture are insurance organizations, the
insurance companies, other private risk pooling organizations, and government agencies engaged in spreading the risks of life and death.

But large organizations and, especially, large corporations buy insurance too, as evidenced by the size of the commercial insurance market.
To date, this corporate insurance market has not figured prominently in
academic analysis or public debate in the corporate law and finance field.
In the academic literature the only strong research thread addresses the
question of why publicly traded corporations buy insurance at all, given
that their shareholders can spread risk simply by holding a diversified portfolio. But this literature has been largely theoretical, and it has not been
followed up by research into what corporations do with the insurance that
they buy and what that insurance does to them.[15] Corporate and securities
law academics, moreover, have largely ignored D&O insurance.[16]

Our research aims at uncovering the relationship between D&O insurance and corporate governance because, as we have already described,

the question of the effectiveness of shareholder litigation as a regulatory device depends upon it. D&O insurance has the potential to insulate corporations and their managers from the consequences of liability rules that are expressly designed to penalize bad governance and encourage good governance. As a result, the D&O insurer thus assumes a pivotal role in the analysis. The question thus becomes, Does the D&O insurer have some means of passing along the deterrent effect of shareholder litigation or does the fact of D&O coverage distort or destroy the accountability mechanisms built into shareholder litigation? In other words, what do D&O insurers do to deter bad acts on the part of their insureds? Since, after all, the insurers are the ones ultimately footing the bill for shareholder claims, they would seem to have ample incentive to control the conduct that might lead to claims.

We hypothesized three ways that the D&O insurer might seek to control the risks posed by its insureds, each with different implications for the effectiveness of shareholder litigation as a regulatory device. First, D&O insurers may screen their risk pools, rejecting firms with the worst corporate governance practices and increasing the insurance premiums of firms with higher liability risk. Second, D&O insurers may monitor the governance practices of their corporate insureds and seek to improve them by recommending changes, either as a condition to receiving a policy or in exchange for a reduction in premiums. Third, D&O insurers may manage the defense and settlement of shareholder claims, fighting frivolous claims, managing defense costs, and withholding insurance benefits from directors or officers who have engaged in actual fraud.

We set out to investigate our hypotheses and, more broadly, to understand the effects of insurance and shareholder litigation empirically by talking to people in the field, asking questions and listening to their stories. We would very much have liked to test our hypotheses quantitatively—for example, comparing premiums against governance terms or the impact of limits on settlements—but the data necessary to study these questions simply are not available. We therefore set out to gather data however we could, applying the qualitative research methods described below.

Research Method

To study the relationship between insurance and shareholder litigation we have used the research tools of qualitative interviews and participant observation that have been employed most effectively in recent years by social scientists outside economics. Following in the footsteps of recent work by sociologists—Richard Ericson, Aaron Doyle, and Dean Barry and earlier work by Carol Heimer—we have sought to illuminate the governance function of insurance, gathering data by interviewing D&O insurance specialists and also by observing and participating in industry conferences on the subject.[17] Our goals were to test our hypotheses about insurance and deterrence as well as simply to learn as much as possible about the role of D&O insurance in shareholder litigation.

From 2005 through 2007, we conducted in-depth interviews with over one hundred people working in and around the interconnected fields of D&O insurance and securities litigation. Our interviews were semi-structured, by which we mean we followed a loosely organized research protocol, which set forth a list of topics to explore with each interviewee.[18] However, our interviews were not designed as cross-examinations. We did not set out in advance to elicit yes or no answers to a predetermined set of questions. Rather, our interviews were designed to engage our interviewees and get them talking about their area of expertise and, from their observations, to begin to compile relevant material on our research questions.

We identified prospective interviewees by beginning with references from leaders of the Professional Liability Underwriting Society, a professional association including underwriters, brokers, claims managers, consultants, and other specialists on professional liability lines of insurance. From these initial interviews, we then proceeded outward to references from our interviewees, thus expanding our set of prospective interviewees with each interview. By the time we were finished, we conducted recorded interviews with

- twenty-one underwriters from fourteen companies, including primary, excess, and reinsurance underwriters;
- twelve claims managers from ten D&O insurance companies;
- twelve lawyers who specialize on the defense side of shareholder litigation;
- eleven lawyers who specialize in bringing shareholder litigation on behalf of shareholders;
- ten lawyers who specialize in representing D&O insurance companies in the monitoring and settlement of shareholder litigation (typically called "monitoring counsel");
- six brokers from six brokerage houses;
- four risk managers employed by publicly traded corporations to purchase their insurance coverage;

- three D&O actuaries from three companies, two of whom were the chief professional lines actuaries in their firms;
- five policyholder coverage counsel;
- three mediators who were among the small group of mediators most actively involved in the settlement of shareholder litigation during the period of our interviews;
- two experts who assist parties in assessing the damages in shareholder litigation; and
- two claims advisors from two brokerage houses.

In addition, we have participated in numerous industry conferences and discussions involving both industry professionals and academic experts, several of which gave us the opportunity to present our work and thus to receive additional comments from our participants on early drafts of our findings.

This method of identifying participants cannot produce a random sample, and some bias may creep into our results from the simple fact that not all potential respondents were equally likely to participate. Nevertheless, in spite of the self-selecting and self-referential nature of this sample, we can describe the interaction of insurance and shareholder litigation with some confidence because the top firms in each part of the field are relatively few and densely connected. As one of our participants said to us, "It's a really small sandbox. You don't want to pee in it."[19] The same is true of the plaintiffs' and defense lawyers working in this area, as one such lawyer described:

> Because the bar is so small, your personal reputation counts. Integrity counts. Saying you are going to do a deal means something. You know, double-crossing someone, maybe you can pull it off once, but you are going to be caught. So there is that, that you trust people within this circle, and of course you do have all the due diligence and documentation and settlement agreements that are a million pages long, but there is some level of trust, some level of candor.[20]

The relevant numbers bear these statements out. The universe of players on the plaintiffs' side has remained small and relatively stable, with the top eight plaintiffs' firms accounting for 75 percent of total securities class action settlement collections.[21] The defense bar is less concentrated than the plaintiffs' class action bar, but the panel counsel lists maintained by the top D&O insurance carriers provide a good guide to that bar, and, perhaps not surprisingly, the top New York and national firms are well represented. D&O insurance, moreover, is a highly concentrated market, clustering around two dominant primary insurers—AIG and Chubb— which together account for more than half of the market for primary insurance.[22] The excess D&O market is broader, but both primary and excess markets are intermediated through the personal connections of relatively few brokerage firms.[23] Moreover, a small number of outside law firms handle the settlement responsibilities of most of the D&O insurers and, thus, serve to bring to claims managers the same breadth of information about the settlement market that the brokers bring to underwriters about the D&O insurance market.

We obtained access to top people in each of these areas. Our requests for interviews were rarely turned down and not disproportionately by any one group such that we would fear a skew in our results, although defense lawyers tended to be the most difficult to schedule. We also countered the problem of bias by interviewing professionals on every side and in every role and by checking their responses against each other. Except as noted in the chapters that follow, our participants provided consistent reports during the interviews, allowing us to conclude comfortably that we are reporting shared understandings of most of those working in the field.

While our research protocol prevents us from identifying the people we interviewed or which companies or firms they worked for, we can say this: We were very mindful of the respective reputations and market shares of the insurers, plaintiffs' lawyers, defense lawyers, mediators, and monitoring counsels working in this area, and with remarkably few exceptions, we were able to interview every person we wanted to. Most of the people we interviewed knew of all or most of the other people we spoke to, and many of them knew one another personally. Risk managers, policyholder coverage counsel, and plaintiffs' lawyers typically were, as would be expected, less well connected to everyone else, and the people involved in the sales process were not well connected to the people involved in the claims process, except within companies and, to a lesser extent, through professional associations.

Through this process we came to have a kind of bird's-eye perspective on shareholder litigation and D&O insurance. Obviously we cannot claim to understand any particular aspect of the field at the level of detail of the active participant. But, because of our access to multiple perspectives, we can develop a holistic understanding of the field that is very difficult for participants to develop. Consistent with that understanding, we have heard from a variety of people in the field that they now recommend as a valuable introduction our earlier articles to new underwriters, brokers, and lawyers working in and around the field.

As a result of having found our way inside these interconnected networks, we are confident that we can accurately describe the interaction of insurance and shareholder litigation on the basis of a number of interviews that may seem small to researchers used to working with large quantitative data sets. We would have liked very much to run quantitative analyses of our research questions, and we hope to one day. But the key data for this kind of quantitative analysis—insurance limits and premiums and detailed information on how settlements are funded—simply are not publicly available. It is our hope that our work can be used to frame more systematic quantitative analyses, should the data one day be made available. In the meantime, the explanatory power of qualitative research depends, like traditional doctrinal and policy arguments, on the persuasive coherence and plausibility of the analysis.

Prior research has used liability insurance as a window on liability,[24] tracked the historical relationship between liability and insurance,[25] modeled that relationship,[26] and explored some of the ways that liability insurance changes behavior in litigation.[27] But the research we report here is the first to systematically explore the relationship between liability and liability insurance through the entire insurance relationship, from underwriting to claims settlement, and to provide a theoretically informed account of the real world impact of this relationship on the particular form of liability that we examine. Thus, our research has both immediate policy relevance for securities regulators and the D&O insurance market and also long-term implications for liability and insurance research.

Roadmap of the Analysis to Come

Looking forward, our account will proceed as follows. We begin, in chapter 2, by exploring the various claims that can be brought by shareholder plaintiffs, examining the legal elements and general characteristics that distinguish each of the basic causes of action as well as those underlying features that the various claims have in common. Because our focus is on the interaction of shareholder litigation and D&O insurance and how insurance both transfers and transforms the risk of shareholder litigation, we proceed from our account of shareholder litigation to a discussion, in chapter 3, of D&O insurance. There we describe the basics of D&O

insurance—what it is, what it does and does not cover, and how the coverage works—and provide an account of important coverage exclusions and the market for D&O insurance. We further discuss how most D&O insurance packages provide several different types of coverage, including coverage for individual directors and officers as well as coverage for the corporate entity itself for losses resulting from shareholder litigation.

This preliminary material leads us, in chapter 4, to our first puzzle. That is, Why do firms purchase D&O insurance coverage for the corporate entity? This strikes us as a puzzle for two main reasons. First, if all that D&O insurance does is spread the risk of loss, this entity-level coverage seems unnecessary since shareholders themselves can spread the risk of loss by holding a diversified portfolio of investments. We therefore devote a considerable portion of the discussion in chapter 4 to analyzing potential explanations for the purchase of the entity-level coverage aspect of D&O insurance. As already noted, this has been a fertile area for economic analysis, and our main contribution here is to highlight an agency cost explanation that has not been emphasized in the prior literature. Second, by transferring so much of the corporation's liability risk to a third-party insurer, entity-level coverage would seem to create a significant moral hazard problem, thus diminishing the deterrent effect of shareholder litigation. Indeed, we find several reasons to suggest that D&O insurance produces significantly greater moral hazard than more traditional corporate property and casualty insurance.

Chapters 5–8 present our empirical results, examining the insurance relationship through the eyes of our interviewees in order to determine whether there is some mechanism to constrain the problem of moral hazard and reinvigorate the deterrence effect of shareholder litigation. As noted above, there are in theory three ways insurers might manage this trade-off. First, by pricing coverage to risk, D&O insurers could preserve deterrence by forcing riskier corporations to pay more for coverage, thus creating an incentive for corporate insureds to improve their governance in order to reduce the cost of D&O insurance. We examine this possibility in chapter 5 and find that corporations do indeed seek to price coverage to risk. Nevertheless, we also describe several reasons offered by our participants to doubt that the differential pricing of D&O premiums deters corporate wrongdoing or provides adequate incentives to optimize corporate governance.

A second means by which D&O insurers might maintain the deterrence function of shareholder litigation is by monitoring corporate insureds during the life of the contract, forcing them to steer clear of risky conduct or to adopt governance practices designed to prevent the kinds of events that lead to shareholder litigation. Yet in chapter 6, we report our finding that D&O insurers in fact do almost nothing to monitor and control the conduct of their corporate insureds. Loss-prevention programs, common in other areas of insurance, are typically not offered by D&O insurers, and when loss-prevention advice is given, it is given as a suggestion rather than as a mandate and is designed, according to our participants, more to promote or market the insurer than to constrain the conduct of the insured. In chapter 6, we seek to account for the absence of monitoring by insurers and emphasize again its implication—namely, moral hazard.

Third and finally, another means by which D&O insurers might reintroduce the deterrence function of shareholder litigation is through control over defense and settlement. At the most basic level, insurers could work to make sure that cases get resolved on the merits and that settlement amounts bear a close relationship to the harm, so that the insurance loss costs that are used in the D&O insurance pricing formulas provide the right signal. In addition, insurers could force defendants in the worst cases— that is, those with greater evidence of genuine wrongdoing—to pay more toward the defense and settlement of their claims, thus incentivizing corporate insureds to avoid the kinds of wrongdoing that will lead to a reduction in coverage. We examine such strategies in chapter 7, where we seek to understand how insurance coverage influences the defense and settlement of shareholder litigation. There we find that, although insurers do have substantial control over settlements, they have almost no control over the conduct of the defense. And although they may occasionally use their settlement control to extract concessions from corporate defendants—how much and how often is impossible to say—there are nevertheless many features of the settlement process, discussed in chapter 8, that prevent D&O insurers from insisting that final settlement amounts track the underlying merits of claims.

From there, we move on to discuss coverage disputes. The coverage dispute is the last opportunity for a D&O insurer to force a bad corporate actor to account for its bad acts. As such, it is the last moment when the deterrence function of shareholder litigation can be reintroduced by an insurer. In chapter 9, we discuss the most common bases upon which insurers assert coverage defenses. In reviewing developments in this area of law, we find a loose correlation between coverage defenses and corporate wrongdoing—the insurer's coverage defenses seem strongest when the plaintiff's underlying claim is meritorious. Nevertheless, as we also discuss in chapter 9, insurers are likely to really press coverage defenses in relatively few cases, for fear of an adverse impact in the insurance market. Instead the insurer may "cash in" the coverage defenses by agreeing to a settlement that is partially funded by the defendant. As a result, the insurer's defenses may function, to an admittedly indeterminate degree, somewhat like a moral hazard coinsurance provision, so that a corporation's contribution to the settlement varies according to the wrongfulness of its employees' conduct. The low value of D&O insurance policy limits in relation to the potential damages in a serious fraud case functions very crudely in the same way. Accordingly, by keeping insurance policy limits low in relation to companies' market capitalization and by cashing in their coverage defenses, D&O insurance companies may preserve some of the deterrent impact of shareholder litigation. Determining how often this actually occurs is yet another quantitative question that we cannot answer because of the absence of insurance data.

We conclude, in chapter 10, by arguing that our findings show that D&O insurance as it is currently structured significantly undermines the deterrence value of shareholder litigation. Nevertheless, we offer a set of three narrowly tailored solutions that we believe both could and should be enacted in order to improve the regulatory effect of shareholder litigation.

Throughout this analysis, our guiding question is the extent to which liability insurance subverts or preserves the deterrence objectives of corporate and securities law. This is a critically important question since its answer should ultimately guide policy makers in debates over the value of shareholder litigation. Deterrence is the raison d'être of shareholder litigation. If shareholder litigation does not deter, it is not necessarily the case that bad corporate acts are utterly undeterred, since a variety of other constraints, such as SEC enforcement actions, criminal prosecutions, and market constraints may still operate to deter the worst corporate misconduct. But if shareholder litigation does not deter, then it loses its core justification and ought, therefore, to be abolished. Yet if we can identify a way to restore the deterrence role of shareholder litigation, notwithstanding the presence of liability insurance, there is no need to consider the more radical solutions of either abolishing shareholder litigation or abolishing insurance. That is what we will seek to do in the pages that follow.

CHAPTER TWO

Shareholder Litigation

U nderstanding the interaction between insurance and corporate and securities law in action begins with an understanding of the basic claims that can be brought by shareholders under corporate and securities law. This chapter reviews shareholder litigation, examining its prevalence and general features as well as the specific elements of each of the basic causes of action. We also pause to consider the common features that, beneath all of their particular differences, enable many such claims to be treated together under the common rubric of shareholder litigation.

Statistical Measures of Shareholder Litigation

Broadly, shareholder litigation may be seen as encompassing state corporate law claims, whether derivative or direct, and federal securities law claims. Federal securities law claims are the most significant, in terms of both settlement values and absolute numbers. Experts estimate that approximately 80 percent of shareholder claims litigated in federal court are securities class actions.[1] Indeed, our participants reported that securities class actions are "head and shoulders above" any other liability exposure,[2] noting that "securities litigation outweighs derivative litigation by far."[3] Much of our discussion therefore focuses on shareholder class actions under the federal securities laws, particularly 10b-5 class actions. Nevertheless, our discussion is applicable to other forms of shareholder litigation as well, especially when that litigation is brought as a derivative action or in conjunction with securities class actions.

The incidence of shareholder litigation may be discussed either in terms of frequency, which measures the probability of suit, or severity, which measures the magnitude of loss. A rough estimate of frequency for securities class actions can be made by dividing all such claims by all publicly traded companies and suggests that companies have roughly a 2 percent chance of being sued in a securities class action in any given year.[4] However, several caveats are in order. First, this 2 percent estimate measures only federal securities law class actions—which, as we describe in greater detail below, are indeed the principal liability exposure—and adding in state corporate law claims to speak to shareholder litigation more broadly would increase the frequency. Moreover, these are averages, and some companies will have significantly higher frequencies than others. Large companies, for example, tend to be sued more often than small ones.[5] Companies in certain industries tend to be sued more than others, although which industries are sued most often fluctuates somewhat from year to year, suggesting a scandal du jour pattern in filings.[6] Finally, Nasdaq companies are typically sued more often than NYSE companies. However, in 2008, for the first time since 2002, companies listed on the NYSE or Amex received more securities class action filings than Nasdaq companies—111 filings against NYSE or Amex companies compared with sixty-eight against Nasdaq firms, reflecting the fallout of the credit crisis on financial firms.[7]

A rough estimate of the second component of liability risk—severity—can be taken by examining settlement amounts. Because the vast majority of shareholder claims are either settled or dismissed, settlement amounts provide a good measure of the total amount paid to shareholders and their counsel. Because they do not include defense costs, however, settlement values represent an incomplete measure of the total cost of securities litigation. At one industry conference we attended, lawyers and claims managers disputed the total extent of the defense costs but agreed that defense costs were at least 25 percent of a typical class action settlement.

Focusing on securities law class actions as the dominant exposure, the numbers are not small. Average settlement values of shareholder class actions exceeded $38 million in 2008, up from $31 million in 2007.[8] The average settlement value for the years 2003–2008 was $45.1 million, significantly higher than the average settlement value of $17.1 million for the years 1996–2001.[9] Comparing median settlement values reveals a signifi-

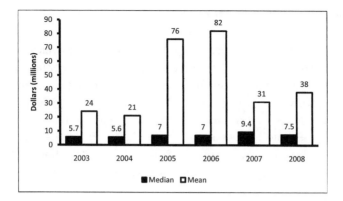

FIGURE 2.1. Median and mean securities litigation settlements, 2003–2008. The data in this figure are derived from Plancich 2008, 9–10.

cant skew in these numbers. Median settlements in 2008 were $7.5 million, in line with the trends over the past five years and significantly lower than the $9.4 million median settlement in 2007.[10] Shareholder suits are thus characterized by a handful of very large settlements, while the typical case settles for a considerably lower amount. Figure 2.1 compares mean and median settlements for the five-year period from 2003 to 2008. To see the sensitivity of average settlement amounts to large, outlier settlements, consider the effect of excluding settlements over $1 billion—such as the $1.08 billion McKesson HBOC settlement finalized in 2008—from average settlements. If these large settlements are removed, the average settlement for the years 2003 to 2008 drops to $26 million.[11] Moreover, the variance of annual settlements from the average is considerably reduced.

All of these statistical measures of shareholder litigation have focused on securities class actions, which are indeed the dominant liability exposure for defendants and therefore worthy of much attention. However, we do not want to lose sight of the other possible grounds for shareholder litigation—in particular, the "tagalong derivative suit" that is likely to be filed in the wake of the 10b-5 claim. Therefore, in this chapter and throughout this book, when we refer to "shareholder litigation," we are referring to all of causes of action, whether under state corporate law or federal securities law, that may be brought on an aggregate basis by shareholder plaintiffs against the managers of the corporation in which they are invested or against the corporation itself. We turn now to an examination of the legal bases of these causes of action.

Legal Bases of Shareholder Litigation

Investors who find themselves wronged by a corporation in which they have invested may have claims under either state corporate law or federal securities law. Although there are differences in focus under either regime—state law focuses on the conduct of the corporation's board of directors, and federal law focuses on corporate disclosures—the two regimes typically proscribe the same acts. As a result, a claim often exists under both state and federal law for the same conduct. In the sections that follow, we discuss the principal causes of action under which a shareholder may seek relief.

State Corporate Law Claims

A firm takes its corporate law—the law relating to its organization, its existence as a firm, and the rights and duties of its managers and owners—from the state in which it is incorporated. For reasons that have long been debated—a subject beyond the scope of this book—more large American companies incorporate in Delaware than in any other state. More than 50 percent of all publicly traded companies in the United States and over 63 percent of the Fortune 500 are Delaware corporations.[12] Moreover, because of Delaware's recognized preeminence in corporate law, many states follow the Delaware model in fashioning their own state law, furthering Delaware's dominance in corporate law and policy beyond its borders. As a result, when we describe state corporate law in the sections that follow and throughout this book as a whole, we will refer primarily to Delaware law, noting important exceptions whenever they arise.

State law enshrines the board of directors as the ultimate authority in the corporation. A key provision of the Delaware code declares, "The business and affairs of every corporation . . . shall be managed by or under the direction of a board of directors. . . ."[13] The board of directors is responsible for the appointment of executive officers who will be delegated the authority to administer the business and affairs of the firm on a day-to-day basis. It is the board, however, that is ultimately responsible for the fate of the company, and it is the board that is therefore ultimately answerable to shareholders. Corporate law thus looks primarily to directors, not to officers. It is the board of directors that is charged with managing on the shareholders' behalf, as fiduciaries. And therefore it is the directors who may be held accountable to shareholders for failing to do so, for having breached their fiduciary duties.

The state law fiduciary duties that directors owe to shareholders have traditionally been understood as dual: directors owe shareholders a duty of care and a duty of loyalty.[14] Under the duty of care, "directors of a corporation in managing the corporate affairs are bound to use that amount of care which ordinarily careful and prudent men would use in similar circumstances."[15] Meanwhile, the duty of loyalty, most basically, is a proscription against director conflict of interest and self-dealing. A more comprehensive statement of duty-of-loyalty principles appears in the old Delaware case of *Guth v. Loft*:

> Corporate officers and directors are not permitted to use their position of trust and confidence to further their private interests. While technically not trustees, they stand in a fiduciary relation to the corporation and its stockholders. A public policy, existing through the years, and derived from a profound knowledge of human characteristics and motives, has established a rule that demands of a corporate officer or director, peremptorily and inexorably, the most scrupulous observance of his duty, not only affirmatively to protect the interests of the corporation committed to his charge, but also to refrain from doing anything that would work injury to the corporation, or to deprive it of profit or advantage which his skill and ability might properly bring to it, or to enable it to make in the reasonable and lawful exercise of its powers. The rule that requires an undivided and unselfish loyalty to the corporation demands that *there shall be no conflict between duty and self-interest.*[16]

In theory at least, each of these fiduciary duties is an available basis for shareholder litigation seeking to challenge board conduct. For example, a bad corporate investment might be thought to violate the duty of care, and a self-interested transaction, where a board member is on both sides of the deal, might be thought to violate the duty of loyalty.

In practice, however, the business-judgment rule often applies to shield directors from duty-of-care claims. As described by an eminent commentator, the business-judgment rule "is simply that the business judgment of the directors will not be challenged or overturned by courts or shareholders, and the directors will not be held liable for the consequences of their exercise of business judgment—even for judgments that appear to have been clear mistakes—unless certain exceptions apply."[17] The business-judgment rule operates both as an evidentiary presumption and a substantive standard. As an evidentiary presumption, it places the initial burden of proof on the shareholder plaintiff. As a substantive standard, however, the business-judgment rule forces plaintiffs challenging the board's actions under the duty of care to allege facts showing that the board's conduct rises (or falls) to the level of "gross negligence."[18] Indeed, given the gross negligence standard of the business-judgment rule, our above formulation of the duty of care, focusing on "ordinary prudence," becomes misleading. Once the business-judgment rule applies, merely negligent conduct no longer violates the duty of care, and the de facto standard of care shifts to something akin to irrationality or waste.[19] As a result, unless the directors have engaged in conduct to which the business-judgment rule does not apply—one of the few exceptions to the rule, focusing on conduct involving fraud, duress, or illegality—the business-judgment rule will typically apply to shield directors from liability for virtually all violations of the duty of care. The effect of the business-judgment rule, in other words, is that "to allege that a corporation has suffered a loss . . . does not state a claim for relief against that fiduciary no matter how foolish the investment."[20]

In the context of loyalty, by contrast, a plaintiff challenging the board's actions does not bear the burden of establishing a *gross* conflict of interest. *Any* material conflict of interest on the part of the board will rebut the board's evidentiary presumption and shift the burden to the defendants to prove that the challenged transaction was either approved by a majority of disinterested directors, ratified by shareholders, or fair to the corporation.[21] As a result, transactions in which board members have some interest on both sides—for example, a transaction in which a board member sells an asset to the corporation and his or her interests as a seller (sell high) naturally conflict with the corporation's interests as a buyer (buy low)—are a much more fruitful source of shareholder litigation. In addition to basic conflict-of-interest transactions, loyalty claims may arise out of pay packages and, perhaps most often, mergers and acquisitions, where the boards frequently are charged with serving other interests over those of their shareholders. Duty-of-loyalty claims arising out of mergers and acquisitions are a steady source of shareholder litigation.

Finally, it is worth noting that Delaware has recently experimented with expanding the dual nature of fiduciary duty by suggesting that a third fiduciary duty, good faith, might exist alongside care and loyalty. The status of good faith as a distinct fiduciary duty arose most notably in the Delaware Chancery Court's 2003 decision in *In re the Walt Disney Company Derivative Litigation*, in which the court allowed a claim to survive the motion to dismiss, in spite of having no basis in either care or loyalty, at least as traditionally understood, because the complaint raised questions of the board's "good faith."[22] In that opinion, the court oscillated between loyalty issues (an imperial CEO involved in a transaction with a personal friend) and care issues (an extremely bad business outcome) in describing lack of good faith as a kind of recklessness.[23] Subsequent opinions, however, have clarified that concerns involving a board's good faith properly belong under the duty of loyalty, albeit under a conception of loyalty broader than some traditional interpretations.[24]

So far, our discussion has gone to the substance of a shareholder plaintiff's claim under state corporate law. To summarize, under state law, shareholder plaintiffs must frame their complaints around some breach of fiduciary duty of the corporation's directors, not its officers. Moreover, although directors owe duties of care and loyalty to their shareholders, application of the business-judgment rule is likely to lead to early dismissal for duty-of-care claims. As a result, a shareholder plaintiff's best chance under state corporate law is to challenge board action under the duty of loyalty. In addition, we must pause briefly to consider a procedural aspect of shareholder litigation under state corporate law—namely, whether the claim will be treated as derivative or direct.

Corporate Law Procedure: Derivative and Direct Claims

Shareholder claims for breach of fiduciary duty may be either derivative or direct.[25] A derivative action is a suit brought by a shareholder when the underlying injury is to the corporation. A direct action is a suit brought by a shareholder on the basis of an underlying injury to himself or herself. Derivative suits are thus brought by shareholders on behalf of the corporation. The shareholder's harm and share of any gain resulting from the suit is only derivative of the harm or gain to the corporation itself. By contrast, although direct suits may be brought as class actions in which one shareholder represents an entire class of shareholders, the underlying claim involves some set of rights that shareholders possess as individuals. Common examples of derivative suits are suits alleging excessive compensation or outright theft by a particular manager. In each case, any amount recovered in the shareholder claim would be paid back into the corporation. The shareholders would gain by virtue of their pro rata interest in the value of the firm, but this gain is derivative of the gain to the corporate entity in the boost to its treasury. The shareholders do not gain directly as individuals. Suits over voting rights or rights in corporate reorganizations, by contrast, are typically direct suits since the underlying right—for example, voting—is a right that each shareholder possesses individually and is not derivative of a right of the corporate entity itself.

The distinction between derivative and direct suits is important because there are special procedural consequences associated with derivative claims. A shareholder bringing a derivative claim must make "demand" on the board of directors—essentially, a formal request that the board of directors bring the claim themselves. Confronted with a demand request, a board of directors may refuse, in which case the claim is dismissed, or they may take control of the claim and prosecute it on the shareholders' behalf. Although the ability of the board of directors to dismiss or take a claim away from shareholders in the demand process may seem jarring, it reflects two basic premises of state corporate law. First, the ultimate authority in the corporation is the board of directors, and second, a derivative claim properly understood is a claim of the corporation itself. Therefore, just as the board has the authority to make decisions regarding the deployment of every other corporate asset, it has the authority to determine what to do with this one, the derivative suit. If the board decides that it would cost more to pursue the claim than the claim is worth, the board can get rid of the claim whether the shareholder likes it or not. A shareholder may challenge the board for wrongful refusal of demand, but in the absence of a conflict of interest, the wrongful-refusal claim is merely a duty-of-care claim, and the board's decision, as in any other business context, will be protected by the business-judgment rule.

Of course, the deference accorded to boards in this context operates on an assumption of disinterest and independence. If, by contrast, the derivative plaintiff can show that there is a conflict of interest infecting the decision making of the board with regard to the suit—if, for example, the underlying harm involves the conduct of the directors themselves—then a court may agree that because demand would be futile—because, in other words, a conflicted board cannot be expected to render a fair decision on demand—demand will be excused. When demand is excused, the derivative suit plaintiff may continue to prosecute the claim. Nevertheless, even when demand has been excused, the board retains yet another extremely powerful means of taking control of the derivative action. A less than wholly disinterested or independent board may appoint a special committee of disinterested and independent directors, or a wholly conflicted board may appoint new directors and immediately name them to a special committee. In either case, the special committee would be charged with making a decision regarding the derivative suit and, just as a disinterested board may refuse demand, may decide that pursuing the derivative action is not cost justified and therefore cause it to be dismissed, again whether the original plaintiff likes it or not.

Although derivative suits were once thought to exert an important constraint on corporate managers—as the U.S. Supreme Court wrote in a famous mid-twentieth-century case, the derivative action, "born of stockholder helplessness, was long the chief regulator of corporate management"—the procedural obstacles associated with demand have substantially limited its usefulness.[26] These procedural obstacles—such as the demand requirement and the requirement of some states (although not Delaware) that derivative plaintiffs post a bond to cover corporate defense costs in the event that the suit is dismissed—were designed to eliminate abusive litigation, so-called strike suits. State law has decided, in other words, that the derivative suit remedy to corporate mismanagement was often worse than the disease. Nevertheless, derivative suits still occur, with a recent spate of derivative suit filings following in the wake of the options backdating scandals of 2006 and 2007. This is not surprising since the backdating of options is, as we have described, a paradigmatic derivative claim—any harm suffered by shareholders is strictly derivative of the harm suffered by the corporation itself.

But the relatively high incidence of derivative litigation following the options backdating scandal proves only that plaintiffs do not choose their injuries. Because the same procedural hurdles—the demand requirement, the special litigation committee, and so on—do not exist for direct suits, shareholder litigation is much more likely to be successful if it can be brought directly as a representative class action. As a result, plaintiffs will seek to bring their claims as direct actions whenever possible. A recent study of litigation activity in Delaware supports this proposition, finding that of all fiduciary duty claims filed in 1999 and 2000, 80 percent were direct shareholder class actions challenging board conduct in the context of an acquisition.[27] They were, in other words, direct, while only 14 percent of all fiduciary duty claims over the same period were derivative suits.[28]

Damages for state shareholder litigation also depend largely on whether the underlying claim is derivative or direct. Damages in derivative claims, as we noted above, seek relief for something of which the corporation has been deprived to the detriment of all shareholders. Damages thus will be keyed to the opportunity the corporation has lost. The damages for an excessive executive compensation claim, for example, will reflect the extent to which the executive's compensation is excessive, requiring that amount to be paid back into the corporation. Although, as we describe in chapter 3, state law bars corporate indemnification for such claims, insurance is available to cover damages in derivative claims. Direct suits, by contrast, often seek injunctive relief, especially when they are brought by individual shareholders aggrieved at the loss of a shareholder right, such as voting. Direct actions may involve cash payments, as when an acquiring company is forced to increase merger consideration as a result of a shareholder challenge of the transaction, a form of litigation that practitioners sometimes refer to as a "deal tax." However, such payments are typically funded directly by the acquiring company and not, with the possible exception of the plaintiffs' attorneys' fees, by the D&O insurer.

Federal Securities Law Claims

The federal securities laws, initially enacted during the Great Depression and regularly amended since then, provide an additional basis for liability of corporate officers and directors and, in some cases, for the corporation itself. Federal securities law liability arises out of two statutes: the Securities Act of 1933 (the "Securities Act")[29] and the Securities Exchange Act of 1934 (the "Exchange Act").[30] Both statutes contain liability provisions, but the basic scheme of the two statutes is different. Securities Act liability attaches to corporate actors in the context of an offering or sale of securities, while Exchange Act liability arises from secondary market activity—that is, the trading of shares and the disclosure of information by publicly traded companies. Under either statute, claims may be brought by private plaintiffs through the class actions mechanism or by the SEC itself. Securities law claims are typically framed around a misrepresentation. Most often, a company releases false or misleading information that has the effect of inflating its share price and inducing investors to buy; when the information is later revealed as false, the company's share price drops, and all investors who bought at the artificially high price lose a portion of their investment.[31]

Securities Act liability can arise under several statutory provisions. Section 12(a)(1) creates liability for corporate issuers by giving securities purchasers a right to rescind if the issuer violates the registration requirements of the Securities Act. Similarly, Section 12(a)(2) creates a rescission right for those who purchase securities from issuers after receiving false or misleading information. Section 11 creates additional liability for fraud, allowing purchasers to recover damages for false and misleading information in registration statements against a number of possible defendants, including not only the officers and directors of the issuer but also the bankers, accountants, and lawyers involved in the offering. Finally, Section 15 allows purchasers to recover not only from the corporation as under Sections 11 and 12 but also from any person or entity in control of the corporation. Although these liability provisions, especially Section 11, are potentially far-reaching, it is important to keep in mind that liability under the Securities Act is limited to a single factual context: transactions in which a company sells securities to the public by means of a registration statement filed with the SEC. Much activity in the securities market occurs outside of this context and, thus, is beyond the scope of Securities Act liability.

The liability provisions of the Exchange Act, however, fill this regulatory lacuna by extending the coverage of the securities laws to secondary market activity. Like the Securities Act, the Exchange Act contains several liability provisions, including provisions relating to stock price manipulation and misrepresentations in the context of corporate elections and tender offers. However, the most important liability provision of the Exchange Act, indeed the most important liability provision of the securities laws in general, is Rule 10b-5, promulgated under Section 10(b) of the Exchange Act.[32]

Rule 10b-5 is the federal securities laws' "catch-all antifraud provision,"[33] proscribing fraudulent conduct "in connection with the purchase or sale of any security."[34] Although the language of the rule itself provides no private right of action, Rule 10b-5 has become the basis of the paradigmatic shareholder class action. Federal courts recognized an implied private right of action in the rule almost immediately after it was adopted and continued to do so with such regularity that, to quote the U.S. Supreme Court, "the existence of a private cause of action for violations of the statute and the Rule is now well established."[35] Indeed, Congress has also abandoned its original reticence and expressly acknowledged a private right of action under Rule 10b-5 in both the Private Securities Litigation Reform Act of 1995 and the Securities Litigation Reform Act of 1998. As a result, Rule 10b-5 has now become, to borrow another oft-repeated phrase of the Court, a "judicial oak which has grown from little more than a legislative acorn."[36] In 2008, 75 percent of securities class actions alleged violations of Rule 10b-5.[37] Sections 11 and 12(a)(2) of the Securities Act are the second and third most common allegations, respectively. In 2008, 23 percent of securities class actions alleged a Section 11 violation, and

19 percent included a Section 12(a)(2) claim. Moreover, 2008 seems to have been an atypical year in terms of allegations, with fewer 10b-5 claims and more Section 11 and 12(a)(2) claims. For the five years prior to 2008, more than 85 percent of securities law class actions alleged a violation of Rule 10b-5, while Section 11 and 12(a)(2) claims peaked at 11 percent and 10 percent, respectively.

Although 10b-5 claims may arise in a wide variety of contexts, 10b-5 class actions are most often brought against companies for misstatements in their public disclosures, especially financial reports.[38] In a typical 10b-5 claim, plaintiffs allege that a company's release of false financial information had the effect of inflating (or deflating) the company's share price, causing investors to buy (or sell) and thereby to suffer monetary loss when the truth was revealed and the share price adjusted. In this prototypical claim, the complaint is then brought as a class action against the nontrading corporation and its managers, alleging "fraud on the market." The plaintiffs bear the burden of showing Rule 10b-5's four basic elements: scienter, materiality, reliance, and causation. They must show, in other words, that defendants, acting with scienter, made a material misstatement on which the plaintiffs relied and that caused a financial loss.

The scienter requirement of 10b-5 can generally be satisfied by recklessness. Because the Supreme Court has never fully elucidated the requisite showing for scienter,[39] circuit courts have fashioned their own standards, with most accepting that the standard has been met when a defendant, unaware of the true state of affairs, can foresee the likelihood of a statement to mislead.[40] The scienter issue, however, was complicated by the enactment of the Private Securities Litigation Reform Act (PSLRA) in 1995, an amendment to the securities laws that was designed to cut down on perceived abuses in securities class actions. The PSLRA included two features that put additional pressure on the question of scienter. First, the PSLRA required that plaintiffs plead facts giving rise to a "strong inference" that defendants possessed the requisite state of mind.[41] And second, the PSLRA instituted a stay of discovery until the motion to dismiss had been decided.[42] The strong-inference showing that was required to support scienter was recently addressed by the Supreme Court in *Tellabs, Inc. v. Makor Issue & Rights, LTD*, in which the Court held that "[t]o qualify as 'strong' within the intendment of [the PSLRA], we hold, an inference of scienter must be more than merely plausible or reasonable—it must be cogent and at least as compelling as any opposing inference of nonfraudulent intent."[43] Plaintiffs, in other words, must equal or beat the plausibility of any nonfraudulent intent claimed by the defendants. Moreover, the stay of discovery means that plaintiffs must meet this heightened standard without depositions or even document discovery. Our respondents told us that this is no small feat, insisting that they "don't really know" the quality of a case prior to discovery.[44] As a result, scienter typically is seen as a significant obstacle to plaintiffs.

Materiality, by contrast, is not a significant barrier to claims. In 10b-5 claims, as in other securities law contexts, materiality depends on a reasonable-investor standard, which is not difficult to show when the release of accurate information causes a corporation's securities values to decline.[45] Almost by definition, information that affects the market value of a security is information that a reasonable investor would regard as material. Similarly, reliance is unlikely to constitute a serious barrier to plaintiffs since, according to the fraud-on-the-market theory, when shares trade in an efficient market, public statements are incorporated into share price and reliance is presumed for any investor trading at the market price.[46] Indeed, apart from scienter, the only significant substantive legal obstacle to recovery for a corporate misrepresentation may be the requirement, recently affirmed by the Supreme Court in *Dura Pharmaceuticals, Inc., v. Broudo*, that the plaintiffs show a causal link between the misrepresentation and the plaintiffs' loss.[47]

Loss causation, as the requirement is known, is not new, but the *Dura* court did change how plaintiffs must address causation in their pleadings. What the Supreme Court said in *Dura*, most basically, is that merely pointing to an inflated security price after a misrepresentation is not sufficient to establish loss causation. Instead, the pleadings must include "some indication of the loss and the causal connection the plaintiff has in mind."[48] What exactly plaintiffs must plead to establish loss causation after *Dura*, however, remains unclear.[49] For claims resembling what we have been treating as the paradigmatic securities claim—plaintiffs purchasing under the cloud of a misrepresentation and holding through to a corrective disclosure that has a significant impact on the security's price—*Dura* does not present additional difficulties. However, the situation is less clear when the market price does not react significantly to the corrective disclosure or when plaintiffs sell prior to the corrective disclosure. Commentators have suggested that it may still be possible to plead loss causation in these situations, perhaps by offering a theory of how the truth leaked into the market (and therefore into the security's price) prior to the corrective disclosure.[50] Leaky-truth theories may support claims when there is no price reaction to the corrective disclosure as long as a price reaction can be shown when the leak occurred. Such theories may also support the claims of plaintiffs who sold prior to the corrective disclosure if they can argue that the price at which they sold reflected the leaky truth, which had the effect of lowering the price and therefore causing their loss. In leaving these and other details to be worked out by lower courts, however, the Supreme Court has not settled the controversy surrounding the pleading of loss causation so much as it has flagged it as an area for future developments. Our participants regularly noted the importance of *Dura* but also acknowledged that it remains to be seen what effect *Dura* and its progeny will ultimately have on securities class actions.

Finally, damages in the typical shareholder class action are measured by the difference between the price the plaintiffs paid (or received) for their shares when they bought (or sold) them and the price they would have paid (or received) but for the defendants' misrepresentations. For a widely held and actively traded security, this measure of damages can easily add up to enormous sums. As we shall see in chapter 7, the vast majority of defendants who fail to dispose of the case on motions choose to settle rather than risk putting these damages before a judge or jury. Indeed, trials of securities class actions are exceedingly rare, and judgments are almost unheard of. The substantive law of securities class actions is thus expressed primarily in the series of procedural steps described below.

Securities Law Procedure: The Life Cycle of the 10b-5 Class Action

Procedurally, the securities class action resembles much large-scale, aggregate litigation. Most claims proceed through predictable stages, including investigating and filing, class certification and lead plaintiff selection, motions to dismiss, discovery, trial preparation, and, finally, settlement.

INVESTIGATION AND FILING. Plaintiffs' lawyers continually monitor the securities markets in search of potential claims. Large plaintiffs' law firms specifically monitor the portfolio companies of institutional investors, keeping them informed of developments and hoping thereby to increase the firm's chances of being selected as lead plaintiff. In the words of one plaintiff's attorney, "We monitor. The research analyst has his general Bloomberg and Dow Jones terminals and access to all the financial news and keeps CNN and CNBC going on a 24/7 basis, etc., etc." [51] Smaller law firms become aware of prospective claims on a more ad hoc basis,

through contacts with former employees, disgruntled investors, or referring attorneys.[52]

Once a plaintiffs' firm is aware of a potential claim, it will begin to
investigate the claim. The firm will engage in a detailed review of the
company's public documents and SEC filings and, frequently, retain a
private investigator to interview former employees or others with inside
knowledge about the corporate defendant.[53] Initially, these investigations
will help the plaintiffs' firm determine whether to file a claim. Once the
claim is filed, however, this informal investigation is likely to continue, and
perhaps intensify, in an effort to unearth facts to support the complaint.
Recall that the PSLRA both raises the bar to survive the motion to dismiss
and stays discovery until the motion has been decided. As a result, the
plaintiffs' firm will often continue the informal investigation of the claim
until formal discovery begins, seeking to amend the complaint with any
new and damning information found along the way.

This dynamic has two important implications, both with the effect of
increasing amounts paid at settlement. First, because plaintiffs invest more
effort in investigating their claims, surviving claims on the whole may be
more likely to include facts that are damaging to defendants, thereby increasing settlement amounts. Second, because plaintiffs expend resources
of time and money in their investigative efforts (including resources spent
on investigations of claims that ultimately are dismissed), they will, on the
whole, be able to collect greater attorneys' fees, thereby increasing the
overall cost of settlement.

CLASS CERTIFICATION AND LEAD PLAINTIFF SELECTION.   As in other class
actions, securities class actions proceed under the nominal direction of
representative plaintiffs but under the actual direction of the lawyers
chosen to represent the class. With the enactment of the PSLRA, Congress sought to alter this dynamic by awarding control over the plaintiffs'
class not to the first to file but to the "most adequate plaintiff."[54] Now, in
place of the old system, under which the plaintiffs' firm that filed the first
complaint had an advantage in the court-directed process through which
the class counsel was selected, the filing of a class action starts a sixty-day
competitive process among plaintiffs' firms to identify and recruit those
plaintiffs who are most likely to be deemed the "most adequate plaintiff"
and thereby endowed with the authority to name class counsel. Although
judges retain some discretion in selecting class council, the biggest investors tend to be deemed the most adequate.[55] As a result, the trick is for the

plaintiffs' firm to represent large institutional investors, and, just as one might predict, plaintiffs' firms actively cultivate such clients.[56] Moreover, since these institutional investors often are public pension funds with politically ambitious managers, the courting sometimes takes the form of campaign contributions. As described by one of our respondents, "The guys who control the business in the public pension funds are all people who stand for election, and I don't have to tell you that somebody who stands for election [is interested in receiving campaign contributions]. . . ."[57]

Although the PSLRA seems to have been effective in ending the freewheeling days when plaintiffs' lawyers had, at best, nominal clients who had no real influence over their claims—days when, as described by a prominent mediator, a plaintiffs' lawyer who was asked to consult with his or her client might be asked to "go to the restroom, look in a mirror, talk to yourself, and come back here and tell me whether you want to accept the settlement or not"[58]—plaintiffs' actual involvement in the litigation remains secondary in most cases. Institutional shareholders were lead plaintiffs in only 20 percent of the securities class actions during the post-PSLRA period.[59] As a result, the plaintiffs' lawyer is still largely in control of the prosecution and, ultimately, settlement of the claim. Moreover, although recent research suggests that cases with institutional settlements settle for a higher percentage of investor loss than other cases, the researchers have not been able to draw a conclusion about cause and effect since the finding may suggest only that institutional investors chose to be involved in the most valuable cases and not that the involvement of an institutional investor makes a claim settle for more.[60]

After the court selects the lead plaintiff and class counsel, defendants have the option of challenging the class certification, but owing largely to the presumption of reliance derived from the fraud-on-the-market theory, class certification has not traditionally been a significant hurdle to plaintiffs' lawyers. But for the fraud-on-the-market theory, where reliance on the defendant's misstatement is presumed due to the ability of efficient capital markets to impound information in price, each individual plaintiff would need to establish reliance. This would have a devastating effect on class certification on the basis of Rule 23(b)(3) of the Federal Rules of Civil Procedure, which provides for class certification only if "the court finds that the questions of law or fact common to the members of the class predominate over any questions affecting only individual members." Requiring individual showings of reliance—each defendant would need to show how he or she became aware of the misinformation and establish that the misinformation in fact motivated the defendant's trade—would cause individual issues to dominate common class issues, thereby preventing class certification. Notwithstanding the fraud-on-the-market theory, defendants have occasionally been able to establish the inefficiency of the relevant market sufficiently to rebut the presumption of reliance, thereby successfully challenging class certification.[61]

Apart from disputing the applicability of the fraud-on-the-market theory, however, a more far-reaching recent development involving class certification is the increasing tendency of courts to hear questions of merit at the certification phase. Arguments over loss causation and other requirements are increasingly heard at the class certification stage.[62] And indeed, although there is some controversy over the degree to which inquiry into the merits of a claim is permitted at the class certification stage—Supreme Court precedent seems to point in both directions[63]—most circuits permit some discretionary weighing of the merits at this stage.[64] This development led our respondents to note that "class certification is becoming much more rigorous than it had been."[65]

THE MOTION TO DISMISS, DISCOVERY, AND SETTLEMENT. Following the tightening of the pleading requirements in the PSLRA, the motion to dismiss has become a very important screen in securities class actions; courts routinely dismiss 25 to 35 percent of securities class actions filed in a given year.[66] Our participants reported that defendants filed a motion to dismiss in every case with which they were familiar; settlement discussions almost never take place until after the motion is filed; and settlement discussions typically do not take place until after the class action has survived the motion to dismiss. After the motion to dismiss is decided, the litigants face "the first genuine settlement opportunity."[67]

Most substantive legal arguments are heard at the time of the motion to dismiss. In deciding a motion to dismiss, courts typically accept as true all well-pleaded allegations as well as all plausible inferences arising from them and view the complaint in the light most favorable to the nonmoving party.[68] In securities class actions, however, the PSLRA complicates this standard. Well-pleaded allegations are still regarded as true, but following the *Tellabs* decision, any inference of scienter must be more than merely reasonable or plausible; it must be at least as strong as any competing inference of nonfraudulent intent. In this way, at least with regard to scienter, the motion to dismiss presents plaintiffs in securities class actions with a stricter standard than other federal claims. Moreover, as also noted

above, *Dura* may pose additional difficulties to some plaintiffs in pleading a theory of loss causation. These facts enable the motion to dismiss to
function as a screen for merit. Nevertheless, a hearing on the pleadings
where the allegations are treated as facts and plaintiffs benefit from a favorable presumption with regard to factual inferences is not the same as a
proceeding that finds facts and forces plaintiffs to prove their claims. The
motion to dismiss does not render judgment on the truth of the allegations, nor does it provide any guide to the amount of the damages that the
defendants ought to pay were the allegations to be proven. Some number
of nonmeritorious suits are thus likely to survive the motion, just as some
number of meritorious suits are likely to be dismissed for failure to meet
the strong-inference standard without access to discovery.

Surviving the motion to dismiss essentially clears the case for settlement. Summary judgment is rare. Our participants reported that class
actions typically do not last through to the stage when they are ripe for
summary judgment, and few of those that go all the way through discovery
are in fact resolved through summary judgment. In the words of one monitoring counsel, "[T]here is a lot of talk in the industry about how some
of these cases need to be pushed to summary judgment and not to settle
until a decision is made at the summary judgment level, but to date I am
literally not aware of a single one . . . [And] I am not aware of any 10b-5
cases that have been dismissed at the summary judgment stage."[69] Trial,
moreover, is virtually unheard of. A recent empirical study going back
to 1980, a period in which thousands of securities fraud cases were filed,
found only thirty-seven securities law cases seeking damages that were
tried to judgment.[70] The Risk Alert service of Institutional Shareholder
Services reports that only seven cases have gone to trial since 1996.[71] The
JDS Uniphase trial in late 2007 would appear to be the exception that
proves the rule. The trial was unusual in that it occurred at all—with the
parties electing to try a financial misrepresentation claim where damages
were alleged to be $18 billion—and perhaps even more rare in that the
jury returned a verdict for defendants on all claims.[72] Any expectation that
this result would lead more defendants to try their luck at trial, however,
does not seem to be borne out in practice since the JDS Uniphase trial,
and thus it remains true that once a claim survives the motion to dismiss,
all involved know that the odds strongly favor an eventual settlement.

Our participants emphasized, nevertheless, that they do prepare for
trial, if only to have a credible threat. This means embarking on discovery,
which, as every lawyer knows, is both laborious and expensive. Our participants reported that the cost of creating the document discovery data-

base in a significant class action is itself a multimillion dollar proposition. The cost of discovery creates an obvious and well-known incentive for defendants to settle. The costs of going forward are high on plaintiffs' lawyers too, if not as high. As one plaintiffs' lawyer explained to us, "[T]rying one of these big huge cases, it's hugely time-consuming, hugely costly, and hugely risky."[73] Or, in the words of another, explaining the tendency to settle rather than push through to trial, "[V]ery few people want to shoot the moon."[74] Moreover, it is worth noting that the defendant's higher costs in discovery do not necessarily give plaintiffs the advantage that one might assume, that is, the ability to threaten the defendant with trial knowing that the defendant's greater costs going forward will bring them eagerly to the bargaining table. In the D&O context, this strategy may not work as well since defense costs reduce available insurance limits. In light of the tendency for these cases to settle within insurance limits, any increase in defense costs may also decrease the total pot available to plaintiffs in settlement. Thus plaintiffs may also have a strong incentive to avoid high discovery costs.

Settlement, of course, is the way out of discovery. And, consistent with this expectation, our participants reported that although it can happen at any point in the process, especially when driven by a change of control or other significant transaction causing the defendant, for business reasons, to seek to eliminate contingent liabilities, settlement most often occurs after the motion to dismiss, when the machinations of discovery are about to begin or have just begun. In the words of one plaintiffs' lawyer, the bulk of cases "will be settled in between the date the judge comes down with the decision [on the motion to dismiss] and the date you start to get heavily involved in discovery."[75] A defense lawyer agreed, noting, "the real opportunity [to settle] is right after the motion is denied."[76]

Settlement, of course, is a subject unto itself, and we examine it separately in two chapters. In chapter 7, we examine the settlement process and how the various parties and their competing incentives interact in the settlement process. In chapter 8, we examine what factors guide outcomes in settlement and the relationship between these factors and what are customarily treated as the merits of a claim.

Shareholder Litigation: Commonalities

Although we have spent the last several pages emphasizing details and distinctions of the various claims shareholders may bring under state corporate and federal securities law, we would like to close this chapter by emphasizing the commonalities among these claims. The state corporate law and federal securities law claims that we have reviewed have more in common than a shareholder plaintiff. Indeed, the underlying concern of all of these causes of action is largely the same—namely, that managers have acted contrary to shareholder interests. Whether the claim is a state law derivative suit charging managers with looting the corporation, a direct action attacking the motives of an entrenched management team in the context of an acquisition, or a securities claim alleging that managers misstated earnings in order to protect their own compensation packages, the basic problem is the same: managers' interests have deviated from those of their shareholders, and, thus, managers have failed to act in the best interests of the corporation's owners. This is perhaps *the* core concern of business law generally, a concern that, in the economics literature, is given the name of "agency costs."[77] Here we see it animating each of the various causes of action included in shareholder litigation.

Seen in this way, it is not surprising that the same conduct can support a multiplicity of state and federal causes of action. For example, a corporate manager who has looted the corporation probably has lied to cover it up, thus giving rise simultaneously to a state corporate law claim for looting and a federal securities law claim for fraud. Or again, a board of directors that manipulates a corporate election creates a state law direct action for disenfranchisement as well as a probable federal securities law claim for misstatements in connection with the proxy materials. The fact that the securities claims are framed around misrepresentations or inadequacies in corporate disclosure should not lead us away from seeing that the basic concern again is that company managers have misused their positions to the disadvantage of their shareholders, the same basic concern animating fiduciary duty in state corporate law.[78] Simply put, the federal securities laws police misstatements because they harm shareholders. That there are some misstatements that might be seen as helping shareholders by keeping the corporation afloat—for example, misreporting earnings when the corporation is approaching insolvency—can similarly be understood as a harm that benefits current shareholders at the expense of those future shareholders who buy their stake under the cloud of the misrepresentation and therefore overpay. Although this may be seen as revealing a temporal conflict between present and future shareholders, it ought not to be seen as altering the basic rationale of the securities laws.[79] Because fraud is bad for shareholders generally, the securities laws adopt an ex ante perspective, asking what all current and prospective shareholders would demand with regard to managerial conduct in order to protect the investor class.[80]

The potential grounds for shareholder complaint are many—a treatise on liability risks faced by officers and directors, for example, lists 170 actions that potentially lead to shareholder litigation, broken down into categories including "Governance, Management, and Business," "Informed Business Judgment," "Unauthorized or Ultra Vires Actions," "Self-Dealing and Conflicts of Interest," "Change of Control Situations," and "Disclosures."[81] Nevertheless, the underlying concern of many of these claims is some sort of managerial departure from shareholders' best interests, and this core concern is policed both by shareholder litigation under state corporate law and shareholder litigation under federal securities law.

CHAPTER THREE

An Introduction to Directors' and Officers' Liability Insurance

Understanding the interaction of insurance and shareholder litigation also requires some basic knowledge of D&O insurance—essentially, what the product is, what it covers, and how the coverage works. This chapter examines these basic details of D&O insurance, looking first at the historical development of D&O insurance and some early problems posed by D&O coverage. It then examines D&O coverage as it now functions, including discussion of the basic structure of the coverage, the purpose of coverage, and various exclusions to coverage. Finally, this chapter examines the market for D&O insurance, focusing in particular on the cyclical nature of the insurance market.

Early History

D&O liability insurance was invented by Lloyd's of London in the 1950s by adapting basic liability insurance policies to the situation of the corporate director. These policies were not widely adopted in the United States until the mid-1960s and, in their early incarnations, did not always fit the special context of shareholder litigation, causing a leading commentator to remark,

> Perusal of the Lloyd's form and its American imitations leaves me with a distinct impression that the draughtsman, though possessed of broad and solid ex-

perience in the field of insurance law, got his corporation law from some rather sketchy recollections of Business Units I (or whatever they happened to call the basic corporation course at his law school) and a quick glance at *Corpus Juris*.[1]

Early D&O policies left gaps in coverage and, because they seemed to clash with public policy objectives, raised issues of enforceability.

The enforceability question centered on the relationship between insurance and indemnification and whether, as a public policy matter, corporations ought to be able to insure directors against losses for which directors could not legally be indemnified. Although indemnification was (and is) broadly permissible under the law of most states, it is generally not permitted for amounts paid in settlement or judgment of derivative litigation. Section 145(a) of the Delaware General Corporation Law, for example, allows indemnification "against expenses (including attorneys' fees), judgments, fines and amounts paid in settlement actually and reasonably incurred by the person in connection with such action" except for actions "by or in the right of the corporation"—that is, derivative actions.[2]

The rationale for disallowing indemnification for judgment and settlement in derivative actions is largely based on the pocket-shifting/circularity critique we have already discussed. Recall from our discussion in chapter 2, that derivative actions are those in which the defendants—typically officers and directors—harmed the corporation and, derivatively, all of its shareholders. Amounts paid by such defendants in settlement or judgment are paid over to the corporation. If the corporation must indemnify these defendants, the amount received by the corporation is simply returned to sender. This is a completely circular wealth transfer. The money travels in a circle—from the defendant to the corporation (in settlement of the derivative claim), then back from the corporation to the defendant (in fulfillment of the company's indemnification obligation). Shareholders, obviously, do not benefit directly from such a wealth transfer. Whatever they gain from the manager defendants is immediately lost as a result of the indemnification payment. It is, in other words, pocket shifting in the extreme, and, to prevent it, state law disallows indemnification for settlements and judgments in derivative suits.

In the early days of D&O insurance, commentators extended this rationale to argue that insurance against amounts paid in judgment or settlement of derivative litigation ought similarly to be disallowed. In the words of a leading commentator, "where the applicable statute flatly prohibits indemnification inconsistent with its terms, it seems to me plainly illegal for the corporation to pay for insurance."[3] Others agreed.[4] Nevertheless, state legislators ultimately mooted the argument by passing statutes that expressly allowed corporations to purchase and maintain D&O insurance even against those losses that the corporation could not itself indemnify. For example, Delaware law provides,

> A corporation shall have power to purchase and maintain insurance on behalf of any person who is or was a director, officer, employee or agent of the corporation . . . against any liability asserted against such person and incurred by such person in any such capacity, or arising out of such person's status as such, whether or not the corporation would have the power to indemnify such person against such liability under this section.[5]

D&O insurance is thus available to protect directors and officers regardless of whether indemnification would be permitted.

This, of course, raises the question of the circular wealth transfer once again. If indemnification for settlement and judgment in derivative claims was impermissible because it amounted to a circular payment from the corporation (to indemnify the director) back to the corporation (to satisfy the settlement or judgment), why is insurance any more permissible since it also involves a circular payment from the corporation (the insurance premium) back to the corporation (to satisfy the settlement or judgment)? Neither the court nor the legislature has ever confronted this issue head-on. Rather, they have simply decreed that insurance is permissible. We address the rationale for corporations purchasing D&O insurance in the next chapter.

Insurance is available to cover settlement for all forms of shareholder litigation, except as limited by the standard insurance exclusions that we discuss below and in chapter 9. As a result, today, nonofficer directors are almost never saddled with personal liability for having caused corporate losses.[6] Officers too are seldom personally liable for their corporate conduct.[7] The purchase of D&O insurance thus operates to transfer risk from individual directors and officers and, as we shall see, the corporation itself to a third-party insurer. How D&O insurance accomplishes this transfer of risk is described in greater detail below.

Coverage

D&O liability insurance is purchased by the vast majority of public corporations in the United States. It may well be the broadest form of liability insurance available. D&O insurance protects officers and directors from almost all liability-related costs arising out of any wrongful acts alleged to have been committed in the course of their duties, with comparatively few exclusions (many of which reflect the availability of coverage under other commonly purchased forms of insurance). D&O insurance coverage is so broad because the risk managers who purchase the insurance care at least as much or more about the breadth of the coverage as they care about the price, as one would expect for insurance that covers the personal exposure of the most senior officials in large, publicly traded companies. The common wisdom, unanimously accepted by the participants in our study, is that people are simply unwilling to serve on public company boards without D&O insurance. The purchase of such insurance generally receives the personal attention of the chief financial officer of the corporation and, in many cases, the board of directors and the general counsel, as well as the corporation's risk manager.

Although there is no single standard D&O insurance policy form, it is possible to describe in general terms the typical features of a D&O insurance program. D&O insurance provides coverage for liabilities arising as a result of the official conduct of directors and officers. Typical policy language offers coverage against "any actual breach of duty, neglect, error, misstatement, misleading statement, omission or act . . . by such Executive in his or her capacity as such or any matter claimed against such Executive solely by reason of his or her status as such. . . ."[8] For private or nonprofit corporations, employment-related claims are the most common source of D&O liabilities. For public corporations, however, the dominant source of D&O risk, both in terms of claims brought and liability exposure, is shareholder litigation. Because our research focuses exclusively on public companies, we treat liabilities arising from shareholder litigation as the basic loss event underlying D&O coverage.

The shareholder suits covered by D&O insurance include both corporate fiduciary duty claims, whether derivative or direct, and securities law claims. Of these, as noted in the prior chapter, federal securities law claims represent by far the greatest liability risk. Covered losses under a D&O policy include compensatory damages, settlement amounts, and defense costs. As regards defense costs, D&O insurance policies typically reimburse insureds for their costs in defending the claim, rather than, as is more common under other forms of liability insurance, such as automobile insurance, directly defending the insured against the claim. D&O insurance, in other words, provides indemnity coverage rather than duty-to-defend coverage. The implications of this policy feature are explored in chapters 6 and 9.

The Three "Sides" of D&O Insurance Coverage

The general label "D&O insurance" is often applied to three distinct insurance arrangements that are commonly provided as parts of a single D&O insurance policy. First, there is coverage to protect individual managers from the risk of shareholder litigation in the event that the corporation is unable to indemnify them. Second, there is coverage to reimburse the corporation for its indemnification obligations. And third, there is coverage to protect the corporation from the risk of shareholder litigation to which the corporate entity itself is a party. The first two aspects of D&O coverage trace to the original Lloyd's of London D&O form.[9] The third form of coverage is a newer development dating to the 1990s. A D&O insurance package may consist of these forms of coverage in any proportion, although typically all three forms of coverage share a single limit (meaning that the amount of insurance coverage provided for all three is identical and amounts paid under one part of the coverage reduce the amounts recoverable under other parts).

The only form of D&O insurance that actually insures individual directors and officers is the first of these, which is referred to within the industry as "side A coverage"[10] for reasons that we could not definitively discover. (One theory is that an early London market D&O insurance policy listed the A and B forms of coverage on opposite sides of the policy form, side A and side B.) Side A coverage essentially provides that the insurer will pay covered losses on behalf of covered managers when the corporation itself does not indemnify them. Typical policy language provides,

> Except for Loss which the Insurer pays pursuant to Insuring Agreement B of this Policy, the Insurer will pay on behalf of the Directors and Officers Losses which the Directors and Officers shall become legally obligated to pay as a result of a Claim first made during the Policy Period or Discovery Period, if applicable, against the Directors and Officers for a Wrongful Act which takes place during or prior to the Policy Period.[11]

Covered losses under side A include compensatory damages, settlement amounts, and defense costs incurred by the individual director or officer in his or her official capacity.[12]

The second form of D&O coverage, side B coverage, does not protect individual directors and officers at all but rather reimburses the corporation for indemnifying its directors and officers. Typical policy language provides,

> The Insurer will pay on behalf of the Company Losses for which the Company has, to the extent permitted or required by law, indemnified the Directors and Officers, and which the Directors and Officers have become legally obligated to pay as a result of a Claim . . . against the Directors and Officers for a Wrongful Act. . . .[13]

Payments under side B coverage are thus triggered when the corporation incurs an obligation to indemnify its officers or directors, which most policies deem to be required in every case in which a corporation is legally permitted to do so.[14] This presumptive indemnification aspect of the D&O policy is aimed at preventing the possibility of opportunism, where a corporation refuses to indemnify solely to cause the payment obligation to fall on the insurer. Finally, it is worth noting that side B coverage has a higher deductible than side A coverage, which typically comes with no deductible at all because "board members are accustomed to a no-deductible coverage."[15]

Together, sides A and B coverage allocates the risk of loss from shareholder litigation as follows. First, when a company is legally permitted to indemnify its managers for their liabilities, as it generally is, it must do so. Second, when a company does indemnify its managers, the insurer will reimburse the company pursuant to the terms of its side B coverage. Third, when a company is not legally permitted or able to indemnify its directors and officers, as in the case of derivative suit settlements and corporate insolvency, the insurer will pay pursuant to the company's side A coverage. The result of all of this is that an insurer's side A coverage obligations are triggered principally when liabilities arise from the settlement of derivative litigation or when the company is insolvent. Otherwise, and in the vast majority of cases, the liability falls on the corporation in the form of an indemnification obligation to its managers. Side B coverage then shifts this liability, albeit with a higher deductible or retention, to the third-party insurer.

Under both side A and side B, coverage obligations arise when a claim is brought against a corporation's officers or directors. Neither side A nor side B coverage is available for liabilities arising directly against the corporation as a defendant in shareholder litigation. Side C coverage emerged to fill this void. Evolving first as a solution to the disputes between insurance companies and corporate defendants over what portion of a securities settlement ought to be allocated to the managers (and therefore reimbursed by the insurer under the corporation's side B coverage) versus to the corporation (and therefore uncovered and paid directly by the corporation), side C coverage moots the allocation issue by insuring the corporation itself against direct claims.[16] Typical policy language provides, "[T]he Insurer will pay on behalf of the Company Loss which the Company shall become legally obligated to pay as a result of a Securities Claim . . . against the Company for a Wrongful Act . . . "[17] To ensure that the company retains some "skin in the game" at settlement, insurers may insist on higher deductibles under side C claims as well as a significant coinsurance percentage.[18] Still, side C coverage is the final step in the process of shifting the cost of shareholder litigation to a third-party insurer. Once these three sides of coverage are in place, the D&O insurer will pay *all* costs associated with the defense and settlement of shareholder litigation, minus deductibles or coinsurance, up to the limits of the policy.

Finally, although each of these arrangements—side A, B, and C coverage—may be referred to generally as D&O insurance, the collective label may be misleading since only side A coverage insures directors and officers. Side B and C coverage insures the corporate entity, reimbursing it for either its indemnification obligations (side B) or its liabilities incurred as a defendant in securities claims (side C). Nevertheless, referring to the arrangement as a whole as D&O insurance underscores the broader point that corporations buy insurance packages and, as we will explore in the next chapter, the entire package is understood by insurance market participants to benefit the directors and officers. The side A coverage benefits them directly, and the side B coverage benefits them indirectly. Hence, the name "Directors and Officers' liability insurance" makes sense in the insurance market context, even though, as a technical matter, the vast majority of D&O insurance payments are made under the side B and C parts of the coverage. We will refer to side B and C coverage collectively as the "entity-level" coverage, to distinguish them from the individual-level coverage provided by side A.

Coverage Exclusions

D&O policies have four kinds of principal exclusions, which we will discuss in more detail in chapter 9: (1) the fraud exclusion for claims involving actual fraud or personal enrichment,[19] (2) a set of timing exclusions that assign claims to the proper policy period,[20] (3) the insured versus insured exclusion for litigation between insured persons,[21] and (4) market-segmentation exclusions that reflect the availability of coverage under other forms of insurance. Significantly, our participants reported that none of these exclusions have a significant practical impact on D&O insurers' overall responsibility to pay for shareholder litigation.[22] In chapter 9, we will explore the coverage litigation and questions arising out of these exclusions and other limits on insurer liability in detail. Here, we simply provide a quick overview so that readers will have a general understanding of the nature of the coverage.

The fraud exclusion prevents insureds from receiving insurance benefits when they have actually committed a wrongful act, often defined as a "dishonest or fraudulent act or omission or any criminal act or omission or any willful violation of any statute, rule or law."[23] Whether an act comes within the fraud exclusion depends on the wording of the policy, which may require "final adjudication" of the fraudulent act or merely evidence that the fraudulent act has "in fact" occurred. Terms requiring a final adjudication of actual fraud benefit insureds because, as we have already noted, the vast majority of D&O claims settle without final adjudication.[24] This has led insurers either to insert the less strict "in fact" language in their policies or, in some cases, to seek to establish actual fraud in collateral proceedings.[25] We suspect that the market forces we describe will inhibit insurers' ability to insist on the broader term and, in time, will result in the standard fraud exclusion stipulating not only final adjudication but also that the adjudication take place in the context of the shareholder litigation itself and not in some collateral hearing.[26]

Interestingly, plaintiffs' lawyers told us that the fraud exclusion leads them to plead strategically, crafting their pleadings to avoid coming within the exclusion. In the context of a 10b-5 class action, for example, where the state-of-mind requirement can be met by showing either intent to defraud or recklessness, plaintiffs' lawyers will plead recklessness since, in the words of one, "why would you want to plead yourself into a coverage denial?"[27] Similarly, another plaintiffs' lawyer told us, "[W]e make sure that we don't use words like 'you intentionally cooked the books' or 'you did this' or 'you did that.' We don't want to provide any sort of out for the insurance carriers. We are careful to emphasize that recklessness can prove scienter and that is not intentional."[28] Another plaintiffs' lawyer described a situation "where the fraud was too good, and the judge voided the insurance policies on grounds of fraud in the inducement. So we end

up arguing and structuring our arguments more in terms of recklessness
because recklessness [is sufficient] under 10b-5." Pleading intentional
fraud would give the D&O insurers a bargaining chip that they could use
in settlement negotiations either to reduce their obligation to fund settlement or, potentially, to avoid the claim altogether. Plaintiffs' lawyers are
not anxious to give liability insurers bargaining chips, so they construct
their case around allegations of reckless conduct, further reducing the effect of the fraud exclusion on D&O policies.

In addition to the fraud exclusion, policies typically contain a related
exclusion for the repayment of moneys to which the insured was not legally entitled—in other words, unjust enrichment. Considering that insurance for unjust-enrichment claims would allow wrongdoers to keep the
benefit of their ill-gotten gains, the unjust-enrichment exclusion is hardly
surprising. It is worth noting, however, that unlike the fraud exclusion,
which rarely seems to operate as written, the unjust-enrichment exclusion
does indeed serve to bar insurance proceeds from being paid in a variety
of claims, including, for example, claims under Section 16 of the Exchange
Act, which require directors and officers to disgorge profits made from
short-swing trades in company shares. Insurers do not fund the losses in
such claims because they are, under most policies, considered to be the
repayment of moneys to which the insured was not legally entitled. The
unjust-enrichment exclusion may thus exist to allow insurers to avoid coverage in a variety of claims that can be similarly construed as involving
the repayment of ill-gotten gains, the details of which we will consider
alongside other coverage defenses in chapter 9.

Next, the timing exclusions carve out any claims noticed or pending prior to the commencement of the current policy, which ordinarily
would be covered under a prior policy. These exclusions reinforce the
insured's obligation to notify its current insurer of any potential claims
activity at the earliest possible date, in order to obtain coverage under the
policy in force when the insured learns of the potential claim (because
such claims are likely to be excluded under any subsequent policy). In addition, the exclusions and related policy provisions make it less likely that
an insured will have access to multiple policy limits to settle shareholder
litigation.

Third, the insured versus insured exclusion withholds insurance proceeds for losses stemming from litigation between insured parties, such
as directors suing the corporation or the officers or the corporation suing
an officer or director.[29] Like the family member exclusion in homeown-

ers' insurance policies, the purpose is to avoid collusive litigation.[30] In the D&O context, however, the insured versus insured exclusion would seem to raise an interpretive difficulty since derivative actions technically are actions of the corporation (an insured party) against its directors (another insured party). D&O policies solve this problem by carving derivative litigation out of the exclusion, with the result that the insured versus insured provision operates to exclude from coverage only those actions that are willfully maintained by insured persons.

Finally, the market-segmentation exclusions remove claims that are covered by other kinds of insurance—such as environmental claims,[31] Employee Retirement Income Security Act claims,[32] claims alleging bodily injury or emotional distress,[33] and claims arising from service to other organizations[34]—from the scope of coverage, leaving shareholder litigation as the principal covered risk.[35]

As already noted, these exclusions do not have much effect on the typical shareholder claim, as important as the exclusions may be to the coverage rights of individual managers or corporations in some cases. Most shareholder litigation avoids the fraud exclusion either on the basis of the actual adjudication language or on the basis of the plaintiffs' attorneys' artful pleading. As long as the claim is promptly noticed, the timing exclusions will have no effect, and given the fact that shareholders are the plaintiffs, neither will the insured versus insured exclusion. Policy exclusions, in other words, are not typically a substantial obstacle to the transfer of shareholder litigation risk from defendant corporations to D&O insurers (as significant as those exclusions might be in the context of specific cases).

The Market for D&O Insurance

The public company D&O market that we researched has sophisticated parties on both the buyer's and the seller's side of the transaction, each with legal counsel at their disposal. In addition, expert intermediaries—specialized D&O insurance brokers—facilitate the transactions. It is worth taking a few moments to discuss the roles of the various participants in the transaction: corporate buyers, insurance company sellers, and insurance brokers.

As already noted, our research is focused on publicly traded corporations—generally the largest and richest businesses in America. Thus, as

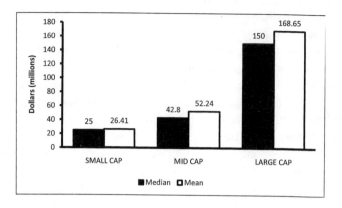

FIGURE 3.1. Annual D&O limits by market capitalization category. The data in this figure are derived from Towers Perrin 2008, 34.

buyers of D&O insurance, we expect most public corporations to have some insurance expertise in-house and also to be well advised by outside lawyers or consultants. The in-house expert on D&O insurance—and all other lines of corporate insurance—typically is the corporation's risk manager, a management position that reports to the treasurer or chief financial officer. As we describe below, however, decisions on D&O insurance and assistance in the marketing of the company to prospective underwriters often involve the firm's legal department and top-level management.

The amount of D&O insurance purchased correlates with the market capitalization of the corporate buyer. This is not surprising because a company's exposure to loss from shareholder litigation is highly correlated with the company's market capitalization. What shareholders have to lose is the value of their shares, and market capitalization is nothing more than the value of all the outstanding shares of a company. According to the Towers Perrin survey, in 2007, small-cap companies—defined here as those with market capitalizations between $400 million and $1 billion—purchased an average of $26.41 million in D&O coverage limits.[36] Mid-cap companies—those with market capitalizations between $1 billion and $10 billion—purchased an average of $42.8 million in limits.[37] And large-cap companies—those with market capitalization in excess of $10 billion—purchased an average of $168.65 million in D&O coverage. Average limits by market capitalization, along with median limits, are summarized in Figure 3.1.

The largest available coverage limit mentioned by the participants in our study was $300 million.[38] And we were told that, in general, insurers prefer not to underwrite the entire limit purchased by any one corporation, especially for the high-limit policies purchased by large- and mid-cap companies. Our participants reported that $50 million was the largest limit available in the late-1990s from a single insurer and noted that, in the late-2005 market, few insurance carriers were offering a policy larger than $25 million and that most policies had limits of $10 million or less.[39] As a result of these constraints, corporations must purchase several D&O policies in order to reach the aggregate amount of insurance they desire. D&O insurance packages are thus said to come in "towers"—that is, separate layers of insurance policies stacked to reach a desired total amount of coverage.

The bottom layer of a D&O tower is called the "primary policy," and the insurance company offering that policy is referred to as the "primary insurer." Primary insurers have the closest relationship with the policyholder. Because the primary insurer's policy is the first to respond to a covered loss and therefore is the most likely to incur a payment obligation, the primary insurer charges a higher premium than those higher up in the tower of coverage. The market for primary insurance was dominated by a small number of companies during the period of our research, most significantly AIG and Chubb.[40]

What will happen to AIG's large market share in the D&O business following the failure of the AIG holding company is an interesting side question that remains very much open. By most accounts, AIG's D&O and other insurance businesses are sound,[41] but some buyers may prefer to move their business to another company out of an excess of caution. Additionally, industry insiders report that some key AIG personnel have moved to other companies and that there has been at least one D&O insurance start-up that principally employs former AIG D&O insurance professionals.

After the primary policy is used up ("exhausted" in the language of the trade), excess insurers—those higher up in the coverage tower—become responsible for covered losses on a layer-by-layer basis as the limits of each underlying policy are successively exhausted by the payment of losses. Excess policies typically are sold on a "following-form" basis, meaning that the contract terms (other than limits and price) in the excess policy are the same as those in the underlying policy. Because all excess policies are less likely to respond to a covered loss than the

primary policy, and each successive layer of excess insurance is less likely
to respond to a claim than the layer immediately beneath it, the premiums
associated with excess policies are lower the higher the policy is situated in
the tower of coverage. As a result, the total premium that a corporate insured pays for its D&O coverage will be a blended amount of several distinct
premiums paid to separate insurance companies. The higher the limits a
corporation buys, the more companies that are likely to make up the tower
of coverage.

Brokers assemble these towers of coverage. The D&O market, like the
corporate insurance market generally, is a brokered market. The largest
retail insurance brokers—Marsh, Aon, Willis, and other national or large
regional brokers—have in-house D&O specialists, while smaller brokerage firms may use a specialist wholesale broker (a broker's broker) to shop
for and assemble a client's D&O coverage. A substantial role for brokers
in the D&O market seems inescapable as a result of (1) the nonuniform
nature of D&O insurance policies, (2) the need to assemble a tower of
coverage from the policies of many different insurance companies, and
(3) the need for a trusted intermediary to convey information between
buyer and seller.

Rounding out our list of the main participants in the D&O market are
reinsurers. Not every D&O insurer uses reinsurance—our participants reported, in fact, that at least some of the market leaders did not use it at all
during the period of our study—but many do. Our participants reported
that most of the leading global and domestic reinsurance companies active
in the U.S. liability insurance market have provided D&O reinsurance in
the recent past and that D&O reinsurance is also offered by some Lloyd's
syndicates and by several of the newer, Bermuda-based reinsurers.

Reinsurers insure the risks undertaken by insurance companies, effectively providing a further means of risk-spreading. D&O reinsurance, like
reinsurance generally, may be provided on either a treaty or a facultative basis. In treaty reinsurance, the reinsurer assumes a portion of all
risks underwritten by the insurer within a defined category, such as public
company D&O, and therefore evaluates the insurer's risk portfolio as a
whole. In facultative reinsurance, the reinsurers assume a portion of a
particular policy and therefore underwrite each risk individually, typically
on an excess-of-loss basis. Reinsurance also provides new entrants with
an easy means of accessing the D&O insurance market and established
insurers with a quick means of increasing their D&O exposure. Similarly,
the easiest way for an insurance company to reduce its D&O exposure

without eliminating existing customers is to reinsure a larger share of its business.

Market Cycles

No description of the D&O insurance market would be complete without some mention of the insurance underwriting cycle. For reasons that have yet to be fully explained, insurance markets follow a boom and bust pattern that is similar to, but not closely correlated with, other business cycles.[42]

More specifically, the underwriting cycle refers to the tendency of premiums and restrictions on coverage and underwriting to rise and fall as insurers tighten their standards in response to the loss of capital or, alternately, loosen their standards in order to maintain or grow market share when new capital enters the market. The tightening of underwriting standards accompanies a "hard market" in which premiums and, eventually, underwriting profits rise. Increased underwriting profits, of course, spur competition, whether from new entrants or established companies seeking to increase market share, and competition leads to another "soft market" of loosening of underwriting standards and declining profits. Industry participants describe this process as cyclical because, in their understanding, each market condition contains the seed to generate the other.[43] Among some insurance economists, the use of the term "cycle" is controversial because economists have not succeeded in creating a satisfactory model for explaining the boom and bust pattern. Nevertheless, we will use that term because that is how our participants talk about their business environment.

All aspects of underwriting are affected by the cycle. In a hard market, underwriters become more selective, less interested in offering insurance in the lower layers of coverage, less willing to offer high limits, less willing to negotiate contract terms, and able to command dramatically higher prices for less coverage. The D&O insurance market went through this hard phase in the mid-1980s and again in 2001–2003. More recently, the D&O insurance market has been shifting to the soft phase,[44] although the recent rise in shareholder litigation following the collapse of the U.S. stock market may permit D&O insurers to raise their prices.

The underwriting cycle has significant consequences for our research. Because of the cycle, no snapshot of the underwriting process can present an adequate basis for understanding insurance underwriting over time.

Our snapshot of the underwriting process took place at a transition period when the underwriting practices of the hard market were largely still in place but prices were beginning to soften. Although we tried to compensate for this snapshot by asking our participants to take a historical view, and not to focus only on the very recent past, it is possible that our research overemphasizes practices more prevalent in a particular phase of the underwriting cycle.[45] In a soft market, for example, D&O insurers may be less selective and may give discounts that reduce the risk-based differences among insureds.

This chapter has reviewed the form and function of D&O insurance, describing the structure both of D&O policies and of the D&O market. Before we move on to consider in greater detail one of the puzzles that has emerged from this discussion—the corporate purchase of side B and C or entity-level coverage—we ought first to look back and consider how the typical shareholder claims we discussed in the last chapter would be covered under a typical D&O policy. First, our prototypical shareholder claim—a 10b-5 class action alleging fraud on the market—would certainly be covered under a typical policy. Unless the company was insolvent, side A of the policy would not be implicated, but side B would cover the corporation's indemnification obligations to directors and officers named in the suit, while side C would cover the corporation's own expenses as a defendant. Second, most fiduciary duty claims would also be covered, with the exception that if the underlying shareholder claim is a derivative suit, the settlement must be funded by side A of the policy. Third, as we discussed above, exclusions will not apply to the typical shareholder claim, although they may apply to bar payment of certain types of claims, such as those involving restitutionary damages for unjust enrichment, as we discuss in greater detail in chapter 9.

CHAPTER FOUR

The Puzzle of Entity-Level D&O Coverage

As we described in chapter 3, D&O policies provide individual-level coverage for directors and officers (side A) and entity-level coverage for the corporation itself (sides B and C), and the vast majority of corporations purchase both kinds of protection. The individual-level coverage is easy to understand as a function of the risk aversion of individual directors and officers. Without insurance, such individuals would either decline to serve or would tend to put protecting themselves from litigation risk ahead of shareholder wealth maximization in their corporate decision making. From the firm's perspective, neither alternative is palatable, and thus the corporation provides them with individual coverage.

Coverage for the corporate entity, however, presents a puzzle. The entity-level aspect of D&O insurance spreads the risk of shareholder litigation from the corporation itself to a third-party insurer. The insurer, of course, does not assume this risk for free, but rather charges the corporation a premium that represents an actuarially determined probability of loss plus a loading fee to compensate the insurer for its efforts. Indeed, an insurance premium can be understood as the sum of the expected claim payment under the insurance contract plus the administrative expenses of the insurance company plus a reward to the insurer for bearing the risk, these latter two additions constituting the "loading" of the contract.[1] Loading fees mean that the cost of buying insurance always exceeds the actuarial probability of loss (otherwise the insurer would go out of business).

The loading of D&O contracts is difficult to assess with precision, given the absence of publicly available data, but insiders have estimated loading costs to be between 20 and 30 percent of the total premium.[2] This estimate is in line with the loading costs of the larger category of liability insurance within which the D&O insurance data are included in the financial reports that all insurance companies in the United States must file with their state insurance regulators.

Even if it is significantly more costly than simply bearing the risk, insurance may nevertheless constitute a wise investment for those with no other means of spreading the risk of loss. But the owners of corporations—the shareholders—have another, cheaper way to spread the risk of loss. They can hold a diversified portfolio of investments.

The basic lesson of modern portfolio theory is that shareholders can eliminate idiosyncratic risk—that is, firm-specific losses not simultaneously experienced by other firms in the market—by holding a diversified investment portfolio.[3] Because the risk of shareholder litigation is idiosyncratic, attaching to a specific firm and not the market generally, it is one of the risks that can be managed through diversification. Although it may be the case that shareholder litigation tends to arise in particular market situations—the deflation of a bubble, for example—it is not the case that every firm in the market at such times becomes a subject of shareholder litigation. Rather, the underlying events leading to shareholder litigation—misrepresentation or fraud—are largely specific to individual firms and therefore diversifiable. What this means is that corporate D&O coverage—sides B and C of the D&O policy—amounts to an expensive way to spread a risk that investors can spread themselves simply by holding a diversified portfolio.

Why, then, do so many corporations buy entity-level coverage? Unless insurance offers some benefit other than mere risk spreading, the purchase of this part of the D&O coverage would appear to be a negative net present-value transaction.

Although the same "Why do they buy it?" question might be asked of a corporation with regard to its other insurance lines as well, such as general liability and property insurance, the question is particularly sharp for D&O insurance, for two reasons. First, most other kinds of insured corporate losses do not lead so directly to declines in share prices, so the ability of shareholders to obtain an alternate form of insurance for those losses by holding a diversified portfolio is not as salient. With D&O insurance, in contrast, the insured losses themselves consist of liabilities to shareholders from declines in share prices, which, apart from systemic risk (which insurance companies cannot manage either), are easily spread by holding a diversified portfolio.

Second, as we will explain in this chapter, D&O insurance presents a moral hazard concern that is less likely to be ameliorated by ordinarily prudent management than other kinds of insured corporate losses. For example, a manager who drives an insured company car will nevertheless avoid accidents out of the fear of being hurt or killed or of having his or her life otherwise disrupted as a result of the accident. Similarly, managers ordinarily will not want their factories to burn down, regardless of whether they are insured, because the fire will lead to business disruptions generally, not just to the cost of replacing the factory. The sorts of conduct that lead to shareholder litigation, however—most obviously, excessive risk taking or overly optimistic financial reporting—are potentially beneficial, and therefore desirable, to individual managers.

Moreover, the conduct that leads to property insurance, workers' compensation, and general liability insurance losses typically takes place at lower levels of a publicly traded corporation than the conduct that leads to shareholder litigation. As sociologists have reported, the lower the level at which the loss-creating behavior occurs in a corporation, the less reactive that risk is to the presence or absence of insurance and, thus, the less moral hazard that the insurance creates.[4] Lower level employees benefit less directly from the insurance, and the corporation has more ways to discipline them. By contrast, D&O insurance claims concern the behavior of the most senior employees in the corporation; these employees benefit directly from the coverage, and they have the greatest control over the corporation. For these reasons, entity-level D&O insurance coverage poses a greater moral hazard and thereby demands a stronger offsetting benefit for its purchase than ordinary corporate property and casualty insurance.

This chapter explores these issues. We begin by exploring the moral hazard problem in greater detail as it applies to D&O insurance. Then we review the standard economic explanations offered for the purchase of corporate insurance, finding that, although these accounts may work well in other insurance contexts, the purchase of entity-level D&O insurance coverage remains problematic. Next we describe what our participants told us they think they are buying when they shop for D&O coverage and, in particular, why they buy the entity-level coverage. Finally, we offer an explanation for the purchase of that coverage drawn from our interviews that focuses on agency costs within the corporation.

The Moral Hazard Problem

We introduced the concept of moral hazard above to refer to the tendency of insurance to increase loss by reducing an insured's incentive to take care to avoid loss. In this section, we discuss moral hazard in greater detail and describe why it is a particular problem in the context of corporate D&O coverage.

The economic analysis of insurance teaches that insurance increases loss whenever the following conditions are met: (1) money compensates for loss, (2) the decision makers are rational loss minimizers, (3) taking care requires effort, (4) taking care is effective, (5) the beneficiaries of the insurance have control over the care-taking activity, and (6) insurance payments are not conditioned on a given level of care.[5] In many other contexts, there are good reasons to doubt that insurance poses a real moral hazard problem because one or more of these conditions are not satisfied. For example, an increase in workers' compensation benefits may not lead to greater on-the-job carelessness since money does not fully compensate workers for bodily injury and workers do not fully control their working environment. By contrast, D&O insurance meets all six of these conditions.

First, in the context of D&O insurance—unlike, for example, automobile accident insurance—most losses are monetary and can therefore be compensated by money. Extreme misconduct may lead to criminal penalties that cannot be insured, and managers may suffer reputational harm—by, for example, lowering their social status and their future employability—that monetary reimbursement cannot compensate. Nevertheless, these consequences do not follow from most acts that give rise to a D&O claim. For the typical D&O claim, the damages demanded by the shareholder plaintiffs represent the only loss seriously at issue. Second, corporate decisions are conventionally regarded as rational, and the incentive effects of liability are, in any event, predicated on that assumption. Third, effort is required to implement corporate governance controls, comply with securities laws, manage loss costs, and otherwise take care. Fourth, such efforts help prevent loss. Good corporate governance ought to correlate to fewer and less costly claims—whether, in fact, it does is a subject we discuss at greater length in chapter 5—and, governance controls aside, the cost of shareholder litigation can be controlled by managing defense costs once a claim has arisen. Fifth, the directors and officers who directly benefit from the insurance are in charge of the corporation and, thus, control the care-taking activity. And finally, as we will discuss in chapter

6, D&O insurers do not condition their coverage on the insured's level of care.

We are not suggesting that D&O insurers do nothing to protect against moral hazard. In fact, they do three things. First, they leave some of the risk on the corporation. Side B and C coverage has deductibles. In a survey conducted by a leading actuarial firm, corporations with $50 to $100 million in assets report median and mean deductibles of approximately $200,000 and $246,000, respectively. By contrast, corporations with over $10 billion in assets report median and mean deductibles of $2.4 million and $5.5 million.[6] Moreover, corporations do face residual liability in the rare but serious event that the settlement amount exceeds the limits of the coverage. As a result of these deductibles and limits, insurance protection is incomplete, maintaining at least some incentive to prevent loss. Yet these deductibles are small in relation to a serious loss under a D&O insurance policy and thus are unlikely to have a significant impact on corporate behavior. These deductibles are larger in comparison with defense costs, yet our participants report that they are not sufficient to encourage corporations to exercise defense cost control, as we discuss in chapter 6. If deductibles do not encourage corporations to exercise control over defense costs at a time when a claim has already occurred, they are unlikely to encourage corporations to take significant measures to prevent a claim that may or may not occur at some point in the future.

The incentive effect of the residual liability is harder to evaluate. Relatively few settlements exceed the available insurance policy limits, but some exceed those limits by a very substantial margin. The deterrent impact of that residual liability depends on the degree to which the conduct that leads to the relatively few massive shareholder claims differs in kind from that which leads to more routine shareholder claims. Our sense is that the truly massive settlements occur in cases in which the managers violated ordinary, business-as-usual norms by a very substantial margin, and thus the fear of residual corporate liability, or criminal liability, most likely does not deter managers who engage in more ordinary financial misreporting. But this would be a worthy subject for more research.

Second, the D&O policy contains a moral hazard exclusion: the fraud exclusion against liability based on a "any deliberately dishonest, malicious or fraudulent act or omission."[7] But, as we described in chapter 3, the wording of the typical D&O policy limits the scope of this exclusion, making it a much less effective means of policing the conduct of the insured than it might at first seem to be. Moreover, our participants confirmed that the fraud exclusion almost never operates to allow a D&O insurer to avoid coverage; even in an egregious case there will be some covered officers and directors whose conduct was sufficiently wrongful to serve as a basis for liability but not so wrongful that it meets the requirements of the fraud exclusion. For example, D&O insurers paid out their limits for claims involving Enron, the poster child for fraud, notwithstanding the eventual criminal convictions of several officers.

Third, as we shall describe in chapter 7, D&O insurance companies do have some control over settlements, with the result that the corporation cannot simply hand money to plaintiffs to make them go away. But strikingly, D&O insurers do not control the defense of claims; they essentially hand a blank check to their corporate insureds to cover defense costs. Defense costs do count against the limits of the policy—thereby reducing the amount available to settle the claim—but the fact that most claims settle well within the total limits of the D&O insurance program suggests that this "defense within limits" feature does not constrain defense costs in most cases. Moreover, as we shall see, the control exerted by D&O insurers over settlement is far from complete.

The failure of these three mechanisms by which insurers might control moral hazard suggests that there remains significant risk of moral hazard in D&O insurance. Insurers of course can account for this risk by regularly repricing the insurance, as indeed they do in the annual policy renewal. Repricing allows the insurer to take any increased hazard (moral or otherwise) into account. Moreover, pricing might itself constrain managerial misconduct. Nevertheless, for reasons we discuss in detail in chapter 5, we suspect that pricing alone is insufficient to change managerial conduct. As a result, regular repricing at best compensates insurers for the increased risk—moral hazard—that the insurance itself creates but fails to provide the serious check on the conduct of management that shareholder litigation is meant to effect.

All of this suggests that D&O insurance does not simply distribute the risk of legally compensable investment losses. Instead, D&O insurance likely increases those losses and, because of the comparatively unmanaged moral hazard in the defense of claims, almost certainly increases the overall cost of those losses. While it is possible to accept this additional cost with regard to the individual coverage of side A owing to the risk aversion of individuals, other explanations are needed for the purchase of the corporate coverage in sides B and C of the typical D&O policy. We begin to explore these explanations in the sections that follow.

Attempted Solutions to the Corporate Insurance Puzzle

The availability of risk spreading through investment diversification has prompted several economists, starting with Mayers and Smith, to seek to solve the puzzle of corporate insurance.[8] Their explanations include (1) tax benefits, (2) bankruptcy transaction costs, (3) credit costs, (4) the cost of external capital relative to internal capital, (5) monitoring services, and (6) protecting investors. As we will demonstrate, these rationales may explain why corporations purchase other forms of insurance, but they cannot adequately explain the purchase of corporate D&O coverage, particularly in its current, pure risk-spreading form.

Tax Savings

The tax benefits of corporate insurance turn on the favorable treatment of market insurance over self-insurance. An insurance premium is a deductible business expense. By contrast, funds put into a reserve are not deductible, and the income earned on those funds is taxable. Losses that actually occur also are deductible business expenses,[9] but these losses are uncertain and in the future. As a result, the tax benefits of deducting an insurance premium today are greater than those of deducting an uncertain amount of similar expected value in the future.[10] Moreover, funds that the insurance company puts into reserves are deductible business expenses; as a result, the insurance company can accumulate funds more cheaply than a corporation and pass these savings along to insureds.

These tax savings make the insurance less expensive to the corporate purchaser than it would otherwise be, but they do not make the insurance free.[11] By contrast, the insurance provided by a diversified portfolio is essentially free. Moreover, the tax savings created by the purchase of D&O insurance must account not only for the higher cost of the insurance relative to diversification but also for the increased risk of moral hazard from the corporate coverage. As a result, we doubt that tax savings alone justify the purchase of entity-level D&O coverage.

Bankruptcy Savings

The bankruptcy explanation turns on the fact that bankruptcy risk leads a corporation's contracting partners to increase their prices. Measures that reduce the risk of bankruptcy therefore have cost-saving benefits across a wide range of corporate activity.[12] Bankruptcy costs are unlikely to explain the corporate protection aspect of D&O insurance, however, because the D&O insurance programs we observed cannot credibly make the difference between a firm going bankrupt and remaining solvent. A corporation seeking bankruptcy protection would have high limits because it is only the very rare massive claim that threatens most corporations' solvency, not the more routine securities class action. By contrast, D&O insurance programs have low limits relative to worst-case scenario losses. As the risk manager of a very large Fortune 500 company explained to us, "[T]he most we could purchase for the corporate side was in the 200 to absolute maximum 300 million available. I mean our balance sheet is billions of dollars. . . . [E]xcess of 300 million or whatever insurance we could buy, we were self-insuring that."[13] By contrast, insurance limits of $1 billion or more are relatively common in the property and general liability insurance programs of large corporations. It thus appears, from this structure of coverage, that corporate managers are not buying D&O insurance to protect shareholders from bankruptcy costs. (Of course, corporate managers do buy D&O insurance to protect themselves from the corporation's bankruptcy; one of the main functions of side A coverage is to protect the directors' and officers' assets in the event of bankruptcy.)

Credit Costs

Creditors may lend at preferential rates to insured borrowers. Just as mortgage lenders insist that borrowers maintain a homeowner's insurance policy, secured creditors will typically demand that corporate borrowers purchase insurance covering pledged assets. Moreover, Mayers and Smith have also demonstrated that even unsecured creditors would prefer to lend to an insured corporation since a significant uninsured loss destroys equity and therefore increases the debt-to-equity ratio of the firm, giving rise to a situation Mayers and Smith refer to as the "underinvestment problem."[14] In this situation, new investment would benefit bondholders, not shareholders, but since shareholders control the firm, the corporation will not make the investment, even if it has a positive net present value. Corporate insurance solves this problem because it reduces the impact of the loss on the debt-to-equity ratio of the firm. As a result, even unsecured creditors will grant better terms to a corporation with insurance, especially if that corporation is highly leveraged.

These reduced credit costs may offset insurance loading costs in some highly leveraged corporations. But, once again, these benefits are unlikely to explain the preference for corporate D&O coverage. Because D&O insurance limits are so low relative to the potential loss, it is hard to see how creditors would place much weight on the presence or absence of such insurance. Indeed, because of the agency cost explanation that we explore shortly, it could well be argued that creditors should prefer to lend to companies without entity-level D&O insurance coverage.

Costs of External Capital

Of course, public corporations engage in a variety of hedging transactions, despite the ability of investors to diversify. Insurance is one such strategy. An important additional reason to engage in such hedging strategies, identified by Froot, Scharfstein, and Stein, focuses on the costs of raising external capital.[15] Because going into the market to raise capital is typically more costly than generating investment capital internally, and because a corporation's ability to generate capital is limited by its cash flow, corporations may not be able to self-fund capital shocks.[16] The comparative advantage of internal capital over external capital means that it can be rational for a corporation to act as if it were risk averse and, thus, to engage in precautionary saving and other risk management techniques undertaken by individuals because of their risk aversion. This is not because corporations necessarily face a declining marginal utility of money (although they may, if we assume prioritization of investment opportunities), but rather because corporations face greater costs of external capital, particularly in times of distress. Insurance solves this problem by guaranteeing a source of capital at a time when cash flows may not be adequate and when the firm will not be able to enter the external capital market on advantageous terms.

We think that this explanation may have substantial force in the D&O insurance context. After all, who wants to invest in a firm that has just been made a defendant in a shareholder class action? The cost of external capital will be higher in this context for the same reasons that create what Professor Park has called the "credibility decline" aspect of the overall decline in a corporation's securities following the revelation of securities fraud. As he explains, "[A]fter a fraud is revealed, the market may no longer trust the corporation's management to tell the truth."[17] If so, the cost of raising capital to pay for the settlement of the securities class action will be higher than raising a comparable amount of capital would have been in the absence of the fraud. Thus, to the extent that the cost of entity-level D&O coverage is less than the additional costs of raising capital externally, the purchase of entity-level coverage adds value to the corporation.

Viewed in this way, the purpose of the entity-level coverage is to protect the corporation from borrowing on disadvantageous terms once a securities claim has arisen. Instead, the funds are promised from an insurer on a clear day when there is no loss on the horizon. We are sympathetic to this account of D&O insurance, but the moral hazard problem raises doubts as to its cost-effectiveness. To the extent that buying the insurance increases the likelihood of a securities class action (in other words, to the extent that the insurance creates a moral hazard), the capital cost reduction benefits of the insurance are reduced. Adding this—admittedly speculative—moral hazard cost to the demonstrably significant loading cost of the insurance leads us to the intuitive conclusion that the entity-level parts of D&O insurance are unlikely to satisfy the Froot, Scharfstein, and Stein analysis. But we would be the first to point out that this is an empirical question that our research methods do not allow us to answer. What we can report is that no one has yet produced this kind of empirical justification for D&O insurance. Moreover, D&O insurance is not sold on this basis. Instead, it is sold—as the name implies—as a way to protect directors and officers.

Monitoring

Economists have also theorized that shareholders or other corporate stakeholders might want the corporation to purchase insurance because the corporation may not have the economy of scale needed to develop loss-prevention or loss-management expertise. Mayers and Smith refer to this as the "real service efficiencies" of insurance.[18] Unfortunately, in the D&O context, this hypothesis is not supported by the central empirical finding reported in chapter 6—namely, that insurers do not in fact monitor their corporate insureds, either through loss-prevention efforts ex ante or through claims management ex post. Demand for monitoring thus cannot explain the purchase of D&O insurance.

Were D&O insurance pricing and contract terms publicly disclosed, the corporate governance component of D&O insurance prices could serve a monitoring role, for reasons that we will describe in detail in the next chapter. Of course, insurance premiums are not publicly disclosed, so this potential monitoring cannot explain the purchase of corporate D&O

insurance at present. It does, however, provide a strong foundation for forcing companies to disclose their D&O premiums and other coverage details, as we argue in chapter 10.

Protecting Investors

If diversified shareholders can eliminate the risk of shareholder litigation by holding a diversified portfolio, perhaps the entity-level D&O insurance is still necessary to protect undiversified investors. After all, not all investors hold the market portfolio. Those who do not might prefer the protection offered by D&O coverage. Perhaps, but it is a tortured interpretation of fiduciary duty that would have directors seek to maximize shareholder welfare by purchasing high-cost insurance against a risk that some shareholders have already eliminated and that all shareholders could eliminate. Those who do not eliminate the risk have either chosen not to or are too unsophisticated to recognize the choice. It is laudable to seek to help unsophisticated investors, but imposing this partial, inefficient, and narrowly targeted cross subsidy on the rest of the market seems an inappropriate way of doing so.[19]

With regard to investors who have chosen to be undiversified, professors Goshen and Parchomovsky and, separately, Fisch have offered a defense of the compensation rationale that applies to "information traders" who invest in acquiring information about companies and trading on that information.[20] As Professor Fisch has explained, "[I]nformed traders are a critical component of the market that enables mandated disclosure to serve as a corporate governance mechanism."[21] Because informed traders explicitly rely on the corporation's disclosures, they are disproportionately harmed when those disclosures are inaccurate. Moreover, because they must target their purchases in order to recoup their investments in information, they are not protected by the insurance that diversification provides.

We find this justification for compensating information traders compelling, but we doubt that it provides an adequate explanation or justification for the D&O coverage that presently exists. To begin with, the existing D&O coverage protects all shareholders in the shareholders class action equally, and thus the bulk of the insurance benefits almost certainly accrue to people who are not information traders. For information traders who have sold all their shares and now seek only compensation, corporate D&O coverage would increase that compensation only in cases in which the corporation is insolvent; even then, side A only coverage would provide the same compensation benefits as long as some officers and directors were individually liable. Moreover, securities class action settlements compensate all traders poorly relative to their losses, making D&O insurance an expensive and very incomplete form of insurance for information traders. Indeed, we suspect these traders would be better off engaging in their own hedging transactions to limit the riskiness of their equity positions. Thus, for all of these reasons, we doubt that information traders would conclude that the entity-level parts of D&O insurance, in light of its costs, are in fact in their best interests.

If the damages rules for securities fraud were changed so that the damages would go primarily to information traders, we would reconsider this analysis. However, because such a change, in spite of its economic rationality, would produce a political aberration—effectively directing settlement dollars away from retirees, pension funds, and other diversified holders and toward hedge funds and other speculative traders—we view its possible enactment rather darkly. Nevertheless, as Professor Fisch points out, the Supreme Court might be able to accomplish the same result by changing its approach to reliance in securities class actions.[22] Were this to occur, we would happily revisit some of the arguments in this section of the book.

Why Don't More Firms Buy Only Side A Coverage?

If the side B and C parts of D&O insurance are problematic for all the reasons we have outlined above, we would expect fewer corporations to purchase them, and we would expect more corporations to buy what is known as pure side A coverage—insurance that protects the directors and officers only in the event that the corporation is unable to indemnify them. In addition to potentially providing a better deal for shareholders, side A coverage offers at least three tangible benefits to directors and officers. First, because most D&O claims are indemnifiable and side A coverage only responds to nonindemnifiable losses, the insurance for the individual insureds will not be eroded by corporate losses. Second, because there is no corporate benefit from side A coverage, there is no risk that a bankruptcy trustee will attempt to deprive directors and officers of the benefits of the insurance in the event of a bankruptcy.[23] Finally, insurers may offer side A coverage without the same carve outs and exclusions as traditional

A-B-C coverage.[24] Nevertheless, the vast majority of public companies continue to buy side B and C coverage.

There are, however, exceptions—corporations that do indeed purchase only side A coverage. The Tillinghast/Towers Perrin D&O Survey reports that approximately one-third of all public companies purchase additional side A limits on top of their traditional A-B-C policies (32 percent in 2007, compared with 38 percent in 2006), while only 2 percent of their respondents purchased side A only policies.[25] Interestingly, however, those companies purchasing side A only coverage tended to be the largest companies in their sample—that is, those with market capitalizations in excess of $10 billion. Moreover, we happened across one such large market capitalization corporation purchasing side A only coverage in our interviews and pursued the subject in a detailed conversation with the company's risk manager, who described his company's approach to D&O coverage as having "evolved from protecting our balance sheet to protecting the individual D&O balance sheets."[26] In the course of our conversation, he indicated that he well understood that his company was the exception to the rule. In his words,

> [P]robably 25 percent or maybe even less of the large corporate buyers have evolved to [side A only coverage]. And again, . . . this is a relatively recent . . . occurrence for us. If you look in the rearview mirror, four years ago we were buying insurance similar to the way a lot of our peers still buy it, which is . . . A, B, C coverages.[27]

In other words, his firm—a major Fortune 500 company—had previously purchased entity coverage and had changed to buying side A only coverage.

We found this exception to be particularly instructive and pursued the conversation in some detail, first exploring the reasons for his company's shift away from entity-level coverage. He offered several reasons, including the erosion of the value of the coverage through bad actors and the inability of his corporation to purchase limits adequate to cover its possible exposure. As he described it, "the value of the B and C coverage was not nearly as great because . . . the size of the limits that [we] were purchasing didn't really protect our [balance sheet] adequately."[28] The shift in value was brought about, in his view, by a shift in the way in which shareholder claims were being brought and in the way in which they were being paid. In his words,

What precipitated this? Enron, WorldCom, . . . all the D&O things that were going on. If you go back and you look in the press and you talk to people in the industry, what was the value of the insurance that was being purchased, and how was it being eroded? It was being . . . eroded by bad guys and the potential for corporate indemnification. You know, it became an issue as to who was first in the door looking to have their claims paid. So the bad guys were getting their claims paid—because they had defense costs—by outside insurers. There were quite a few bad guys that were eroding the good guys' insurance, and then there was the idea, you know, coming out of some of those major financial meltdowns, that . . . these policies are assets of the corporation [and therefore at play in a bankruptcy proceeding], when in fact the original intent of D&O insurance was to protect directors and officers, not the corporation. . . . We basically said we are going to go back to its original purpose.[29]

He went on, further describing the issues then under consideration:

There were certainly pricing pressures, and when we review our coverages up with the board and the finance committee of the board, you know, we do have price in there, but I don't think it was a price issue. I really think we went back to, what's the intention of the purchase of this insurance product? Who is it protecting? And how do we get the most value out of it for those individuals?[30]

In light of this conversation, we found the rarity of side A only coverage particularly puzzling. We thus continued to press our other respondents on why they bought D&O insurance to cover the corporate entity. As we describe below, the explanations we received tended to focus on a perceived mispricing of side A only insurance or on the greater value our respondents attached to side B and C coverage. In the sections that follow, we reject the mispricing explanation and ultimately offer our own explanation, culled from our interviews with D&O professionals, for what really is going on in the purchase of entity-level coverage.

Mispricing?

Several of the participants in our study reported that corporations do not buy side A only policies because those policies are too expensive relative to the protection that is provided and the additional cost of purchasing side B and C coverage is less than the marginal benefit of entity-level coverage. They suggested, in other words, that the discount offered for side A only coverage is not large enough. Following the numerical example offered by one of the risk managers we interviewed, if 85 percent of claims paid are under sides B and C of a traditional insurance policy, the price for equal limits under a side A only policy should be approximately 15 percent of the cost of a traditional A-B-C package.[31] Side A only coverage, however, is not offered at this discounted price. Indeed, our respondents reported that the discount offered for side A only coverage does not compensate the corporation for the forgone coverage. In their words, "the credit that you get for dropping [B and C side coverage] is not worth what you are actually getting if you are losing coverage."[32]

Most of the risk managers in our study supported this explanation. When asked why his firm purchases side B and C coverage, one responded,

> [W]e evaluate it every year. But I would say that . . . maybe 70–80 percent of large companies still do the A, B, and C. We have heard of a few companies just going out and doing a side A, bankruptcy protection. . . . [B]ut we haven't seen it done, because when it all comes down to it, you know, you really are protecting the asset[s] of the corporation. . . . You could [buy side A only]. I am not arguing against that. It is a decision you truly go through each year. . . . And you think about it, but there is no patent answer for that. It depends on the price.[33]

Another replied,

> [F]rom my perspective as a risk manager, the reason why I buy side C coverage or I recommend that we buy it here is because I feel that it would be negligent not to buy it. . . . There is not enough credit for excluding it out of the policy. If there was, we would probably [not buy] it because philosophically we don't agree with the coverage.[34]

These answers support a view that the value of balance sheet protection to the corporation is greater than the cost of the coverage, at least when compared with the discount offered for buying a side A only policy.

Nevertheless, this is an odd explanation since it suggests a long-term failure in the market for side A only coverage. If it is true that the discount for purchasing side A only coverage is not commensurate with the insurer's reduced risk, why don't insurers sell side A only coverage for less? Is it because they want to discourage this line of coverage in order to maximize premium dollars? That would seem to be a losing strategy since a competing insurer could appropriately price side A coverage and thereby gain market share.

Moreover, given that shareholders can spread these risks costlessly (or nearly so) simply by holding a diversified portfolio, sides B and C coverages are really only a bargain if the insurer is essentially giving them away. Do insurance companies always get the pricing right? Clearly not.[35] But if insurance companies always underpriced the product, one would expect losses to drive them to abandon the product. Thus, although our research methods do not permit us to conclusively reject this explanation, we view it as a particularly weak explanation for entity-level coverage because it depends upon persistently irrational pricing by sophisticated companies in a competitive business with low barriers to entry.

Agency Costs

Having considered the various explanations for corporate insurance by economists and by our own respondents, the purchase of entity-level D&O insurance coverage remains problematic. Judging from the perspective of shareholder wealth maximization—the customary frame of reference for corporate law theorists—the entity-level coverage is difficult to justify. But perhaps the focus on shareholders has blinded us to a more basic reason for the purchase of this coverage—namely, agency costs.

Agency costs result from the divergence of interests of the firm's managers and its owners.[36] The purchase of entity-level D&O coverage fits the pattern of an agency-cost problem if there are some within the firm who view the purchase of side B and C coverage as a good investment regardless of how the decision ought to be viewed from the shareholders' perspective. Corporate managers, unlike shareholders, cannot eliminate the risk of shareholder litigation through diversification. After all, they only work at one firm, and if that firm is sued, they suffer. For these people, insurance may be the only available means to spread risk. Since these are the people in charge of making the insurance decision, they are likely to purchase insurance that is in their own best interests, rather than in the best interests of the shareholders.

We believe the agency-cost problem works better than any of the other explanations we have explored in explaining the pure risk distribution form of D&O insurance that we have observed. Indeed, we found that the agency-cost problem operates at two levels: first among senior managers and secondly among risk managers. We review each in turn.

Executive Agency Costs

Executives, unlike shareholders, are not able to avoid the idiosyncratic business risks generated by the firm they manage since their investment in human capital is not easily diversified. Their jobs and, perhaps more directly, their incentive pay packages remain at risk from shareholder litigation regardless of how many different corporations' stocks they hold in their individual investment portfolio. D&O losses thus threaten executives in two ways. First, large losses may push the firm toward insolvency (and lead to job loss) or, short of actual insolvency, may make the firm a takeover target (and lead to job loss). Insofar as it keeps shareholder litigation from pushing a firm to insolvency, corporate D&O insurance protects managers against this risk.

Second, even if the losses are not large enough to threaten the financial stability of the firm, losses may have a significant impact on accounting measures of performance and the compensation packages tied to those performance measures. An uninsured corporation that must suddenly pay millions of dollars to settle shareholder litigation may not go out of business, but it is likely not to make its numbers for one or more accounting periods. Buying side B and C D&O insurance coverage allows managers to avoid these shocks to the firm's accounting statements, essentially exchanging large but infrequent expected losses for a smaller, regular annual cost, thus reducing the volatility of corporate earnings. The entity-level coverage, in other words, is a form of earnings management. Managers buy it to protect their compensation and their jobs in spite of the fact that it may often be a negative net present-value investment for the corporation.

Moreover, when the managers select D&O insurance, the insurance they select does not provide monitoring. This too represents an agency cost. Buying D&O insurance without monitoring increases the freedom of managers to take financial reporting and other risks that improve accounting measures of performance and, hence, their compensation but not the long-term value of the firm. If these risks lead to shareholder litigation, D&O insurers step in to pay the claim.

Econometric research supports the agency-cost explanation for this corporate D&O coverage. John Chalmers and colleagues studied the relationship between the amount of D&O insurance purchased in connection with an initial public offering (IPO) and the later price of the stock that was offered, investigating the hypothesis that managers are willing to buy large amounts of D&O coverage at high premiums because they receive all of the benefits of the coverage but bear the costs only in proportion to their fractional ownership of the firm's equity.[37] They found a significant negative correlation between the three-year post-IPO stock price performance of the company and the amount of insurance that the company purchased just before issuing the IPO. They concluded that "managers choos[e] abnormally high D&O insurance coverage based on their belief that their shares are priced too high."[38]

Similarly, John Core studied the relationship between director pay and D&O insurance limits in Canadian firms, investigating the hypothesis that more entrenched managers are more likely to purchase D&O insurance.[39] Unlike U.S. firms, Canadian firms are legally required to disclose their D&O insurance limits. He found that "firms with higher excess director pay . . . are more likely to carry D&O insurance coverage and purchase higher limits," suggesting that managers bundle compensation and insurance because they do not internalize the cost of either.[40]

Risk Manager Agency Costs

Risk manager agency costs exist if the corporation's risk manager has an incentive to purchase D&O insurance notwithstanding the fact that such insurance may be a negative net present-value investment from the shareholders' point of view. The basis for this divergence in incentive is obvious: the risk manager may suffer adverse career consequences if he or she does not buy insurance against a loss that ex post seems costly to the firm. One of the risk managers in our study candidly suggested this explanation:

> I guarantee you that no matter what anybody says or anybody tells you, a big loss comes in to a company and it is 100, 200 [million]. You say . . . "I have bankruptcy protection over there, but . . . I don't have anything for [this 200 million thing against the company]" . . . So there is an element of making sure there is comprehensive protection.[41]

From a strictly ex post point of view, insurance against a significant loss may seem like a good idea even if the ex ante value of the insurance is less than its cost. If his or her superiors will tend to view loss from an ex post point of view, a risk manager may purchase D&O insurance in order to protect his or her own career regardless of the shareholders' preferences. This incentive is compounded if the organization is rife with the executive agency costs we just explored.

This emphasis on an ex post perspective and compounded incentives helps explain the nearly pure risk distribution form of existing D&O insurance, especially the absence of defense cost management. Managers and directors facing securities litigation prefer the maximum autonomy, blank-check approach to D&O insurance coverage and will not be pleased with a risk manager who agreed in advance to hand over the defense to an insurance company, even if that decision might have made sense from an ex ante perspective. The following excerpt from an interview with the head of the claims department in a leading D&O insurer illustrates this point:

> They got a D&O policy to pay for it, and the general counsel, the last g-d damn thing that he wants to do—excuse my language—is to walk into the CEO's office and say, "Oh, I cut their bill in half." The CEO is going to say, "Wait a second. In other words, I am not getting the best possible defense because you are pissing them off? Oh, I don't think so. You know, I've got a huge house in Greenwich. I want to keep that huge house. I've got the mistress. I've got the Mercedes. . . . Why the hell are we doing this?"[42]

We thus have happened upon an account that explains the prevailing form of D&O coverage but still does not justify it. Our essential story is simple enough: managers want corporate protection included in D&O insurance, shareholders don't, managers win. Not a cheerful story.

In order for shareholders to benefit from entity-level D&O coverage, there must be some benefit to the coverage other than pure risk distribution, which shareholders could accomplish more efficiently by themselves (leaving aside the information traders we addressed earlier). Although some plausible explanations have been suggested—including offsetting tax advantages and the benefits of low-cost contingent financing—every such explanation is only partial and ultimately proves unsatisfactory once the cost of the moral hazard of D&O insurance, as currently structured, is factored into the analysis. Indeed, none of these explanations accounts for the pure risk distribution form of D&O insurance that we observe. Any benefit offered by, for example, low-cost contingent financing must overcome not only the insurer's loading fees but also the cost of moral hazard.

Accordingly, within the economic framework that dominates research on insurance and corporate law and finance, we are therefore left with only one satisfactory explanation for the form of D&O insurance that we observe: agency costs. Managers do not want insurers monitoring their decisions ex ante, and they do not want them managing their defense ex post. Both monitoring and defense management would reduce managers' autonomy and, relatedly, their ability to profit at the shareholders' expense. Thus, our research strongly suggests that the prevailing form of D&O insurance benefits management at the expense of shareholders. Only firms that purchase side A only coverage, a relatively rare coverage package, are not susceptible to this charge.

CHAPTER FIVE

Pricing and Deterrence

The story we have related so far has largely been a theoretical one. In chapter 2 we outlined the legal framework governing shareholder litigation. In chapter 3 we introduced D&O insurance, describing the three parts of the customary insurance policy and the nature of the coverage. Then in chapter 4 we raised the foundational theoretical concern that undergirds our research: the possibility that D&O insurance undercuts the deterrence function of shareholder litigation, quite simply by paying for it.

We now turn to our empirical research, reporting the results of our efforts to evaluate whether, in fact, D&O insurance undercuts deterrence. Our efforts were focused on evaluating whether, and how, D&O insurers use the traditional tools of the insurance trade to offer liability insurance protection that facilitates, rather than undercuts, the deterrence function. In this chapter we explore the first opportunity for the D&O insurer to reintroduce the deterrence function of shareholder litigation: through the underwriting of D&O coverage. In the next chapter we will explore the second opportunity: monitoring the policyholder during the course of the insurance relationship. In chapters 7 and 8 we will explore the third opportunity, defense and settlement of shareholder claims. Then in chapter 9 we will explore the final opportunity, insurance coverage disputes.

During the process of underwriting, insurers decide which risks to cover and how much to charge for that coverage. If D&O insurers use a prospective insured's risk of incurring shareholder litigation to decide whom to insure and how much to charge for coverage, then these decisions will, in turn, have an effect on prospective insureds. For example, if insurers refuse to cover very high risk corporations—for example, corporations that follow extremely aggressive accounting or lax corporate governance practices—then these firms must either change their practices or go uninsured. Similarly, if insurers charge higher premiums to higher risk firms, then those firms must either alter their practices or face higher insurance costs. Thus, if insurers are successful in their underwriting, higher risk firms will pay systematically more for their D&O coverage than lower risk firms. The D&O premium, in other words, becomes the annualized present value of shareholder litigation risk for any particular corporation. Because D&O insurers pay for all or most shareholder claims, they have a great incentive to get that price right, and, in contrast to insurers who sell products sold to ordinary individual consumers, there are no regulatory restrictions on their ability to price the coverage as they see fit.

Paying higher costs for D&O coverage is like paying higher damages in shareholder litigation. Firms have an incentive to avoid both. In this way, the pricing of D&O insurance could reintroduce the deterrence function of shareholder litigation. Firms paying systematically more for D&O insurance than their competitors have a natural incentive to lower their risk of shareholder litigation. Simply put, the need to control costs in order to compete more effectively in product and capital markets ought to induce firms to improve their corporate governance, thus decreasing their risk of shareholder litigation and, with it, their D&O premiums. This incentive to improve conduct is the very meaning of deterrence. It arises from shareholder litigation and is preserved, even in an environment in which the risk of shareholder litigation is thoroughly insured through the pricing of D&O coverage.

This chapter collects evidence from our participants to explore whether the underwriting and pricing of D&O insurance preserves the deterrence function of shareholder litigation. It asks, first, Do insurers evaluate the riskiness of the insured in underwriting D&O insurance? If so, what risks do underwriters assess? What are their proxies for risk, and how do these coincide with traditional notions of shareholder litigation? Next it asks how insurers price risk and addresses the relevance of these findings for the question of deterrence.

Ultimately we conclude that, although D&O insurers do seek to price on the basis of risk, their efforts are unlikely to be sufficient to reinvigorate the deterrence function of shareholder litigation. All is not lost, however. As we will explain in chapter 10, D&O insurers' risk-based pricing would be much more effective at preserving the deterrence function of shareholder litigation if corporations were required to disclose their D&O insurance details.

Do Insurers Risk Rate in Underwriting D&O Insurance?

Across the spectrum of insurance products, insurance companies commonly charge different prices on the basis of risk for two simple reasons. First, the risk of loss of the entities seeking insurance coverage typically differs in observable ways, with the result that insurers have the ability to price on the basis of risk. Second, an insurer that does not price on the basis of risk will quickly find itself insuring the relatively high-risk—and therefore most expensive—entities in the pool, because its competitors will identify and pick off the low-risk entities by offering them slightly lower prices. Indeed, risk-based pricing can be a potent competitive tool. An insurer that finds a better way to classify risks gains an edge over the competition by simultaneously decreasing the average risk relative to price of the entities that it insures while increasing the average risk relative to price of the entities that its competitors insure. For this reason, it was hardly surprising that our respondents confirmed that screening and selecting risk is a key aspect of D&O insurance underwriting.

Underwriters spend considerable time and effort analyzing risk factors, and risk assessment was typically referred to as the critical judgment underlying all underwriting decisions. A senior reinsurance underwriter abbreviated the basic goals of the underwriting process with an acronym: SLAP—selection, limit, attachment, and pricing.[1] "Selection" refers to selecting which risks to insure and which risks not to insure. Underwriting involves picking and choosing among the many risks of firms seeking to purchase insurance at any one time. "Limit" refers to the amount of coverage any given insurer is willing to sell to a prospective insured. As we described in chapter 3, no single D&O insurer covers a company's entire risk, and so each insurer in deciding how much to offer in terms of limits determines how much or how little of its own capital to expose to the risk. "Attachment," similarly, refers to where in the tower of coverage an insurer's policy will attach. Is the insurer selling the primary policy or an excess policy? If it is an excess policy, where does coverage attach? The higher the layer of coverage sits in the tower, the less risk each insurer faces. For example a $10 million policy that attaches after $80 million in insured losses (in industry terms, a "10 × 80" policy) is less risky from an insurer's perspective than a $10 million excess of $20 million in insured losses (a 10 × 20 policy).

"Pricing" then is the final piece of the underwriting puzzle. After selecting the risk and choosing limits and attachment point, the insurer must decide on a price that will reflect the risk borne by the insurer. That is, price depends not only on the attributes of the insured but also on the various ways in which the policy allocates risk. Thus, a high-limits policy is more expensive than a low-limits policy, and the farther down the tower an insurer's layer of coverage sits, the higher the price will be. Each of the SLAP decisions turns on the underwriter's assessment of risk. Risk assessment is thus the core feature of underwriting. The underwriter's assessment of the riskiness of a prospective insured guides the decision not only whether or not to sell coverage but also how much coverage to sell, at what layer within the tower, and at what price.

All of the underwriters we talked to emphasized the importance of individual risk selection in addition to risk rating. We had expected at least some insurers to take more of an index approach and, following the analogy to mutual fund indexing, to seek to diversify their risks by underwriting a small portion of the entire D&O market rather than concentrating their underwriting in particular risks. Although some described underwriting strategies that are consistent with these ideas—for example, limit management strategies that seek to reduce the insurer's exposure to any one D&O risk by reducing the maximum limits available to any one insured and risk pool diversification strategies that emphasize underwriting across different industries and market capitalizations[2]—no underwriter claimed to use such strategies in place of traditional risk selection. Indeed, all D&O underwriters stressed individual risk selection. And several adamantly rejected the idea that indexing might be a better approach. In the words of one,

> That is not enlightened thinking. If you followed that through to the end, why wouldn't you just simply regress to the mean . . . ? I mean, if your actuary assumes that you are just going to do average and he is going to make you price the business for average, right, how do you get more aggressive on the better business?[3]

Every underwriter in our sample sought to underwrite better business— that is, better D&O risks. One participant frankly described his firm's goal to "out-select [its] peers."[4] Whether, in fact, this can be done, or whether, instead, D&O underwriters simply succumb to the Lake Wobegon illusion—where all the children are above average—we leave for another day.

All of the underwriters we interviewed had their own methods of assessing D&O risk, the precise details of which they were unwilling to share—"I would have to kill you if I told you," one quipped.[5] In the words of another, "we spend a lot of time studying [what factors correlate to D&O risk]. We know quite well, but again it is private."[6] Others, however, were willing to talk generally about their underwriting process. And with regard to their processes, we found wide variation among underwriters, some being driven by mathematical models and others by much less formal discussions around a conference table. In the words of one underwriter, "[D&O underwriting is not like] auto insurance or these other lines of insurance where an underwriter can actually plug numbers into an actuarial model. We didn't do that. We literally sat at a round table and, just based on the experience of the more senior folks, we would say this is a great number. We drew a number out of the hat."[7]

With regard to the risk-assessment process, we can report that underwriters have access to both private and public information concerning the riskiness of the insured. Underwriters told us they make use of a wide variety of publicly available information in assessing the risk of a prospective insured, such as news reports, analyst estimates, SEC filings, and corporate governance reviews and accounting studies. This is much the same information that would be available to any investor. Additionally, however, insurers take information from prospective insureds in the form of applications and questionnaires, often targeted to specific industry categories, and at underwriting meetings. Any additional information gained through these channels is, of course, private information, not publicly available, and often passes between the applicant and the insurer by means of a nondisclosure agreement to assure the applicant of confidentiality.

The typical D&O application solicits much basic information that is likely to be available elsewhere. Indeed, the application typically requires prospective insureds to attach recent SEC filings to the application. But more than simply rehashing this publicly available information, the application contains an important bonding mechanism. D&O applications contain a provision requiring the applicant to aver to the veracity of all representations made in the application and all written statements and documents furnished in connection with the application. For example, a Chubb D&O application provides,

The undersigned . . . declare that to the best of their knowledge and belief, after reasonable inquiry, the statements made in this Application and in any attachments or other documents submitted with this Application are true and complete. The undersigned agree that this Application and such attachments and other documents shall be the basis of the insurance policy . . . ; that all such materials shall be deemed to be attached to and shall form a part of any such policy; and that the Company will have relied on all such materials in issuing any such policy.[8]

Because, as we shall explore in chapter 9, an insurer's reliance on false information in underwriting the policy forms the basis for a subsequent rescission action, any untrue document furnished to the insurer in connection with the application may potentially destroy coverage. Attachments typically called for in D&O applications include organizational documents, recent SEC filings, and copies of any correspondence between outside auditors and management. The bonding mechanism would also capture written answers to interrogatories and any other information provided in connection with the underwriting process. We should also note, however, that, as we will explore in chapter 9, insurers are typically reluctant to bring rescission cases and that even good cases are difficult for insurers to win. For example, recent attempts to rescind against Dennis Kozlowski (Tyco) and Richard Scrushy (HealthSouth) failed. The bonding mechanism created by the potential to rescind may not be as powerful as it first seems.

D&O applications typically elicit the name and experience of each of the officers and directors covered under the policy, as well as a full description of any claims history of the individuals or the corporation itself. The applications ask whether any covered individual has ever been involved in securities or antitrust litigation, criminal or administrative actions, derivative claims, or other representative proceedings. Some of the information elicited in the application may not be publicly available. For example, the D&O application inquires into the prospective insured's plans to make acquisitions or issue securities, plans that the prospective insured may not yet have disclosed to the public. Additionally, applications ask whether the prospective insured's insiders have knowledge of conduct likely to give rise to a claim. Such insider knowledge obviously is not public knowledge.

In addition to the information gained in the application itself, underwriters have private access to officers and directors of the prospective insured in underwriters' meetings, in which "underwriters are posing questions to officers of the company in regard to business practices, in regard to their current activities, and in regard to their future plans."[9] The meetings often involve the prospective insured's chief financial officer or treasurer as well as members of the accounting and legal departments and occasionally, for smaller or exceptionally risky companies, the chief executive officer. The executives of the prospective insureds typically present information about their business model, strategies, and risks, while underwriters ask questions and gather further information. An insurance broker compared the meeting to a "first date" and described the process: "Generally, an insured's CFO or general counsel or maybe even the [CEO] might give a presentation. There will be questions asked by the underwriters. I think that insureds for the most part are pretty forthcoming."[10] Much of the information gathered during the underwriters' meeting and in any subsequent inquires is not publicly available, and underwriters sign nondisclosure agreements to protect confidential or otherwise sensitive information. Insurers then compare the information gathered in the underwriters' meeting to what is publicly known. Thus, private and public information is combined to generate the insurer's assessment of risk.

Finally, we should note that many of our respondents described risk assessment as highly detailed and, from the prospective insured's point of view, onerous. Corporate risk managers are typically in charge of preparing the prospective insured for the meeting, and their perspective on the process was therefore especially interesting to us. One risk manager at a corporate insured observed that "there is a very thorough review and research into the guts of the finance [and] the guts of the operation of the company."[11] Another risk manager noted,

> I can recall probably fifteen years ago where a D&O renewal might take me a half hour to fill out the applications. It [now] takes me about a week to do all the financial [projections], just to get them assembled and to determine where I need to go for information. . . . They want detailed information. . . . [A presentation to incumbents and potential markets] is followed by an interview process and sometimes followed by another set of application questions.[12]

It was also suggested, however, that the insurer's level of scrutiny in the underwriting process varies with the cycles of the insurance market. "Prior to [the corporate] meltdowns," one risk manager quipped, "[D&O] was a cake coverage."[13]

To summarize, all of our respondents reported that underwriters engage in risk assessment, and many provided some detail on the process, including what sources of information underwriters examine to assess risk. Underwriters start with much the same information that is available to traders and other market participants, but they also have access to private information through the application process and the underwriters' meeting. So, what exactly do underwriters look for in all of this information? What information is most relevant in underwriting D&O risk? What particular features of prospective insureds do underwriters look for? What information do they value most? And what do they believe best predicts the risk of shareholder litigation? We turn to these questions in the sections that follow.

What Is the Risk?

What underwriters value in assessing risk is an especially telling question. The insurer, after all, is ultimately on the hook for losses stemming from shareholder litigation. This means that whatever an insurer uses to assess the risk of loss is, to borrow a phrase from economics, a "revealed preference." Because insurance companies pay out their reserves when they get their risk assessments wrong, of all parties, they are the most motivated to get it right. In this regard, insurers are unlike other third-party evaluators of corporate risk, including equity analysts, Institutional Shareholder Services, and ratings agencies such as Moody's and Standard and Poor's, all of which operate on a fee-for-services model and therefore do not directly suffer when a rating is incorrect. Such other evaluators of risk may of course suffer harm to their reputation if they are repeatedly incorrect in their assessment of risk, and such harm to their reputation may lead, over time, to a decrease in subscriber revenue. However, these harms seem likely only if the risk evaluator is incorrect repeatedly and its customers are aware of its mistakes, two conditions that are not always met and thus render such third-party evaluations of risk considerably less reliable. D&O insurers, by contrast, suffer immediately for their incorrect assessments of risk by paying the losses of the bad risks they have insured. To state it more plainly, insurers put their money where their mouth is.

This suggests that what D&O insurers consider important in evaluating the risk of shareholder litigation must really be important. As a result, one ought to learn a substantial amount about what matters in corporate governance by considering what insurers think about when underwriting D&O coverage. So, what matters to D&O insurers in assessing risk?

We will begin this discussion with an extended quotation from a leading D&O underwriter in which he describes what his company looks at in
evaluating risk:

> We look at the industry that the company operates in trying to figure out if we
> are in a mature industry, a growth industry, a start-up section of the industry,
> whatever. Are we working with proven technology, new technology, proven
> consumer goods, new consumer goods[?]
>
>   ... We look at the history of the company and see if M&A [mergers and
> acquisitions] is a prominent part of their planning process for the future or not.
> We look if there are takeover risks. We look if there is a restructuring perhaps
> necessary in the future of the company. We examine the type of securities filings
> they did at the [SEC]. . . . We look at any SPEs, SPVs [special purpose vehicles],
> joint ventures that they are using to grow strategically.
>
>   Then we dive into the corporate governance. We examine who the direc-
> tors and officers are, their applicable experience. We look at interlocking board
> relationships. We actually keep a separate database here. Since 1996 we can
> run our database and tell you if any one director or officer was a defendant in a
> securities class action or derivative action.
>
>   ... [W]e record which company they were serving in when they were sued,
> but what we can then do is go back and look to see if the folks that we are un-
> derwriting now were sued in what was a fender bender or if it was a complete
> corporate meltdown. So we have a driving record in this.
>
>   We look at the . . . organization of the corporate governance committees and
> [the] independence of those committees and . . . how active they are and then
> we look at insider ownership [and] compensation packages. Then we move into
> a broader understanding of the entire ownership of the company and . . . what
> conflicts may or may not may exist within the ownership interest.
>
>   We take a serious look at the equity trend of the company over recent years
> and what made its price earnings multiple what it is. We examine insider trades.
> We look at any intellectual property that the company may be relying on. We
> look at the regulatory structure and who the regulators may be and how the
> history with the regulatory relationships was. We look at both former existing
> director and officer litigation as well as general litigation that the corporation
> may be involved in that could be a threat to the future value of the company. We
> look at how they handle corporate investor communications. We look at how
> they are handling legislative or environmental issues that may face the com-
> pany. We look at how they may handle employment practices and bankruptcy
> of course. We have an entire dedicated review of the bankruptcy and potential
> emergency or liquidation.

Then we go into a very meticulous breakdown of the financials of both the balance sheet and the cash flow statement and profit and loss statement. You know, your typical ratio analysis is supported by about fifty-five or so different ratios. Underneath those ratios we look meticulously at who the auditors are, what the revenue recognition policies are, how they manage accounts receivable, inventory, payables, valuing intangibles, you know, formulating debt and appreciation, capital expenditures, pension obligations, and we look even at vendor financing if it exists. Then we take all that stuff and we rate it for risk. We summarize, you know, what makes us want to write the account and what makes the necessity of the insurance relevant to the risk of the company, and then we price it.[14]

As this quotation illustrates, when underwriters assess the risk of a D&O policy, they consider a wide variety of firm-specific features, including industry, business strategy, accounting policies, who the officers and directors of the company are, what corporate governance structures are in place, and finally the firm's financial statements, which are carefully scrutinized. Starting from this list of basic variables, we sought greater detail about how underwriters seek to understand and assess D&O risk. We sought to learn, for example, why each variable is on the list. What information lies behind each factor? And what is the relative weight of each factor? In seeking answers to these questions from our participants, we discovered that we could divide the major factors considered by D&O underwriters into two large categories: financial risk factors and governance risk factors, each of which we discuss in greater detail in the sections that follow.

Financial Risk Factors

Insurance underwriters think of risk in terms of frequency and severity. What is the likely frequency of an insured loss? And what is the probable magnitude of the loss once incurred? All of the underwriters we interviewed agreed that D&O insurance "is a high-severity, low-frequency game."[15] And all of them glean an initial estimate of frequency and severity from financial analysis. The reason is simple: virtually all shareholder litigation stems from investment loss. Thus, a major part of assessing the risk of shareholder litigation lies in assessing the risk of investment loss.

The financial acuity of D&O underwriters has increased over time, as illustrated by a story told by one broker:

[I]nitially these policies were rated by the number of people on the board. So if you had a larger board, you had more risk. It was sort of a per-person type

of rating scheme. Then people thought about it and said, well we really need a
proxy for decision making. What are the size of the decisions and the frequency
that decisions need to be made in a corporation? The first proxy they came up
with was assets. . . . That has evolved as we look[ed] at the tech companies in
the nineties and we said to ourselves, wait a minute. This tech company has very
little revenues, very little assets, but a huge market cap. Therefore, the potential
for liability is not necessarily correlated with assets for that industry. We saw
carriers moving toward using market capitalization now as a basis for the initial
premium. Once the initial premium is determined, though, we can factor out
mildly or dramatically depending [on a variety of qualitative factors].[16]

Although they may once have focused on the number of directors or the
overall amount of corporate assets, underwriters now focus their financial risk assessment on such factors as the prospective insured's industry
and maturity, market capitalization, volatility, and various accounting
ratios.

Industry and volatility are associated with frequency: some industries
are sued more often than others, and shareholder litigation tends to coincide with sudden declines in share price (volatility). Market capitalization,
meanwhile, is used to predict both frequency and severity: larger firms are
sued more often, and larger capitalization firms have farther to fall with
regard to damages. These financial factors enable underwriters to form an
initial estimate of a prospective insured's exposure to shareholder litigation risk.

Although underwriters and investment analysts consider some of the
financial considerations, an underwriter's evaluation of these financial factors differs from an investment analyst's. Insurers, unlike investors, do not
look favorably on high-growth companies. They do not favor highly vola-
tile earnings. As one broker explained,

They don't want [an earnings chart that looks like a] hockey stick. The hockey
stick, I think, causes them to believe that if there's such a spike, then can a company accommodate that? Can it grow like that without getting to the top of that
hockey stick and then dropping like a rock? So they want to make sure that the
company is on a platform of sustainable growth, they feel comfortable with the
management, understand all of the compliance issues that are in place.[17]

Insurers, in other words, focus more on downside risk because they have a
fixed return (the policy premium) that is modest in relation to their exposure to loss (the policy limits), while equity investors have a fixed exposure

to loss (their initial investment) and a potentially unlimited upside (their share of the business's growth). D&O risk, in other words, is not the same as investment risk. In the words of an underwriter,

> [Evaluating D&O risk] is not the same as [evaluating] investment risk . . . .
> [T]here are companies that would be terrific companies [to invest in] that would be terrible D&O risks. There are companies that you would never ever put a penny of investment in, but they are great [D&O risks] because they are just not going to have this kind of class action lawsuit.[18]

Risk selection, in the words of one underwriter, "is not about picking winners as much as avoiding losers. . . . If I avoid three or four bad claims a year, we had a great year."[19] D&O insurers screen prospective insureds with a view toward avoiding sudden investment loss, irrespective of the potential for gain.

An underwriter's financial analysis seeks to assess the potential for a prospective insured to suffer sudden losses, regardless of the cause of those losses. The second key consideration in underwriting—the evaluation of the prospective insured's corporate governance—seeks to assesses the probability that the investment loss will be linked to corporate or securities law violations and is described in greater detail below.

Governance Risk Factors

One participant in our study remarked that there are two pillars of D&O underwriting: "Number one is the financial health of the [company, and n]umber two is how good that company [is] at governing itself."[20] The second most important factor, in other words, is corporate governance.

The term "corporate governance," as we described it in chapter 1, can be used to refer not only to specific charter terms or board structures but also to any aspect of the system of incentives and constraints operating within a firm. Indeed, as we shall see, the participants in our study tended to give corporate governance this broader definition.

When asked what corporate governance variables were most important in underwriting risk, our respondents repeatedly emphasized the importance of culture and character. Typical remarks included, "I believe that really what it comes down to is the culture and the people,"[21] or, "Ultimately the insurance underwriter is really betting on the ethics and confidence of the management of the company."[22] Similarly, we were told that "the only way you are ever going to be able to underwrite this stuff is through people. . . . It is your ability to assess character."[23] And, "there's one [underwriting] model that works, and it's the best model. It's the people. It's simply the people. Who are you dealing with? And how do they act?"[24]

Culture and character, we were regularly told, are at least as important as and perhaps more important than other more readily observable governance factors in assessing D&O risk. In the words of one underwriter,

> I don't view my [underwriters] as financial experts to begin with, but if I am going toe to toe with a CFO of X Corp. . . . am I getting to the bottom of what is going on here? The answer is no. To me, my style in terms of underwriting has been to look for the way people deal with certain issues and how they view their goals and how they are going to achieve them.[25]

Concepts such as culture and character, however, require interpretation. As described below, we took "culture" to refer to the system of incentives and constraints operating within the organization, including both formal rules and informal norms. We took "character" to refer to the likelihood that top managers would defect from corporate interests when given an opportunity to do so.

CULTURE: INCENTIVES AND CONSTRAINTS. The system of incentives and constraints operating within a firm may be based on formal rules, informal norms, or, most likely, some combination of the two. Participants in our study emphasized each of these aspects of corporate culture. Several underwriters cited executive compensation as a key indicator of intrafirm incentives. An equally large number also emphasized the constraint of internal controls. In their discussion of these incentives and constraints, it was clear that underwriters looked past the formal rules, seeking a sense of how strong the norm of compliance is within the organization or whether, by contrast, there is a norm of defection. As one senior underwriter described,

> [N]o company ever just dropped out of the sky. There is a history which is a narrative of how they got in [this business]. Who are the players? Who founded them? What is their culture? You might get to the ethics of the culture of the company, but you [need to] understand how it got put there, into the state it's in now. . . . [W]ho are they? And where did they come from? . . . [H]ow did they know each other? In a fraternity? Did they know each other in business? . . . I mean, there is a story. They didn't just all land out of the sky.[26]

One frame through which underwriters examine corporate culture is executive compensation. In the words of this same underwriter,

> You have a hard time convincing me when a guy makes a fortune and the board signs off on the increases or the other demands or the perks or the airplane flights or the bonus packages, severance packages, or the balloons, or whatever it is. You have a hard time telling me that that board has a real grip on that CEO.[27]

It is interesting to note, however, that, notwithstanding all the recent controversy surrounding executive pay packages, executive compensation alone itself does not create liability risk. Shareholders cannot sue simply because the CEO is making too much money. Instead, they must argue that the board was grossly negligent in setting the compensation, a claim that, in the absence of some kind of fraud or deceit, shareholders are unlikely to win. The insurers' focus on executive compensation thus suggests a deeper concern about the incentives operating within the firm.

Just as D&O underwriters review a firm's internal incentive structure, they also review the firm's internal constraints. Indeed, if there was one central corporate governance variable that our respondents sought to emphasize, it was the quality of the prospective insured's internal controls. In the words of a prominent risk manager, "The one word that really captures the heart of [the] process is evidence that there is controllership."[28] An underwriter elaborated on this point:

> You need to understand some of the accounting issues that were driving claims, particularly revenue recognition procedures at companies. . . . [E]ach of those industries had different . . . revenue recognition issues. You need to be able to drill down, see if the answers were there, and if not, ask the right questions to get them.[29]

Indeed, revenue recognition procedures, because they can lead to restatements and thereby to securities claims, were repeatedly emphasized as a core concern, as illustrated by our respondents in numerous anecdotes:

> Division president is having a bad quarter and says, you know what? We will fix it next quarter. He brings in temps. They ship more product. Their revenue recognition, which is a huge question in these interviews, is if it is shipped, you can book the revenue, so we make the quarter. The next quarter we don't recover. . . .

We say, we'll make it up next quarter. We ship more product and we make our numbers. Now we are in quarter number three, and I'm having trouble as division president making my numbers. Things have not recovered in my sector, so I start to look into my reserve for returns. I say, you know what? That's pretty high. I am going to take down my reserves[,] which translates into more dollars[,] which allows me to make my numbers. I tell my accountant, if anyone asks about this, don't talk to them. Send them to me. Well, you know then in the fourth quarter everything blows up.[30]

And again,

Harley-Davidson got sued because they were channel stuffing motorcycles. . . . [T]hat wasn't happening at the board level. That was probably the VP for sale[s] had a monthly sales target that he was desperate about making because his [bonus] compensation was tied to meeting his target, and so they started [channel] stuffing motorcycles.[31]

Channel stuffing is an attempt to force more inventory through a distributor than the distributor can handle. It is an attempt to manipulate results that typically fails since, if the distributor cannot handle the sales, the inventory will ultimately come back to the manufacturer. Because pressures to manipulate results may exist throughout the firm, as these examples suggest, the question of internal controls is really the question of whether the organization can constrain these temptations throughout the firm.

Underwriters view board independence as an aspect of controllership. In the words of one, "There is a lot of cronyism still. . . . I mean, you still have entrenched boards, boards that only work for the CEO as opposed to vice versa. It is a fundamental underwriting question we ask people, who works for whom."[32] The firm's ownership structure is taken into account for similar reasons.[33] But the investigation into internal controls does not stop at the board level, nor does it end once underwriters are given a corporation's statement of controllership principles. Instead, our participants noted that underwriters investigate how information flows throughout the firm: "How does 'bad news' flow upward within the organization? Does the corporate culture encourage such news to be brought to the attention of senior management? Are significant developments shared with the board of directors as they become available?"[34]

Underwriters investigate who reports to whom within the corporation.[35] They inquire into the actual practices underlying formal policies. The

When Mr. Wirthmore began wearing a crown at
board meetings, no one said a word about it...but they
did vote unanimously to up their D&O policy limits.

FIGURE 5.1. When Mr. Wirthmore began wearing a crown at board meetings, no one said a word about it . . . but they did vote unanimously to up their D&O policy limits. Courtesy of the artist, Charles Pugsley Fincher. C.06CharlesFincher11.22 Scribble-in-Law at LawComlx.com.

corporate risk managers, sitting on the other side of the table from the underwriters, confirmed this inquiry. As one risk manager described, underwriters ask not only whether there is a process of controls in place, "but how are you exercising the process and what evidence do you have to support your controllership process. . . . [A]ll the questions are around that subject."[36] To inquire further into a corporation's internal controls, underwriters reported that they also retain forensic accounting consultants to detect inadequacies in internal controls before they lead to fraud, which has led to the blooming of a "cottage industry" in forensic accounting.[37]

In this way, underwriters investigate corporate culture by uncovering the buried structure of incentives and constraints operating within the firm. They do not confine their investigations to the presence or absence of big-picture structural features, such as an independent board or a formal controllership program. Instead they dig beneath the formal rules in an effort to unearth the firm's internal culture of compliance or defection. The very fact that they make this effort suggests that such measures of corporate culture affect the risk of shareholder litigation.

CHARACTER: "IT WAS A SMALL AQUIFER." The other major governance feature emphasized by our respondents was the character of a prospective insured's executives.[38] "Ultimately," one broker said, "the underwriter is really betting on the ethics and confidence of the management of the company."[39] Character, of course, is an amorphous concept. Character, one underwriter quipped, can be understood in terms of the seven deadly sins, but "greed, stupidity, and ego" most often lead to D&O claims.[40] When we pressed underwriters to define it, they often responded by emphasizing arrogance and excessive risk taking.

Arrogance, our interviews suggested, may apply to individuals who hold themselves above rules and norms. Several underwriters described warning signs, such as the amount of perquisites consumed by managers[41] or a CEO's drive "to be king of the world and . . . roll up other companies,"[42] or "a CFO who has got all the answers, doesn't want to listen. . . . Or a senior management team where all you see is the CEO and no one else. . . . [J]ust one person out front and no one else. You never see them, and it is I, I, I."[43] Others offered anecdotes, including the following:

> I am interviewing . . . a CFO once at a company, and they were a manufacturing company. . . . I said, "Do you have any pollution issues?" He said, "Well . . ." "You know, recent problems?" He said, "What do you mean by problems?" Stuff like that. . . . I said, "Have you ever polluted an aquifer?" And to my surprise he says, "It was a small aquifer." And then he goes on to rationalize . . . how small three parts per billion is, or whatever the number was. He said it was ridiculous. . . . To my way of thinking, this is a bad insured. This is a guy who looks at his problems, [and] he doesn't look at solving the problems or doesn't look at what the law says. He is extemporizing on how he thinks the law ought to be applied. That is very bad. Because when things go wrong, those things will cause you to pay big time.[44]

Understood in this way, arrogance indicates a lack of restraint, as well as the ability and willingness to rationalize one's conduct in a way that makes the rules seem not to apply.

With regard to risk taking, insurers seek to avoid those executives whose appetite for risk exceeds the norm. As one actuary explained,

> [M]aybe the most important questions you can ask a CEO [are] how many speeding tickets do you have? What kind of car do you drive? How many times have you been married? How often do you drink? How much do you drink? . . . [D]o you have extramarital affairs? Simply because you're looking for risk takers. *Risk takers above the norm*—those are the people that get in trouble. . . . [I]n a lot of situations, [that kind of information is] more important than how much cash [they have] or what their balance sheet looks like or what new products they have coming out.[45]

But what risks are excessive? Risk, after all, is a good thing in private enterprise, and it is certainly possible to distinguish fraud (which involves lying or deceit) from risk taking (which does not). Because the underlying exposure is securities fraud, not business risk, we would expect insurers to be focused on fraud in particular, not on risk taking generally.

Pressed on these points, underwriters indicated that they look for evidence that the company is overcommitted to growth, because in such situations there will be a strong temptation to misstate results when reality falls behind expectations. Excessive risk taking, in other words, can lead to fraud. An underwriter illustrated this situation as follows:

> [O]ne company . . . [said] they were going to grow 20 percent. . . . Some people [said], "I'm not sure how we are going to grow 20 percent, but the CEO said we are going to grow 20 percent." You know, but without that clear articulation of *how* we are going to grow 20 percent, in the absence of really great controls—and maybe they had them, maybe they didn't—you are going to have somebody who [when] the pressure is on [starts thinking], "I had better make my numbers."[46]

Underwriters derive much of this information from their meetings with management. "We talk to people," one underwriter said. "We stare down a lot of people, and if their comfort level is starting to get very solidified with a group of [managers], we will follow them around."[47] As with the evaluation of corporate culture, this character aspect of risk assessment in D&O underwriting reflects a broader conception of corporate governance that goes well beyond formal charter provisions.

Pricing the Risk

All of the factors discussed above, our participants reported, are considered in the risk assessment and ultimately the pricing of a prospective insured. In the words of the underwriter we quoted at the outset, "We take all that stuff and we rate it for risk. We summarize what makes us want to write the account and what makes the necessity of the insurance relevant to the risk of the company. *And then we price it.*"[48] Our question, of course, was, How? How do D&O underwriters derive a price from this extensive list of risk factors?

As we learned, D&O underwriters begin with a simple algorithm, which differs from company to company, and then employ a highly discretionary, largely unobservable (even for the companies' own pricing actuaries) system of credits and debits. As described by one of the underwriters in our study, "[T]he market cap and the volatility and some of those easily observed things will get you your first price. [Then the question] is whether . . . the risk is 'clean' enough to make the next cut, [where] some of these other more qualitative factors will come into play."[49] This section explores each of these aspects of pricing in turn.

The Base Algorithm

Each of the underwriters and actuaries we spoke to reported that their companies have developed algorithms to generate an initial price. No underwriter or actuary would provide us with their company's precise algorithm, but they did tell us the factors used in their algorithms: market capitalization (all insurers), industry sector (most insurers), stock price volatility (many insurers), accounting ratios (many insurers), and age/maturity of the applicant corporation (some insurers). A senior reinsurance underwriter described the pricing algorithm as "a merging of . . . corporate finance concepts and actuarial pricing concepts" and noted that "writing a D&O insurance liability policy [is] very[,] very similar to a put option for stock."[50] That is, D&O underwriting involves the same basic bet one makes in connection with an option to sell shares—namely, taking a position on the likelihood that the underlying share price will decline.

Aspects of the insurer's basic pricing algorithm are disclosed to state insurance commissioners. In a rate schedule filed in the state of California, for example, Chubb disclosed that base rates depend first on a combination of market capitalization and volatility (beta) with specified increases from the base rate factored in on the basis of limits and industry. The rate schedule then lists a large number of rating modifications—including "risk relative to industry," "financial trends," "board/management architecture and controls," "individual qualifications," and "overall board/management quality"—most of which require a qualitative (as opposed to purely quantitative) analysis.[51] Indeed, this filing illustrates the two aspects of D&O pricing—a quantitative base rate adjusted by qualitative factors.

Filings with state insurance regulators, however, do not provide good guidance on what insurers actually do. The plans include such a broad range of underwriter discretion that they would provide very little guidance even if the companies actually used the plans to generate premiums.[52] But, in fact, underwriters do not use these plans to generate their premiums.

Not one underwriter whom we interviewed described starting the pricing process with the formula in the rating plan. Instead, they described a process in which premiums that were in fact generated by assigning credits and debits to various governance features were then checked against the plan on file only as part of a regulatory compliance process. Moreover, a senior underwriter at the most heavily quantitatively oriented firm said that the actual algorithm "is very different" from what is in the plan. He explained that they file and use "a traditional rating method to see if we comply with the state or not from a guidelines standpoint, because . . . we don't want [our proprietary algorithm] in the public domain."[53] Thus, in order to understand D&O pricing, we must understand the system of credits and debits, described in the next section.

Credits and Debits

All underwriters reported using some form of debit and credit system to arrive at an ultimate price, which, as a result, can vary widely from the output of the basic pricing algorithm. As described by one of our participants, "[A]ctuaries set the overall rates for an insurance company, but then within that rating system, an underwriter has a lot of leeway. I mean, they probably have judgments that are plus or minus 40 percent."[54] The influence of actuarial science thus declines once underwriters begin to issue credits and debits.

Insurers differ widely on how they determine their system of credits and debits. A small number of insurers use quantitative guidelines based on the presence or absence of specific governance features. An underwriter from an insurance company with a highly quantitative model described the process as follows: "So, for example, if you are in a certain industry class, you are going to get debited between 5 and 10 percent or credited between 5 and 10 percent. If you have got a very poor board score, you are going to pay anywhere from 10 to 20 percent more."[55] However, even for such "quantitative" models, the range of credits and debits grants underwriters significant discretion.

Most insurers are not rigidly quantitative in their adjustments to price, thus allocating even more discretion to individual underwriters in setting premiums. As described by one such underwriter, "An underwriter ultimately consciously or unconsciously formulates an opinion about a risk, and that opinion leads him to make a certain decision" about price.[56] Insurers often subject these opinions to additional layers of consultation and approval, depending on the size of risk, with ultimate authority typically residing in a small group of experienced D&O underwriters.[57] But regardless of the process, which varies widely across insurance companies, the ultimate goal of the process is to adjust the base price up or down on the basis of less quantitative, more qualitative factors.

In sum, the pricing algorithm sets an initial price range on the basis of financial factors that seem geared to capture the likelihood of sudden investment loss of any kind, while the debit and credit process may be seen as linking investment loss to specific features of the firm. It is through this credit and debit process that an insured's corporate governance "works its way into pricing."[58] However, the degree of influence that governance features have on the ultimate price of the insurance, given the wide degree of discretion built into the system, is uncertain.

Pricing and Deterrence

The basic finding of our interviews on this question is that D&O insurers have designed a system for pricing D&O risk that looks to both financial risk factors and governance factors of prospective insureds. D&O insurers, in other words, do indeed attempt to price corporate governance risk. Moreover, as we described at the opening of this chapter, this pricing of such risk factors is a necessary first step in the reintroduction of the deterrence function of shareholder litigation into an environment of insurance. If the system works, higher risk firms will pay systematically more for their D&O coverage than lower risk firms, and this cost will serve as an incentive, just as shareholder litigation serves as an incentive, for higher risk firms to improve their corporate governance and thereby reduce risk. A firm that does not improve will face higher costs than its better-governed competitors year after year, which will either reduce profit margins or be passed on to consumers. If profit margins are reduced, capital market participants will prefer the firm's higher profit rivals, leading to higher costs of capital for the worse-governed firm. Conversely, if costs are passed on to consumers, the firm will be at a disadvantage in price competition with its rivals and may lose market share. Either way, such firms would seem to have real incentives to reduce annual D&O costs.

It would be a leap, however, on the basis of underwriters' attempts to price governance risk, to conclude that this deterrence system does in fact match the theoretical ideal. Indeed, for shareholder litigation to preserve its deterrent effect in the presence of liability insurance, the D&O insurer must not only take risk into account and attempt to price it, but the insurer must also do a good job of it, appropriately pricing the various risk factors and successfully passing these costs to the insured in the price of the policy. Moreover, in order for shareholder litigation to deter corporate misconduct, the price of the D&O insurance must provide an incentive for insureds to change their behavior. If either of these conditions does not hold—if D&O insurers either misprice governance risk or otherwise fail to pass the cost of this risk on to the prospective insured or if the cost of D&O insurance is not sufficient to cause bad corporations to change their ways—the deterrence function of shareholder litigation may fail, notwithstanding the efforts of underwriters to price their product.

The sections that follow explore reasons that either or both of these conditions might fail to hold.

The Price May Not Be Right

Our respondents told us that insurers try to price risk in underwriting D&O policies. They did not tell us that they always succeed. Underwriters are, of course, fallible. They may make mistakes in estimating governance risk and, more specifically, may be influenced by individual career incentives to generate ever greater premiums without regard to greater risk. Moreover, underwriters operate in a highly cyclical insurance market that may constrain the ability of insurers to charge the correct price to the prospective insured.

First, on the question of whether underwriters do a good job of pricing D&O risks, several of our respondents were openly skeptical. It is worth noting on this point that the worst corporate frauds are perpetrated by precisely those who are accustomed to deceiving others. If a CEO or CFO is able to deceive a board of directors, outside accountants, investment analysts, and sophisticated investors, it is not unlikely that they will be able to deceive insurance underwriters as well. Additionally, underwriters have such leeway in pricing that personal incentives to generate underwriting revenue may infect their decision making, leading them to be less cautious with regard to risk. The actuaries in our sample frequently suggested as much about their colleagues in the underwriting department. In addition, the actuaries we interviewed doubted that underwriters have a consistent system of evaluation that applies the same factors in the same way over time.[59]

Several of our respondents also pointed out the substantial short-term pressures on underwriters to generate premium volume, notwithstanding possible losses in the longer term. "If an underwriter is under pressure to write a premium," a broker told us, "he is going to deal with cognitive dissonance a lot differently than if he isn't under pressure."[60] The same broker noted that even the largest insurance companies can be inconsistent in their approach to risk depending on how they are doing with regard to underwriting revenues: "[I]f you come to [a major insurer] with a tough account at the end of the month and they haven't made their budget, guess what? You can get a really good deal."[61] This suggests that underwriting departments are not perfect agents of the insurance company as a whole and may face incentives to generate revenues that will lead to losses later. Of course, those who underwrite too aggressively may have to answer for the losses their risks generate down the line, but our respondents emphasized the fact that the losses from an underwriter's portfolio often materialize years later, after which time the underwriter may have moved on, having been either promoted within the company or hired on by another firm, leaving a trail of losses in his or her wake for which he or she is never called to account.

In other ways, D&O insurers operate in a highly competitive and transparent market. Underwriters are keenly aware of the price the competition has quoted or is likely to quote for the risk in question. They know historical premiums paid by a prospective insured and are finely attuned to prevailing market conditions. They can draw on their personal networks for information and in some cases will simply be told by the broker what prices other carriers are quoting both on the particular risk and on similar risks in the market. Moreover, the primary insurer's quotation is disclosed to all excess carriers before they provide their final quote, putting them in an even better position to predict the prices charged by their competitors. Insurers thus have ample opportunity and incentive to adjust their pricing on the basis of market factors that are not strictly relevant to the assessment of risk. An underwriter that charges significantly more than its competitors for the same risk will find that it has relatively few underwriting opportunities. The product market thus constrains the ability of underwriters to factor risk into price. If a D&O underwriter attaches a very high risk premium to a particular account, it may not have the opportunity to underwrite that account.

But, for present purposes, the single most important aspect of the insurance market may be its cyclical nature. Insurance markets follow a boom-and-bust pattern that forms the basis of what is referred to as the underwriting cycle—the tendency of premiums and restrictions on coverage and underwriting to rise and fall as insurers tighten their standards in response to the loss of capital or, alternately, loosen their standards in order to maintain or grow market share when new capital enters the market. The tightening of underwriting standards accompanies a hard market in which premiums and, after a lag, underwriting profits rise. The lag occurs because, at the start of a hard market, insurers increase the reserves set aside to pay claims under policies that were previously sold, suppressing profits for at least one year. Once profits begin to rise, however, competition is spurred, whether in the form of new entrants or established companies seeking to increase market share. This increased competition leads inevitably to another soft market, in which profits begin to decline and, often, underwriting standards are loosened to maintain underwriting revenues. The process is described as cyclical because each market condition contains the seed to generate the other.

An observation from a participant from a leading reinsurance company pithily describes the impact of the underwriting cycle on insurance pricing. When we asked him to read our article on D&O insurance pricing to verify that we had accurately described the D&O insurance underwriting process, he said that we had but added the following observation: "This is all theater around a price list. And what is the price list? At one moment there is a happy hour and everything is half price."[62] In other words, although insurers may attempt to price on the basis of risk, there are market realities that can lead to dramatic price cuts that have little or nothing to do with the risk of the particular corporation. The underwriting cycle is one reason for such "happy hours."[63]

All aspects of underwriting are affected by the cycle. In a hard market, underwriters become more selective, more interested in higher attachment points, less willing to offer high limits, less willing to negotiate contract terms, and more able to command dramatically higher prices for what amounts to less coverage. The D&O insurance market went through this hard phase in the mid-1980s and again in 2001–2003.[64] Beginning roughly in 2004, the D&O insurance market began shifting to the soft phase, such that underwriters in our study regularly commented that pricing is "pretty much inadequate across the sectors."[65] The Tillinghast/Towers Perrin survey corroborates this perception, with repeat respondents reporting a 14 percent drop in premiums from 2006 to 2007 and a similar drop in retentions (deductibles).[66] The increase in shareholder litigation following the collapse of the stock market in 2008 and the accompanying decline in the investment portfolio held by insurance companies appears to be moderating the price cutting, although as of this writing, the insurance market has not yet hardened.

Of course, hard and soft markets are relative, and D&O premiums do not have to be consistent over time in order to work as deterrence. All that is required is that in any given market, higher risk firms pay more. However, our respondents reported that the cyclical nature of the market complicates more than pricing. It also affects risk assessment, since underwriters scrutinize risk to a much greater degree in hard markets than in soft ones. The cyclical nature of the insurance market thus diffuses into risk rating. Indeed, if underwriters pay close attention to risk selection only in hard markets, the price of D&O insurance may differentiate comparative firm risks only in hard markets. Some of our respondents suggested as much, noting that scrutiny of formal governance factors in D&O underwriting is relatively new. In the words of a D&O actuary, corporate governance "might have crossed people's minds, but I don't recall it being part of the discussion [prior to 2002]."[67] In the words of an underwriter, speaking in the midst of a softening market, "The problem in the market the way it is, the guy who asks the hard question gets put [at] the back of the line. And we don't get answers that we used to get. You know, the last soft cycle, if you asked this question and nobody else was asking it, somebody [else] would write the business."[68]

The cyclical nature of the insurance market may thus suggest that D&O pricing incorporates risk cyclically and that it is not consistently attuned to differences in the governance quality of firms. Moreover, underwriters make mistakes, and there are strong reasons to suspect, given insurance company agency problems and the strong career incentives for underwriters to sell more insurance, that these mistakes are biased in favor of underestimating the risk of prospective insureds. All of this suggests that the price insurers generate at any particular moment may not always be right, but it does not mean that prices on average and over time are wrong. Moreover, because these problems are likely to increase the insurance company's losses, it is very much in the interest of insurance companies to solve them. If greater constraint is exercised over underwriting departments, there is no reason to believe that the cycle alone will distort the ability of D&O pricing to deter since, as we have argued above, deterrence does not require an absolute number in order to be effective; it requires only that in a given market, higher risk firms pay more than lower risk firms.

Why Price Alone May Not Deter

In addition to the distortions introduced by underwriters' errors and mis-
aligned incentives and the underwriting cycle, there are several reasons to
doubt that the price of D&O insurance alone will be enough to deter corporate misconduct. That is, even if the underwriters always got the price
right and the market never failed to incorporate the underwriters' risk assessment in the ultimate price of the insurance, the deterrence function of
shareholder litigation still might not be preserved by D&O insurance for
the basic reason that D&O expenses may not be large enough to change
corporate behavior. This could be so either because D&O expenses are
an insignificant portion of a large corporation's total costs or because the
marginal difference in D&O expense between good firms and bad firms
may not be large enough for bad firms to change their ways.

First, D&O insurance expenses might be so small, given a corporation's
overall costs and cash flows, that companies fail to take them into account
as a significant source of cost savings. Without firm-specific information,
we cannot comment on whether D&O insurance costs are large enough,
relative to market capitalization or cash flows, to affect firm behavior. We
can, however, point out that D&O premiums are nontrivial. Average annual premiums are summarized in figure 5.2 below. These costs may be
large enough to affect the behavior of some firms.

Nevertheless, our respondents suggested that, taking into account a
public corporation's overall budget, D&O premiums simply may not be
large enough to induce insureds to change their behavior. In the words
of one underwriter, "[I]t seems to me that however high D&O premiums
climb, they are not going to climb high enough to get the companies to really, really pay attention. . . ."[69]

Second, even if D&O expenses are nontrivial and therefore noticeable
to corporations, the difference between the premiums paid by good and
bad firms may not be sufficiently large to force bad firms to improve. Good
firms might pay too much while bad firms pay too little. This could be because underwriters make mistakes or the liability system makes mistakes
or, as is most likely, both do. As a result, although there may be some difference in the prices charged to firms with differing corporate governance
practices, good firms would cross-subsidize bad firms to some degree, and
deterrence would therefore be blunted.

Interestingly, liability insurers may play a part in the failings of the liability system by keeping the costs of shareholder litigation artificially low.

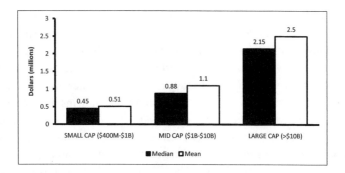

FIGURE 5.2. Annual D&O premiums by market capitalization category. The data in this figure are derived from Towers Perrin 2008, 34. We derived the "Mid-Cap" category as a weighted average of three market capitalization classes ($1–2 billion, $2–5 billion, $5–10 billion), reported by Towers Perrin.

To see this, consider the fact, already discussed, that shareholder claims typically settle within the limits of available insurance. This alone is unsurprising since plaintiffs' lawyers typically prefer to be paid by an insurance company that is contractually obliged to pay, rather than to expend extra effort seeking recovery from individuals who will do everything they can do to protect their personal assets. Now consider what happens if the real cost of securities litigation grows at a faster rate than insurance limits, which, by many accounts, seems to have occurred in the 1990s when market capitalizations grew exponentially but D&O limits remained relatively stable. In such a case, because plaintiffs' lawyers are often willing to settle for insurance proceeds only, settlements will not reflect the real cost of liability but rather a lower amount—the growth rate of insurance limits. In this situation, bad actors will pay significantly less in liability costs than the harm they cause. They will, in other words, be underdeterred. Damages will be effectively capped at typical policy limits. This compression of damages may lead to an inadequate spread between the liability costs of good and bad actors. When these liability costs are converted into an ex ante insurance premium, they will be similarly compressed, leading to further cross subsidization of bad firms by good firms and therefore less deterrence.

In sum, although this chapter has shown that D&O insurers do indeed attempt to price corporate governance risk, we cannot conclude that this pricing of governance risk is sufficient to reintroduce the deterrence function of shareholder litigation. Not only may underwriters make mistakes and be led astray by the desire to generate ever greater underwriting premiums, but even more significantly, defects of either the underwriting system or the liability system may lead to little difference between the premium charged to high-risk firms and to lower risk firms. If there is not much difference in the price paid by these two categories of firms, then there will be little incentive for the worse-governed firms to improve. Instead, all firms will simply pay their D&O premiums, whatever they are, and continue with business as usual. This is, to us, the most serious obstacle to the ability of D&O insurers to reintroduce deterrence through pricing, since it suggests that however carefully the underwriter works to understand the risk, the paltry difference in price charged to good versus bad firms will not be enough to induce the bad firms to be good. As a result, although we can report that underwriters do indeed try to get the price right, we cannot conclude that price ultimately deters in the same way that shareholder litigation might in a world without insurance. We will defer discussion of our suggestion for enhancing the deterrence effect of risk-based pricing—mandatory disclosure of insurance premiums and other D&O policy information—until chapter 10 and, in the intervening chapters, continue with our account of the other ways in which the D&O insurance relationship might preserve the deterrence function of shareholder litigation.

CHAPTER SIX

Insurance Monitoring and Loss-Prevention Programs

In the prior chapter, we explored the first means by which insurers may reintroduce the deterrence signal of shareholder litigation in the context of D&O insurance—namely, by pricing insurance to risk and thereby forcing corporations to internalize, through the insurance premium, the cost of their actions. It is worth emphasizing, however, that this is not the only means at the D&O insurer's disposal in controlling risk. In addition, insurers may seek to monitor the conduct of insured corporations and require them to establish specific practices to minimize the probability of loss. They may, in other words, develop loss-prevention programs.

This chapter explores the possibility of such insurer monitoring, exploring loss prevention in other insurance contexts and examining why such programs might be expected in the D&O context. Next, it reviews the empirical evidence collected from our participants on their experience with insurance monitoring and loss-prevention programs, finding, contrary to some expectations, that D&O insurers neither monitor nor provide loss-prevention programs to the corporations they insure. Finally, we explore explanations for the absence of insurer monitoring and loss prevention in the D&O context.

Why We Expected D&O Insurers to Monitor Insureds

Prior work provides three reasons to expect that D&O insurers would play a monitoring role in corporate governance as broadly defined in the prior chapter. First, economic theory asserts that liability insurance companies should work to prevent and manage insured losses. Second, historical and sociological research demonstrates that insurance companies do prevent and manage insured losses in some other contexts. Third, some work has claimed that D&O insurance companies do so as well. For these reasons, we began this research expecting to find corporations that treated D&O insurance companies as trusted suppliers of loss-prevention services, D&O insurance premiums that provided significant loss-prevention incentives, and D&O insurers that conditioned coverage on loss-prevention behavior. As we have just explained in the preceding chapter, D&O insurance premiums do not, in fact, provide specific loss-prevention incentives, but perhaps they do these other things, or at least so we thought at the outset of our research.

Economic Theory

As we explored in chapter 4, one of the standard explanations that economists give for why corporations buy insurance is monitoring. In theory, corporations do not need the risk spreading that insurance provides. Instead, they buy insurance for the other services that are packaged with the risk spreading: tax avoidance, lower credit costs, bankruptcy avoidance, potentially cheaper external capital, and, most importantly for this chapter, monitoring.

Again, in theory, insurance companies provide monitoring services not only for their customers' benefit but also because monitoring saves insurance companies money. In other words, monitoring is not only an important part of economic theory's answer to the question of why corporations buy insurance, it is also an important part of the answer to the moral hazard problem of liability insurance more generally. Indeed, Steven Shavell, perhaps the leading theoretical economist to have studied this question, concludes, "Although the purchase of liability insurance changes the incentives created by liability rules, the terms of the insurance policies sold in a competitive market would be such as to provide an appropriate substitute (but not necessarily equivalent) set of incentives to reduce accident risk."[1]

Institutional economists have reached the same conclusion after comparing the ability and incentives of different suppliers of loss-prevention services. They conclude that insurance companies have the best incentives to provide good loss-prevention advice because, alone among all possible providers of loss-prevention programs, insurers fund the losses. Insurance companies are, in other words, bonded to their advice. As George Cohen explains, "[L]oss prevention services by an insurance company come with a stronger guarantee than loss-prevention services by lawyers. The insurance company bonds its appraisal by agreeing to indemnify the insured for losses that occur; lawyers guarantee only nonnegligent appraisals."[2] This bonding should give insurance companies a comparative advantage in providing loss-prevention advice, and for that reason, customers should trust advice from insurance companies more than from institutions that do not bond their loss-prevention advice.

Historical and Sociological Research

There is a growing body of historical and sociological work documenting the loss-prevention role of insurance in other contexts. For example, historians have documented the long-standing role of insurance in the ship building industry, with the risk of insured losses providing the motivation for significant advances in ship safety.[3] Sociologists have similarly documented insurance companies engaged in loss prevention in the building industry, in home security, and in managing physical disabilities.[4] Industrious law students have provided fascinating accounts of insurance industry loss-prevention efforts in the motion-picture business and of insurer efforts to combat sexual harassment (which is covered by employment practices liability insurance).[5] Professor Jonathan Simon has provided what may be the most entertaining account of insurance industry–led loss prevention: the effort by insurance companies to eliminate keg parties at college fraternities.[6] Finally, one of us has gone so far as to place insurer-led loss-prevention efforts into a larger context of the social construction of responsibility by insurance organizations, describing loss prevention as a way that insurance organizations make their customers more trustworthy:

> Workers compensation insurance provides a number of useful examples of how insurance institutions structure situations in this manner. One common approach is designing and maintaining workplaces so that it is difficult for workers

to behave in an unsafe manner, thus making it easier to practice safety. Workers compensation achieves this in a direct, command-and-control manner through teams of inspectors employed by insurance companies and consulting firms. It also achieves this in an indirect manner through experience-based premiums that give employers an incentive to prevent injuries.[7]

Indeed, it is out of all this research that the concept of "insurance as governance"—the title of the Ericson team's landmark study[8]—has emerged.

Prior Writing on D&O Insurance

The first scholar to apply the economics of insurance to directors and officers insurance was Clifford Holderness. In a 1990 article he wrote,

> Insurance companies monitor their customers' directors and top managers in a number of ways. When it decides to issue a policy, the insurer investigates the firm's past actions, occasionally requires changes in the board, and sets conditions for directors and officers to observe. When allegations of misconduct arise, the insurer through its defense efforts can serve as an independent external investigator of not only the accused official but the entire board and top managerial team.[9]

Requiring changes in a board, setting conditions for directors and officers to observe, and serving as an external investigator are precisely the kinds of D&O insurer monitoring that we expected to learn more about from our interviews. Strengthening that expectation, Noel O'Sullivan reported in 1997 that he had supported Holderness's monitoring thesis in the United Kingdom (which, unlike the United States, requires corporations to disclose the purchase of D&O insurance). Finding a correlation between the number of outside directors and the likelihood that the corporation purchased D&O insurance, O'Sullivan reasoned that inside directors are better able to monitor the corporation and, thus, do not need the D&O insurer to serve that role.[10] We think that this empirical result can be more persuasively explained by outside directors being more likely to demand that the corporation purchase D&O insurance to protect them. But in any event, the modest prior literature on D&O insurance has claimed that D&O insurance provides a monitoring function, and, as we explored in chapter 3, this monitoring function is consistent with the theoretical literature on the corporate purchase of insurance.

How Do D&O Insurers Monitor Corporate Insureds?

Having set out some of the reasons why we expected to find that D&O insurers monitor their corporate insureds with the goal of reducing the frequency or severity of shareholder litigation, we now turn to the question of what D&O insurers in fact do. The question has a short answer and a longer answer. The short answer: D&O insurers do almost nothing to monitor the public corporations they insure, and D&O insurers do not condition the sale of insurance on compliance with loss-prevention requirements in any systematic way. Although D&O insurers do occasionally provide loss-prevention advice, underwriters report—and brokers and risk managers confirm—that this advice is not highly valued by public corporations, nor is it in any way binding on corporations as, for example, a condition of policy renewal. Finally, in sharp contrast to the liability insurance norm, D&O insurers do not actively manage defense costs. We take up the defense-cost topic in the next chapter, but we observe here that defense-cost management is an important after-the-fact loss-prevention effort practiced by liability insurers in all other contexts of which we are aware (one of us having practiced, researched, and actively consulted in the field for over twenty years). Indeed, Kenneth Abraham documents the continuous involvement of insurers in liability defense, from the birth of liability insurance in the 1880s to 2001, in his highly regarded recent book, *The Liability Century*.[11]

The longer answer, described in the sections that follow, seeks to account for what exactly D&O insurers do and why they do not do more.

No Loss-Prevention Programs

With only one exception (discussed in detail below), none of the underwriters or brokers we interviewed could tell us about a single situation in which a publicly traded corporation had changed a business practice in response to a governance concern from a D&O insurer. In fact, the consensus was that this rarely, if ever, occurred. One underwriter described his view in more vivid terms than the rest, but his basic point represents the common understanding of those we interviewed: "You had asked me on the phone whether companies . . . changed their behavior . . . for the benefit of the D&O insurers. I don't think they [do]. I think the brokers sometimes can put lipstick on the pig, but that is [a marketing feature]."[12] Our participants were nearly unanimous in reporting that insurers are not

successful at getting public companies to change their governance practices, and indeed that they rarely ever try. By contrast, loss-prevention
conditions and advice are frequently provided in the private and nonprofit
D&O insurance market. In that market, D&O insurance is sold as part
of a policy package that also insures against employment liability risks.
Employment liability is a more significant risk in the nonprofit sector, and
the insurers' loss-prevention efforts reflect this fact, focusing above all on
employment practices.

The public company D&O underwriters we talked to did seem to
understand why one might expect them to be actively involved in monitoring corporate governance. Some even reported that they had tried.
For example, the assistant D&O product manager for a leading insurer
reported,

> At one point we wanted to go in with accountants and governance experts and
> have them do a rigorous review, an interview with management and everything
> else in exchange for—assuming the report comes back positive—in exchange
> for much better terms and/or price, and we started to try to do this and send out
> feelers probably [in] early '03 when the hard market was still, you know, roar-
> ing along, thinking, "OK, clients will be open to this, if they can get significant
> reductions in their D&O prices," [but] they were very, *very* reluctant, I should
> say. [It was like trying to get through a brick wall] and that is still very much the
> case for two reasons I think. One, the companies don't want you in there and
> two, the brokers don't want you in there because they feel part of their value
> proposition is giving . . . the customer some risk insights on that front, so you are
> kind of conflicting with their value proposition.[13]

Here again it is worth emphasizing the cyclical nature of the insurance
market. As described in greater detail in chapter 3, liability insurance is a
cyclical business with recognizable periods of tight supply, high prices, and
other factors demonstrating that insurance sellers have the upper hand. If
D&O insurers cannot introduce serious loss-prevention programs at these
periods in the market, they will almost certainly be unable to do so during a soft market when greater bargaining power lies in the hands of the
insured. Their inability to do so, in other words, is proof that there is no
demand among public companies for loss-prevention programs. Advice
from the insurer thus appears as an imposition. Buyers do not demand
these services and, it would appear, are willing to push back or switch carriers in the event that their insurers seek to introduce them.

A few of the insurance companies we talked to do have D&O loss-prevention booklets and newsletters. One of the more detailed examples we received comes from Chubb.[14] Written by a highly regarded lawyer who regularly advises insurance companies about D&O insurance and related litigation, the brochure consists of general, practical advice for corporate directors and officers. Without in any way meaning to be critical, we can understand why underwriters and brokers uniformly described this literature as marketing material with no discernible impact on their clients' business practices. The statement from this underwriter for a major insurer is typical: "We have a newsletter, but it doesn't really . . . say, 'Look, if you do this, you'll get a better price.' What we do [say] is, 'Look, here are some issues.' . . . It goes in one ear and out the other."[15]

The product manager of a leading D&O insurer concurred: "We produce publications on [good governance], and we subscribe and participate in the best practices and conferences with directors, directors' conferences and things like that. We sponsor things that are the best practices and we publish stuff. . . ."[16] But he also reported that his company does not condition coverage on any governance practices, provide governance or related loss-prevention audits, or even provide identifiable discounts for adopting what his firm might regard as good corporate governance practices. The company's general support for improved corporate governance is a long way from the bundled package of monitoring and risk distribution services seen in other types of insurance.

Nonetheless, in the course of conducting our research interviews, we did hear the story of one insurance company that seemed to be an exception to the norm and perhaps the exception that proves the rule. This small, rather specialized, excess D&O insurer had developed a reputation in the market for emphasizing loss prevention. Upon learning this, we talked to people familiar with the company and ultimately secured an interview with a senior official in the company. He confirmed that, in the past, the company did have a business plan that focused on loss prevention. In his words,

[W]e felt strongly that there were certain things that, if the companies did [them], would reduce their likelihood of being named in a securities class action lawsuit, and those would be things like controlling insider trading, controlling your disclosure and corporate reporting, having policies and procedures in place in advance in case they have to report bad news. If they do so, they do it in a controlled way that does not exacerbate the situation and wind up in and of itself causing the source of the class action lawsuit. When we first started it, what we were telling people was, "And if you do these things, we will give you a discount. . . ."[17]

He shared with us their loss-prevention guide, which was prepared in the mid-1990s. The guide addressed a variety of topics: analyst communications, insider trading, bad news disclosure, and the mechanics of the protections provided by the then recently enacted Private Securities Litigation Reform Act (PSLRA). For each topic, the guide provided what appeared to be sensible background explanation and concrete procedures, forms, and practices for companies to use to reduce the likelihood of securities litigation. The guide was much longer and more detailed, with a more concrete practical orientation, than any of the loss-prevention materials we obtained from other D&O insurance companies or brokers. For example, the section on insider trading explained the legal rules governing insider trading, how plaintiffs' lawyers use insider trading as evidence of fraudulent intent, and how companies can defend against the use of insider trading as a fraud litigation weapon. In particular, the guide provided "recommended procedures for preventing improper insider trading/tipping and reducing securities fraud exposure."

This loss-prevention guide had received substantial attention among D&O insurers and brokers and was a large part of the reason that the company had developed its reputation for providing credible loss-prevention services. The only problem was that this loss-prevention effort did not work.

As the senior official at the company described, "It was a lesson in both directions."[18] From the customer side, what he learned was, "we don't value your message enough."[19] And from the insurance company side, he learned that "we couldn't show the discount." They could not demonstrate, in other words, that following the guide reduced loss and therefore justified a discount in premium. "We had to learn the value of humility too," the company official told us, continuing, "I still think they are good practices. I still think they work, too. I think what it will do—if you have a lawsuit, it will make it more defensible."[20]

But because the company could not prove the connection between their loss-prevention program and reduced loss, it could not offer reduced premiums to firms that were willing to follow their loss-prevention guidelines. And without a bundled premium discount, companies were unwilling to follow the insurer's loss-prevention program, especially when competing insurers were offering the same insurance without any loss-prevention requirements. "Look," the official said, describing the sales pitch of his competitors, "those guys will make you jump through a bunch of hoops; we can get the insurance for you cheaper . . . without all the fuss and bother."[21]

As a result, the company was forced to drop its loss-prevention program. "It was costly to maintain, and it was not economically supported."[22] Subsequently, the company left the D&O insurance business entirely. While we have no reason to believe that the failure of the loss-prevention experiment explains this decision, nevertheless this experience cannot provide much encouragement for future efforts to adopt a D&O business model emphasizing loss-prevention services.

What about the Brokers?

It occurred to us that if D&O insurance carriers were not providing loss-prevention programs, then maybe insurance brokerage firms were. Indeed, the broker has at least as much access to the details of a customer's corporate governance as the insurer, and the broker could obtain at least as much institutional knowledge about what factors tend to lead to D&O losses. Nevertheless, we discovered that brokers do not provide loss-prevention programs either.

Several brokers reported that they often do offer advice about which governance features are likely to count as negative factors in an insurer's underwriting assessment. For example, one broker from a major brokerage house reported,

> There have definitely been points . . . where we would say to our clients, "This is going to be a negative from an underwriter's perspective," and why. But I guess I would say, we really don't have the authority or position to turn around and say to them, "You need to change this." I think it is really up to them and, frankly, their board and audit committee as to what they end up doing, but we definitely point out what we would view to be a negative.[23]

As the quotation suggests, advice about how to avoid a negative underwriting assessment and put one's best foot forward in the market for insurance is relatively piecemeal—a far cry from a comprehensive program about how to implement structures that will avoid D&O losses. Brokers principally offer marketing advice, and they explain which governance features will be viewed as positives by underwriters and therefore ought to be emphasized and also note which features will be viewed as negatives and ought therefore to be deemphasized or explained. For example, one major D&O broker provided us with a document he circulated to prospective clients in the aftermath of the Enron and WorldCom scandals. The document was entitled "Examples of Questions Being Asked by D&O Underwriters" and listed a series of questions addressing specific hot button governance concerns.

1. Does the Parent Company or any Subsidiary act or intend to act as a general partner to any limited partnership?
2. Does the Parent Company or any Subsidiary utilize any off-balance-sheet entities for financial transactions?
3. Does any member of the Board of Directors have any outside affiliation or any common business interest with any major shareholder (10 percent or more)?
4. Within the past three years, did the Parent Company or any Subsidiary engage in any related-party transactions?
5. Has the Audit Committee received legal advice that dealing with Special Purpose Vehicle or Entity does not present any conflict of interest?
6. Has the Parent Company or any Subsidiary suspended its dividend payment within the past year, or is it currently anticipating such a suspension?
7. Has the Parent Company changed auditors or restated its financials in the past three years?
8. Please discuss the extent of the experience of the Audit Committee Members. How often do they meet? Does the Internal Audit Function have a direct report to the Audit Committee/Board of Directors?
9. Has your external auditor approved revenue recognition practices?
10. What is the length and scope of the company's relationship with its outside auditors? What percentage of fees has the company paid for auditing versus consultant fees? Are there any planned changes to this mix going forward?
11. In the past three years, has any executive officer or member of the Board of Directors resigned or been forced to resign for reasons other than retirement, poor health, or promotion?
12. How does the succession plan work in the event the CEO is nearing retirement age or in poor health?
13. How is management ensuring that the highest levels of integrity and ethical values are maintained?
14. How does "bad news" flow upward within the organization? Does the corporate culture encourage such news to be brought to the attention of senior management?

15. How are key executives compensated to ensure that they are properly motivated and still committed to ethical behavior?

16. Are significant developments shared with the Board of Directors as they become available?

17. How does the company select a new member of the Board? How does the search process take place?

18. Has the Parent Company or any Subsidiary been involved in any of the following within the past five years: any material civil, criminal, or regulatory action or any complaint, investigation, or proceeding relating thereto, including but not limited to actions rising from violations of federal, state, or local securities, environmental, antitrust, fair trade, employment practices, copyright, or patent infringement statutes or regulations?

19. Please provide any reports prepared by outside financial or investment analysts or consultants within the last twelve months, including any report directed to the Audit Committee of the Board of Directors on internal controls or financial reporting issues?

20. What is the company's response to SAB 99 (Materiality) and SAB 101 (Revenue Recognition)?

21. What has been the company's response to Reg FD?

22. Do you report earnings on a Pro Forma basis?

23. Has there been any violation of insider trading policies in the past twenty-four months?

24. Do you anticipate having to take a significant one-time charge to earnings or restatement of earnings, within the next twelve months?

25. As the economy continues to be unstable, what measures have you taken to manage market fluctuations/volatility in relation to your operation?

26. What are 2003 projections for Operating Expenses and Compensation and Benefits?

27. How does management cope with pressure to meet "street" expectations?

28. Have personal performance targets been adjusted to reflect current economic and risk conditions? Are management expectations clearly established, communicated, and understood?

29. Do the company's reported results make real sense, in view of prevailing business conditions and the current economy?

30. Where might the company be subject to criticism, if at all, for "earnings management?" How strong are internal controls over the financial reporting process?

31. Are you anticipating any unusual charges to earnings, including write-down of goodwill?

32. Have you ever recognized "Swaps" or "Barter" transactions as revenue?

33. Have you ever recognized as revenues a transaction that was paid for by means other than cash?

34. Are mechanisms in place to identify and address emerging crisis risks, such as terrorism, brought about by economic or social changes? Who is responsible for monitoring those mechanisms? How often are those mechanisms tested?

35. How have you addressed the Client Privacy Issues relating to Internet activities?

36. Does the company have written policies on sexual harassment and diversity? How are those policies communicated to all employees? How is training conducted in these areas?

37. How does the company review potential mergers and acquisitions?

The obvious purpose of this document is to flag areas of concern for the prospective insured and, with the broker's help, to prepare answers to the questions in order to "deliver a risk profile that is desirable to the underwriting community."[24]

Such advice is, in other words, marketing advice. The broker helps the prospective insured put its best foot forward in purchasing insurance, but the broker does not counsel his or her client on how to modify its corporate governance structure. As an insurer explained, "For a broker, an insurance broker to get in there and say, 'Let me have eight hours from your board' . . . It is just not taken particularly well. . . ."[25] Thus, like D&O insurers, brokers provide little in the way of loss-prevention programs. Brokers may provide other valuable services—including negotiating with insurers to structure the insurance tower and, in the event of a claim, using their market power to pressure insurers to settle—but these services do nothing to monitor the conduct of corporate insureds.

Why Don't D&O Insurers Monitor?

There are a number of reasons why it may not be feasible for insurers to provide loss-prevention programs. First, loss-prevention advice may be a public good, and as a result one might well expect that it would be undersupplied.[26] Public goods are those things that society as a whole needs but that individuals, by themselves, are unwilling to provide because individual producers typically cannot recoup their investment in providing the good. It is difficult to recoup one's investment because public goods have two basic characteristics: (1) they are nonrival—in other words, one person's consumption of the good does not reduce the supply available to others—and (2) they are nonexcludable—that is, it is difficult to exclude those who have not contributed to the cost of the good from enjoying the benefits of the good. The classical example of a public good is a lighthouse. One mariner's use of the light does not reduce its usefulness to others, nor can those who have not contributed to the expense of building and maintaining the lighthouse be excluded from the benefit it bestows.[27] Likewise, national defense is a typically considered a public good.

General loss-prevention advice may also be a public good. Loss-prevention advice is nonrival in the sense that one corporation's use of information about how to avoid D&O losses does not diminish the supply or usability of the same information by another corporation. Similarly, it is difficult to exclude others from the use of such information since, once known, it can easily be transmitted by parties other than the producer. So if loss-prevention advice is produced by D&O insurers, it may easily be transmitted by the insured or by their lawyers or their insurance broker to a larger group, who may in turn pass the information along. This inability to exclude others from the value of the advice is, of course, a disincentive to invest resources in the production of such information, since it impedes the producer from recouping those resources by charging for the information. As anyone who has followed the decline of the recording industry knows, it is difficult to get users to buy something from you when they can obtain it elsewhere for free. This means that insurers (and everyone else for that matter) will underinvest in research about general loss prevention.

But even if general loss-prevention advice is likely to be undersupplied, it may still be possible for insurance companies to extract value by tailoring their loss-prevention program to the unique circumstances of particular insureds. A tailored loss-prevention program does not have the same public good features as loss-prevention programs generally, because information specific to a particular company's situation is, by definition, not broadly useful and thus less likely to be passed on by parties other than the producer of the information. The producer can therefore exclude others from use of the information and charge users for its production. However, a tailored loss-prevention program is likely to be expensive to produce, requiring not only knowledge of how companies in general may reduce their shareholder litigation risk but also detailed knowledge of the unique situation of a particular corporation, including how its corporate governance and accounting controls work. Such knowledge is far from the typical one-size-fits-all corporate governance discussion, in which commentators debate the merits of isolated features such as board independence, poison pills, and various compliance committees. Because this requires a thorough and detailed review of the finer points of how the corporation is managed, as well as a high level of legal, financial, and accounting expertise to assess this information, such tailored advice is extremely expensive.

Nevertheless, D&O insurers may be in a unique position to provide such a service. As we have already noted, alone among all possible providers of loss-prevention advice, insurers fund the losses. They are, in other words, bonded to their advice. In addition, insurance companies are less subject to cooption by the client than fee-for-service professionals because the insurer is less dependent on any one client for business.[28] Moreover, as the ones ultimately at risk for losses, insurers are likely less susceptible to the ideological biases of corporate governance "policy entrepreneurs."[29] For all these reasons, D&O insurers should be, in theory, among the most trusted suppliers of loss-prevention expertise.

As we have already described, D&O underwriters undertake a thorough examination of the deep governance features of prospective insureds, mining variables of culture and character along with financial risk factors and structural governance features of firms. They could extend this underwriting analysis to provide the basis of loss-prevention guidance. That they do not do so is a puzzle. D&O insurers do not seem to be capitalizing on their comparative advantage at providing corporations with tailored loss-prevention programs. Moreover, according to our sources, corporations largely ignore D&O insurers' occasional loss-prevention advice and do not look to D&O insurers for monitoring services of any kind. Why not? Why are insurers unable to offer a service—monitoring—that their corporate purchasers seem to need and that they are uniquely situated to provide? We address this question in the sections that follow, focusing first on the institutional barriers to monitoring by D&O insurers and then on a possible agency-cost explanation.

Institutional Barriers

A handful of institutional barriers may prevent D&O insurers from bundling loss-prevention programs with D&O insurance. These include (1) a lack of underwriter knowledge and experience; (2) characteristics of securities misinformation losses that may make monitoring futile or prohibitively costly; (3) the layered, excess-of-loss structure of D&O insurance programs; and (4) the insurance underwriting cycle. We consider each of these potential explanations in turn.

UNDERWRITER KNOWLEDGE AND EXPERIENCE. Perhaps an obvious explanation for the D&O insurer's failure to engage in ex ante monitoring is the claim that D&O insurance companies cannot competently monitor because they do not employ people with the necessary knowledge and experience. Insurers simply do not have the skill sets of investment analysts, lawyers, and accountants. While we tend to agree that most current D&O insurance personnel lack the requisite skill set to be competent monitors of corporate governance, we feel that this explanation inverts cause and effect.

Accounting firms, law firms, and consulting firms all sell compliance and other securities loss-prevention services to public corporations. For example, former SEC Chairman Harvey Pitt has organized a consulting firm to advise both on corporate governance and risk management. What this suggests to us is that there are at least some individuals with skill sets that enable them to convincingly market their expertise in providing loss-prevention services.

The most obvious candidate to provide these services may be the accounting firms that every public company retains to audit their financial statements. Accountants are currently well situated both to gather and to analyze this information, but unlike D&O insurers, they do not bond their advice by agreeing to pay for a loss. This fact that has led some commentators to suggest that the best way to monitor and distribute the risk of fraud might be for accounting firms to insure the financial statements of the firms they audit. Professors Ronen and Cunningham, for example, have recently advocated the creation of a new product, financial statement insurance (FSI), to guarantee the accuracy of financial statements.[30]

Whoever ultimately provides the package of loss-prevention and risk-spreading services, the existence (and apparent profitability) of corporate governance consulting firms suggests that there are indeed experts who can gather and process information relevant to the risk of shareholder litigation. It may be expensive, but the fact that it is being done suggests that information costs alone cannot be the principal bar to the creation of robust loss-prevention programs. Moreover, if it can be done, D&O insurers should be able to do it, either by developing these areas of expertise or, at the very least, hiring individuals who have them. And we can think of no reason why such individuals, if adequately compensated, would not be willing to work for D&O insurers.

In this way, D&O insurers could easily acquire the knowledge and expertise to offer these services, and, indeed, if there are in fact efficiencies to bundling risk distribution and loss prevention as we suggest, then we would expect D&O insurers to do just that. Thus, the current lack of knowledge and experience on the part of D&O insurance personnel seems more likely to represent a revealed preference of the managers buying D&O insurance policies than a significant institutional barrier. It must not be worth it for insurers to acquire the skill set to sell these services because the market will not compensate them for doing so.

THE FUTILITY OF INSURANCE MONITORING.   Perhaps D&O insurers do not provide corporation-specific monitoring because it would not be cost-effective. There are at least three reasons to suspect that this might be so. First, it may be that shareholder litigation is a truly random event—uncorrelated with any identifiable predictive factor—in which case it would be impossible to advise a prospective defendant on what sorts of actions they ought to take to mitigate their risk, since no such precautions would in fact reduce risk. Alternately, shareholder litigation may not be random, but business risk may so outweigh governance factors in determining the frequency and severity of claims that additional monitoring of corporate governance is not worth the candle. Finally, getting sufficiently inside the corporation to provide effective monitoring may be prohibitively expensive even if governance risk really is significant. While the structure of our research does not allow us to answer any of these possibilities definitively, we can offer the following observations on the basis of our research.

First, the question whether shareholder litigation is a random event, rather than the consequence of poor governance, is a variation on the "do the merits matter?" question so hotly debated in corporate and securities law circles. We focus on this question more directly in chapter 8. For now we note that there is a substantial amount of empirical research supporting the proposition that the merits matter—at least to some degree—in shareholder litigation. Studies conducted since the enactment of the PSLRA in 1995 have found that securities lawsuits are now more often dismissed and that the securities claims now take longer to settle, suggesting perhaps that plaintiffs' lawyers are bringing better claims and pushing them harder.[31] Perhaps most significantly, studies find that claims featuring clearly identifiable indicia of wrongdoing or fraud—such as earnings restatements, insider selling, and concomitant regulatory investigations—settle higher than claims without such features.[32] Insofar as such indicia correlate with the merits of a securities claim, these studies may support the proposition that at least some meritorious claims settle higher than nonmeritorious claims. Moreover, as we described in the preceding chapter, D&O insurance underwriters believe that corporate governance—properly and broadly understood using their metaphors of culture and character—does correlate with securities liability risk, as demonstrated by the fact that they consider corporate governance in deciding whether to sell D&O insurance and on what terms.

Second, even if shareholder litigation is not wholly random and completely uncorrelated with merit, it is possible that factors other than fraud or bad governance so dominate corporate governance risk that the savings from a loss-prevention program focusing on corporate governance factors would not be worth the cost. Indeed, as we described in the preceding chapter, D&O underwriters focus extensively on financial factors in pricing insurance. This suggests that factors such as a firm's market capitalization, the number of shares that regularly trade, and volatility, as well as the firm's industry sector and maturity, are critically important in gauging D&O risk. These factors, of course, cannot form the basis of a loss-prevention program. No insurer would ever tell a prospective insured to reduce its market capitalization or change industries merely to avoid shareholder litigation. If business and financial risk factors are much more important in determining liability risk than idiosyncratic factors such as a firm's unique governance structure, then it will not be worthwhile to design a loss-prevention program focusing on governance factors.

This may well be, but there is more that we would like to know before drawing such a conclusion. First, as we have argued elsewhere in this book, it is critically important to know how much D&O risk can be predicted on the basis of financial or general business risk factors and how much D&O risk attaches to specific governance items. The most we can say about this on the basis of our research is that those involved in the D&O industry claim that both financial or business risk factors and governance risk factors are significant. Ideally, we would compare the effect on D&O pricing of various financial and business risk factors—such as market capitalization, volatility, industry, and maturity—compared with a firm's specific governance features. However, without corporate disclosure of D&O premiums, it is impossible to determine the relative importance of finance and corporate governance risk in D&O insurance pricing. Therefore, it is impossible to draw a strong conclusion about whether financial and business risk so dominates governance risk that there is little marginal benefit to be gained by designing and adopting an expensive loss-prevention program. It is, in other words, presently unclear whether merits matter enough to justify loss-prevention programs. As we will argue in the concluding chapter, this is one reason to require public companies to disclose the details of their D&O insurance programs.

Third, with regard to the expense of getting sufficiently inside the corporation to do effective monitoring, accounting firms already are deep inside the corporation. For that reason, the most cost-effective way to bundle monitoring and risk distribution may involve a combination of accounting and insurance functions. One possible approach is the financial statement insurance concept we mentioned earlier, in which insurance companies offer insurance that would guarantee the accuracy of financial statements.[33] This idea has received considerable attention in legal academic writing,[34] but insurers and accounting firms have not embraced the idea. One reason may be that the proponents have emphasized both the novelty of their idea (a plus for an academic audience but not for existing firms) and the legal and institutional change required for implementation. In addition, they have predicted that it would lead to dramatic improvements in the accuracy of financial statements that may seem unrealistic to firms.

In our view, the concept of bundling monitoring and risk distribution is simpler and less novel than they suggest. As we described earlier, economists have long understood that monitoring can be an important benefit that corporate insurance provides to shareholders, and the obvious candidates to perform monitoring in the D&O insurance context are the accountants who are already deep inside the corporation. Accounting firms already provide a limited amount of "insurance" (in the form of professional liability), and D&O insurance companies already provide a limited guarantee of financial statements (in the form of coverage for securities violations related to inaccuracies in the statements). The challenge is to identify incremental ways to bring these two functions closer together, without the need for legal reform or dramatic changes in existing institutions.

Developing a realistic set of incremental steps requires further work, including consultation with experts in the accounting industry. Nevertheless, to illustrate the kind of innovation we have in mind, we note that an accounting firm could agree by contract to provide a warranty that a particular financial statement does not contain material misrepresentations. The warranty could be drafted so that it provides protection that is equivalent to existing D&O insurance. For example, the warranty could be limited to a specified dollar amount (recognizing that the firm would remain potentially subject to additional liability on a traditional malpractice basis), and the warranty could be made subject to conditions similar to the exclusions in D&O insurance policies. The firm could obtain contractual liability insurance coverage from an insurer that would indemnify the firm for any warranty payments. From an underwriting perspective, this contractual liability insurance coverage would be similar to D&O insurance and thus could be offered by D&O insurance companies with relatively little change in their operations. This limited warranty would bring the monitoring and risk distribution functions closer together without the need for legal change.[35]

THE LAYERED, EXCESS-OF-LOSS STRUCTURE OF D&O INSURANCE PROGRAMS. D&O insurance programs consist of layers of insurance coverage provided by different insurance companies on an excess-of-loss basis. This arrangement is often conceptualized as a tower, with the primary insurer—that is, the insurer whose limits are first reached in the event of a claim—at the bottom and each excess insurer becoming responsible for a claim only after the lower layers of insurance are exhausted. All insurers within the tower thus bear a part of the risk of the total policy limit, and each insurer's risk can be greater or less depending on their position in the tower (or, in the language of the insurance trade, their "attachment point"). Similarly, the total policy premium is divided among all insurers within the tower, with those who bear greater risk receiving a greater share of the proceeds. The primary insurer receives the greatest share of the premium, in line with its position facing the greatest risk.

This excess-of-loss structure might be seen as an obstacle to the development of loss-prevention programs, since the benefits of such programs would accrue to the insurance program as a whole—that is, to all insurers in the tower—while the costs would be imposed on a single monitoring insurer. And indeed, the one company we found that had designed a serious loss-prevention program had designed its program in precisely this way, conducting its own research into the firm's governance practices and offering discounts if specific corporate governance practices were followed. If this program improved the governance quality of the insured and thereby reduced its D&O risk, that risk reduction was a benefit that the rest of the insurers in the tower shared without any contribution to its cost.

Nevertheless, we doubt that this feature alone explains the absence of loss-prevention programs. Insurers incurring additional costs as a result of their loss-prevention programs could demand an additional share of the D&O premium to compensate them for those costs. Indeed, the primary insurer would be well positioned to fill this role. Moreover, if their loss-prevention efforts provided value by decreasing the risk borne by other insurers in the tower, we would also anticipate that those insurers would accept lower premiums when they participated in D&O insurance programs in which primary insurers provided valuable loss-prevention programs. That such an arrangement has not been struck suggests to us that some other explanation must lie at the core of this problem.

THE INSURANCE UNDERWRITING CYCLE.   The insurance underwriting cycle provides one final potential explanation for the absence of loss-prevention programs. Recall from our discussion in chapter 3 that underwriting premiums and coverage restrictions increase and decrease as insurers tighten or loosen their standards in response to capital losses or, alternatively, the influx of new capital in the insurance market. This regular oscillation through hard and soft markets affects many aspects of the insurance relationship, most notably price, but also coverage terms and underwriting standards.

In soft market conditions, underwriters are eager to sell insurance contracts and, in addition to lowering their prices, often loosen their standards on risk. It would not therefore be surprising if soft market conditions also eroded the ability of insurers to insist on the adoption of loss-prevention programs as a condition to underwriting an insurance policy. Monitoring, as we have said, is likely to be considered intrusive by the insured and, were it ever to be seriously considered, may well be one of the first items to go in a soft market. Indeed, the story we have already related about the one company that attempted to establish a loss-prevention program supports this proposition. As we noted above, when this company insisted on loss prevention as a part of coverage, it found itself undercut by competitors emphasizing that "those guys will make you jump through a bunch of hoops; we can get the insurance for you cheaper . . . without all the fuss and bother."[36]

Although we accept that the market may appropriately discourage loss-prevention programs with high costs and low marginal benefits, we suspect that if loss-prevention programs could be shown to enhance value by reducing risk, insurers would be competing to provide the best such program. Moreover, we would not be surprised if insureds eagerly sought coverage with the provider with the best such program since, even if the insurance policy insulates them from financial loss, shareholder litigation can have negative reputational consequences that, we expect, managers would be eager to avoid by reducing their risk. Again, the absence of such programs cannot be explained by this factor alone.

Agency Costs, Again

As the preceding discussion makes clear, none of the institutional barriers adequately explains why D&O insurers do not in fact bundle loss-prevention programs with D&O insurance, which brings us back again to the agency-cost story we first considered in chapter 4. Consider the following: When an accounting firm, a law firm, an outside director, or a consulting firm provides securities loss-prevention advice, the downside is the potential for a loss that—in the vast majority of cases—will be insured. When that advice is provided as part of a bundled package of monitoring and risk distribution services, however, the downside is much bigger: ignoring that advice could lead to an uninsured loss for the corporation.[37] If taking the advice is likely to have no impact, or a positive impact, on share prices, then a manager whose compensation is linked to those share prices should be willing to take it. But in at least some circumstances, the advice will be bad-tasting medicine—a disclosure, a revenue recognition decision, or some other accounting judgment that means that the company will not "make the numbers" for the quarter and, thus, share prices will decline. In that case, the manager may prefer not to take the advice. Linking that advice to D&O insurance protection—so that ignoring the advice means that there is no insurance for any resulting loss—would significantly constrain the manager's autonomy. Who wants that? The answer may be, the shareholders.

Here is the heart of the issue: if managers knew best, and if managers could be trusted to act in the best interests of the shareholders, then the shareholders should want their managers to purchase flexible loss-prevention advice—advice that the managers can ignore, in their best judgment, without losing D&O insurance protection. Even then, however, shareholders should want their managers to get the insurers' best loss-prevention advice, because that advice is, as we have emphasized, more fully bonded than the advice from any accountant, lawyer, or consultant. There is no reason to believe that insurance companies would be unwilling to provide that advice, with no strings attached (other than the right to charge a higher price if the advice is ignored). Yet the evidence suggests that managers do not want that advice from insurance companies.

It is true that D&O insurance companies are not presently structured to provide excellent, tailored loss-prevention services, but they could be. Indeed, a longtime top official in the D&O insurance industry described a time that he and another senior official prepared a detailed set of loss-prevention recommendations for a customer in the early days of what was then their new company. (Because the D&O insurance industry is so small, we cannot provide more information about the backgrounds of these two officials without revealing their identities to the insiders who, we very much hope, will read our book. But we have talked to many people in the industry, and we are confident that these two officials are very highly regarded, with more than enough technical accounting and legal competence—and wisdom—to undertake this task.) Very pleased with their work, they mailed it off to the customer. "We got it back," he reported, "almost like it was something we sent them in a brown envelope. They didn't want it. And they didn't want it in their files. We learned that's not what they want from us."[38]

Conclusion

This chapter tells a complicated story. In theory, loss prevention should be a routine part of the package of services that any insurer provides. The insurers have the right incentives. They have the means to hire the necessary expertise. And their customers should highly value that service. In other contexts, insurance companies sometimes do, in fact, provide loss-prevention services, but in the D&O context, they do not. Clearly insurers understand that they could attempt to offer loss-prevention services in the D&O context, yet for some reason they are reluctant to do so.

Why?

Here again, we find the agency-cost explanation most compelling. Top executives buy D&O insurance, with their shareholder's money, so that all but the most extraordinary securities class actions will be a "nonevent" in the life of a publicly traded company. And, it would be easy to argue, they do not want to allow an insurer's concern about the possibility of a securities class action to be an event that interferes with their freedom. Thus, the absence of insurer monitoring, like the existence of the entity coverage itself, is an agency cost—a "perk" that managers buy to make it easier, and more profitable, for them to keep their jobs, at the expense of the shareholders who own the company. Top executives in public corporations are thus able to purchase income-smoothing insurance without ceding any governance authority to insurers because this purchase, like all such decisions, is insulated from shareholder challenge by the business-judgment rule. Insurers are willing to sell this coverage because, in most markets, they can do so profitably; they cannot be blamed for providing a product that customers are eager to buy. Most basically, corporate governance arrangements that cannot place reasonable limits on CEO compensation can hardly be expected to place reasonable limits on a far less visible (and less expensive) insurance product that is not widely understood.

CHAPTER SEVEN

The D&O Insurer at Defense and Settlement

In the last two chapters, we examined the influence exerted over public corporations by the third-party insurer at the time insurance is purchased and later, during the life of the insurance contract. We found, first, that D&O insurers do seek to price policies on the basis of risk and, second, that one of the factors they consider in assessing risk is the governance quality of the insured. Nevertheless, we expressed doubt that the pricing of the D&O policy succeeds in deterring the kinds of bad corporate acts that lead to shareholder litigation. D&O insurance makes the risk of shareholder litigation visible within the corporation by putting a price on it. But the pricing process does not present clear choices that provide a basis for corporations to engage in loss prevention in order to obtain a lower price. Moreover, in examining the role of the insurer during the life of the policy, we found that insurers do not monitor their corporate insureds, exacerbating the moral hazard problem. Indeed, were we to end our account of the relationship between D&O insurance and corporate governance on these points, we would be tempted to conclude that insurance very nearly severs the relationship between shareholder litigation and deterrence.

But our account does not end there. Once a claim has arisen, the insurer can attempt to exert control over the progress of the claim, defending some claims more vigorously than others or, alternately, moving some claims more quickly toward settlement. As the party that ultimately funds settlement, the D&O insurer has significant say over settlement amounts. Insurers could vigorously fight and stubbornly refuse to settle nuisance claims and, in the event that genuine corporate wrongdoing is uncovered, insist on a greater contribution to settlement from the corporate insured. In this way, the insurer's control over defense and settlement offers another potential avenue for the insurer to reintroduce the deterrence function of shareholder litigation. And it is in that vein that we examine, in this chapter, the role of the D&O insurer in defending and settling shareholder litigation.

The D&O Insurer's Role in Defending Shareholder Litigation

Shareholder litigation, of course, is not the only context in which insurance proceeds fund the defense and settlement of claims. Insurance companies are the true party at interest in a wide variety of tort claims, from automobile accidents to medical malpractice. There are, however, several important differences between D&O coverage and these other forms of coverage. We explore these differences in the sections that follow, with an eye toward how these differences in the form of coverage affect the D&O insurer's influence in the defense of claims.

Duty to Pay as Opposed to Duty to Defend

Liability insurance generally provides two related kinds of protection: protection against the costs of defending a claim and protection against the costs of judgment or settlement. Traditionally, liability insurers have not simply paid the costs of defense and settlement; rather, they have assumed control over the defense and settlement.[1] Put in terms of the standard automobile or general liability insurance policy, insurance companies have the right and duty to defend a covered claim, and they have the discretion to settle that claim.[2]

This structure makes sense because insurers are repeat players with significant claims-processing and defense expertise and also because allocating control to an insurer mitigates an additional risk of moral hazard. Just as a person who knows he is insured may be more likely to engage in risky conduct prior to a claim having arisen, so too is a person who knows she will be fully indemnified for her expense costs likely to over-consume services used in her defense. To distinguish this aspect of moral hazard from the one we addressed in chapter 4, we will refer to it as "ex post moral hazard." Because moral hazard makes insurance more costly across the board, many consumers of insurance would prefer a mechanism to control this risk and therefore reduce their cost of insurance.[3] In other words, when buying insurance, consumers ordinarily would prefer to allocate considerable control over defense to the insurer because that structure would reduce the price.

In this regard, D&O insurance differs significantly from auto and general liability insurance. D&O insurance policies provide the insurance company with the right to "associate" in the defense of the claim, meaning that the insurer is entitled to receive information about the defense of the claim and to provide input to the defense lawyers, but the clear understanding and practice are that the policyholder, not the insurance company, controls the defense of the claim. Indeed, we learned that some defense counsel treat D&O insurance companies as adversaries when defending a securities class action. The better approach, our participants agreed, was to maintain cordial, cooperative relations with the insurance company, but the existence of this alternative view provides one demonstration of the limits of the insurers' control over the defense.

Moreover, D&O insurance policies do not give the insurance company the traditional control over settlement reflected in the standard "discretion to settle" provision in other liability insurance policies. Instead, D&O insurance policies put the policyholder in charge but obligate the policyholder to obtain the insurance company's consent before settling a case. This creates a very different settlement dynamic than in an auto or general liability case. In an ordinary auto or general liability case, the insurance company controls the defense and settlement, keeping the policyholder informed enough so that its employees will do what the insurance company's lawyers need in order to maintain the defense. The insurer most likely will consult with the policyholder before settling the case, especially if people involved have good relationships and the insurer's claims manager values the in-house counsel's judgment. But the insurer is not obligated to do so. In shareholder litigation, in marked contrast, the policyholder is in charge, subject only to the need to obtain the insurers' consent to settlement.

When we asked the defense lawyer and risk manager participants in our study why D&O coverage was structured this way, the typical response was that D&O insurance companies are not trusted to act in the insured corporation's best interests once a claim has arisen. As a senior lawyer in the general counsel's office of a Fortune 100 company pointedly asked us,

"Would you trust an insurance company to defend you?"[4] To him, at least, the obvious answer was an emphatic "No."

While we do not doubt the sincerity of that view, we think it provides only a partial explanation. We do understand where that view came from. Many corporate policyholders have had poor claims experiences with the liability insurance industry over the last twenty-five years.[5] Liability insurance coverage disputes routinely follow in the wake of any significant environmental or product liability claim, with the result that litigation with customers has become an acceptable, normal state of business relationships for the major commercial insurance companies. Coverage litigation is not as common in the D&O context—nor is it entirely unheard of, as we describe in chapter 9—but nevertheless, many of the same carriers whose reputation has suffered as a result of their claims conduct under other lines of insurance also sell D&O coverage. And the history of their claims conduct under other lines of insurance may have a negative effect on their perceived trustworthiness with regard to the defense of securities class actions and other shareholder litigation covered by D&O insurance.

Nevertheless, we think there are important differences between D&O coverage and other lines of liability insurance that could provide a basis for greater trust in the D&O insurance context. The environmental and products liability claims that arose under general liability policies were brought years and even decades after the policies were sold, at a time when no underwriter could have predicted either their frequency or severity. Thus, insurance company leaders may have felt that they had some justification for contesting these claims on the grounds that the policyholders had not paid premiums consonant with the coverage demanded years after the fact. By contrast, D&O insurance claims typically relate to recent behavior of a kind that D&O insurance underwriters cannot reasonably claim to have been a surprise.

This is especially true given that D&O insurance policies are "claims made" policies—meaning that they apply to *claims* made during the policy period regardless of when the underlying injury took place (as opposed to the "occurrence" form that is followed in commercial general liability policies, which covers *injuries* incurred during the policy period, regardless of when the claim for relief is eventually made) and are typically renewed each year. In other words, insurers have ample opportunity to perform due diligence and to circumscribe their D&O risk. Perhaps as a result, litigation between insurance companies and their policyholders has traditionally been less common in the context of D&O insurance claims than in similarly sized product liability claims. Moreover, the D&O insurance market has been very responsive to customer demand. The interested customers here include the directors and officers of the very largest corporations. They buy D&O insurance every year with their shareholders' money; they are willing to pay more to get better coverage; and they get relatively rapid feedback from their brokers on whether the product is performing as advertised.

As a result, we are very reluctant to conclude that D&O insurance coverage gives policyholders so much control over the defense and settlement of claims because insurance companies could not provide trustworthy coverage in the traditional duty-to-defend manner. Instead, we conclude that D&O insurance coverage is structured the way that it is— with policyholders choosing and directing their own lawyers—because that is the structure that D&O insurance buyers prefer.

Claims Management

Even within the duty-to-pay structure of D&O insurance policies, insurers might still exercise some control over claims costs. Indeed, as George Cohen has observed in the context of legal malpractice insurance, some of which is structured similarly to D&O insurance, "After diversification, the risk reduction method most used by legal malpractice insurers, as well as by other liability insurers, is ex post loss reduction."[6]

Typical measures taken by insurers in this context include negotiating preferred rates with particular law firms, maintaining a list of approved counsel providing an adequate defense at a relatively low cost, monitoring counsel to reduce unnecessary discovery or motion practice, and managing the settlement process to minimize the sum of defense and settlement (or judgment) expenses.[7] Because of the insurer's direct control over the defense in automobile insurance, medical malpractice insurance, and general liability insurance, these kinds of ex post loss reductions measures are the norm in those lines of insurance.

Similar results could be obtained, at least in theory, through the D&O insurer's right to associate in the defense and the power to refuse to pay for unreasonable defense costs. Nevertheless, D&O insurance personnel reported to us, with some frustration, that they exercise little or no practical control over defense costs.

We did find that two leading D&O insurers maintain lists of preferred counsel, but when we obtained copies of these lists, we found that almost every prestigious securities law firm we could think of was on the list. For example, both lists contain prominent and very high priced New York firms such as Sullivan and Cromwell and Cravath, Swaine and Moore. The first list that we obtained contains 552 law firms, 257 of which are multiple offices of the same national firms. The second list is significantly shorter, with 182 firms, of which 77 are multiple offices, suggesting that this insurer did exercise more control. However, we soon learned that insurance buyers can and often do insist on retaining preferred counsel regardless of whether the firm appears on the list, either by prearrangement during the application process or through waivers after the fact, as long as the policyholder can demonstrate that the lawyer and the lawyer's firm have substantial experience defending claims. We learned of only one case in which a recognized securities defense law firm was rejected, and our source explained that the claims manager refused to hire the law firm in retaliation for that firm having engaged in aggressive litigation against the insurer in the past.

The lists and the waiver process do serve the important function of channeling the defense of securities class actions to law firms with substantial experience. We learned of situations in which an insurer would not allow inexperienced, regional law firms to defend a case. But even here the insurer's role may have been less significant than it first appears. One participant suggested that the general counsels at the corporations in question may not actually have wanted those law firms to defend the case, knowing that the firms did not have adequate experience, but arranged to have the insurance company make that decision to preserve their close relationships with lawyers in the firms.

There were two other situations in which we learned of a D&O insurer asserting some control over the selection of defense counsel. First, a D&O insurance claims manager reported that insurers sometimes prevent claims from being defended by the same law firm that handled the issuance of the securities in question on the grounds that the law firm and the policyholder have a conflict of interest. In these situations the claims managers reported that insurers proceed by persuasion and negotiation and that they are not always successful. Second, a variety of participants reported to us that claims managers closely scrutinize and sometimes refuse to approve requests that separate counsel be appointed for individual officers or directors or subgroups of individual defendants. The claims managers try to proceed through persuasion and negotiation, but they do have the authority to refuse to pay the fees of the individual firms—an authority that we will discuss shortly—on the grounds that there is not a sufficient conflict of interest among the defendants and that the additional defense costs are therefore not "reasonable" within the meaning of the D&O insurance policy. In any event, the D&O insurers do not control who is appointed as the main defense counsel, or even who would be appointed as the secondary defense counsel, but simply whether the secondary counsel can be appointed.

In short, D&O insurers have relatively little control over who conducts the defense. In addition, our participants reported that insurers have very little control over how the defense is conducted. The insurers have no control over strategic litigation decisions and not much more control over defense costs, except in some cases with regard to the decision about whether to appoint separate defense counsel for some or all of the individual defendants. Insurers do occasionally require insureds to submit litigation budgets, but senior insurance company officials assured us that these budgets are largely pro forma and that very little is done to control costs. As one insurance company executive summarized,

> Generally speaking, the way this works is that the defense firms that are picked by the insureds are people that are qualified to represent the insureds in these sorts of cases and don't have conflicts. There are repeat players, and we see them over and over again, and we don't object to their retention, and we consent ultimately to incurring defense costs.[8]

Occasionally an expense item might raise an insurer's eyebrows—for example, we were told a story about lavish expenses charged by a defense lawyer who, rather than use the hotel gym, ordered a treadmill to be brought to his room—but typically the expenses are paid. As another top insurance executive explained, "[In other lines of insurance,] insurance companies are known for negotiating lower rates and not letting people fly first-class. Well, that is not the case here. Now the lawyers are selected by the policyholders, and they fly first-class."[9]

It is worth noting that defense costs are not insubstantial, even in relation to total losses under a D&O policy. While there are no definitive, publicly available defense cost data as there are for auto insurance, medical malpractice insurance, and other coverage lines, the Towers Perrin D&O insurance survey includes questions about defense costs. Excluding claims that were closed with no payment to the claimant, Towers Perrin reports that the median and mean defense costs in shareholder litigation were

$800,000 and $3,042,159 per claim.[10] Compared with the median and mean settlement amounts reported in the same survey ($1.6 million and $26.5 million), this suggests that defense costs fluctuate between 50 and 11 percent of the cost of paid claims, declining in percentage terms as the settlement amount increases. Our respondents confirmed this back-of-the-envelope estimate. One senior underwriter reports that defense costs commonly rise to 25–35 percent of the settlement amount and sometimes go as high as 50 percent.[11]

The head of the claims department of a leading D&O insurance company described the defense cost situation as follows:

> We don't have a high level of control. . . . [T]he policy suggests that we will pay for reasonable and necessary defense costs. The case law on that is pretty funky and is not positive to insurers. . . . So the situations where you can absolutely reject it—the behavior has to be incredibly egregious behavior.[12]

The D&O product manager at another leading D&O insurance company described the incentives somewhat more bitterly:

> On the defense side, and again, this is not an accident, this was totally predicted, with the insureds not having an economic participation, they don't really care, and so it is no accident that the rates for securities firms have gone from $40 and $50 per hour to $750 per hour in the last five years. That is not photocopy inflation, okay. That is the fact that they can charge that amount and that the companies will pay it. Increasingly, we get boxes of bills, so to speak—you know, "Here, sort through it and pay it." So, you know, the inflation on the defense cost side is huge, probably much faster than the overall settlement as a whole, but nobody has really studied it . . . I just think that it is a function of, "You get what you can," and I think the defense firms can charge $700 per hour because nobody cares. I mean, it is staggering to me.[13]

The same product manager provided an example that clearly illustrated his understanding of the ex post moral hazard, although without using that term:

> I will give you two customers, both Fortune 500 companies, both in 10b-5 securities class actions. One customer spent $75 million in the course of eighteen months, and another one spent $3.5 [million], and the difference was the deductible. In one case it was our money, and in the other case it wasn't; it was

their money. And the difference was how they watch-dogged it, how they went through the bills, how they leaned on these guys and pushed back. In the case of the $70 million bill, they had a $250,000 deductible, and the insured stopped caring a long time ago, and, literally, it boiled down to us opening boxes, you know, exercise bicycles, things in hotel rooms, I mean, you couldn't believe the stuff that was in that box, but it was all billable, it was all defense expenses. On the other case, they had a $20 million deductible, and they were pounding on that law firm in terms of the bill. Think about that difference, though. I mean, that's a huge, exponential difference in the cost of the case.[14]

Two features of D&O insurance programs reduce insurance companies' incentive to control defense costs in very large cases. Defense costs count against the limits of a D&O insurance policy. And D&O insurance programs are layered, very often with a $5 or $10 million primary (first-layer) policy. In combination with the high cost of defending securities class actions, these two features mean that the defense costs alone may well exhaust the first layer of coverage and sometimes even additional layers of coverage. Once it is clear that the defense costs will ultimately consume the policy limits, an insurer has little incentive to try to reduce the fees in that case. As a claims manager described, "You sometimes observe those carriers as kind of going to sleep, not doing anything, just kind of rubber-stamping."[15]

The D&O Insurer's Role in Approving Settlement

As we have noted, virtually all U.S. public corporations purchase D&O insurance, and shareholder litigation is largely funded by insurance proceeds. What this ultimately means, to both plaintiffs and corporate defendants alike, is that their settlements are funded by other people's money. And other people's money, our respondents confirmed, is often viewed as easy money. As one defense lawyer candidly pointed out, "You know, the [defendant] company doesn't care about the insurance company's money."[16] Others agreed: "[I]t is much easier to [talk settlement] when you can play with somebody else's money."[17] Even the claims managers agreed: "I think it is easier to get money out of an insurance carrier than it is out of an insured. Why? Because it is a third party's money. We are in the business of paying claims. That is what we do for a living."[18] This point was made most clearly in the following story, related to us by a monitoring counsel:

[T]he meeting of the board of directors to decide how to resolve these securities class actions goes something like this: Defense counsel comes in, makes a presentation that's very erudite about the nature of the case and the defenses that are available. At the end of the presentation he says that "we believe it would be recommendable and it is appropriate and highly recommended that the board approve a resolution that allows us to pay $60 million to resolve this case."

"Gasp, gasp, that's $60 million." . . . "How are we going to pay for $60 million? We just had a presentation with the finance committee, and they said we need this, this and this. How are we going to pay for $60 million?"

The general counsel says, "OK, fine. We have $70 million in D&O insurance and every dollar is coming out of D&O."

The next question is, "What time is lunch?"[19]

But insurance money is not easy money for everyone, most notably not for the insurers whose reserves fund the settlement. Their foremost concern at settlement, obviously, will be to minimize claims payments. Secondarily, they may be interested in delaying settlement, since the longer they delay paying out their reserve accounts, the larger the investment return on their reserve accounts will be. That is, other things being equal, the faster an insurance company pays out its reserves, the less investment return it realizes. Every insurance carrier thus has an incentive to delay paying claims in order to maximize investment returns.

The claims managers we spoke to in our study denied that they intentionally delay settlement in order to increase their companies' investment return on the reserve accounts. In the words of one claims manager, "[Y]ou wouldn't have to look too long or hard to recognize that you are not making money by investing with interest rates the way they are. That's not anyone's motivation from the insurer's side. The insurer would be far better off making a reasonable settlement at an early time and building good will."[20]

Yet many other participants in our study, on both the plaintiff and the defense side, confirmed this tendency. "Insurance carriers' profitability is driven by two things," one defense lawyer pointed out, "their payout ratio and what are they earning on their investments. They can have a very high payout ratio and be very profitable [because of their investments]. So they're never in a hurry to pay out."[21] And again, in the words of a prominent plaintiffs' lawyer, "Most [insurers] in my view will set very high reserves on these claims internally and then decide when they have to reserve them by really settling the case for less than the reserve, OK, so that they can report a higher income."[22] Although it is impossible to gauge precisely a D&O insurer's profits from the investment of reserves (since the aggregate financial statistics insurance companies must disclose to insurance regulators do not segregate their D&O lines), we note that the insurance financial reporting category that includes D&O insurance along with other lines—the "other liability" category—reports income from the investment of reserves that has recently varied from a high of 28 percent of net premiums in 1999 to a low of 11 percent of net premiums in 2002.[23]

Whatever their investment returns, common sense suggests that the longer a carrier is able to keep its reserves invested, other things being equal, the better its results will be. This may well create an incentive for them to delay payment on claims, offset of course by the reputational risk from being seen as more recalcitrant than the norm. This does not mean that claims managers consciously drag their heels in order to delay settlement. Indeed, we are inclined to believe that they, like traditional claims managers, would like to close their files.[24] The mechanism is more systematic. The layered nature of D&O insurance slows down settlement.

The sections that follow explore the impact of insurers and insurance on the settlement process, first by looking at the incentives and bargaining power of the insurer in the settlement process vis-à-vis other parties, especially plaintiffs' lawyers and defense counsel, then by examining how certain structural features of D&O insurance policies—notably limits and layers—affect the settlement dynamic and, ultimately, the outcomes of claims.

The Insurer's Leverage at Settlement

The insurer's leverage over settlement is rooted in the insurance contract. D&O policies typically provide that the policyholder must obtain the insurers' consent before agreeing to a settlement. As expressed in a basic policy form, "The Insureds shall not admit or assume any liability, enter into any settlement agreement, stipulate to any judgment, or incur any Defense Costs without the written prior consent of the Insurer."[25] Insurers might be able to use this authority to cut off the flow of easy money to plaintiffs (and their lawyers) and also to prevent defendants (and their lawyers) from simply buying their way out of trouble.

The insurer's authority, however, is not all powerful, for two reasons. First, refusal to settle entails the risk that the insurer could be liable for the entire judgment that results, not just the limits of the D&O insurance policy. As described by our participants,

[I]f there is a demand to settle within the limits and then the insurer takes on a very great risk in refusing that demand to settle within limits and saying that they are going to seek to go to judgment. . . . They risk bad faith action or some other kind of action that will make them responsible for the whole amount and not just the limits. So the defendant wants to settle and the insurer needs to settle in order to avoid the bad consequences of refusing to settle.[26]

Under long-standing principles of insurance law, a liability insurer that refuses to accept a reasonable offer of settlement within the limits of its policy has, in effect, waived the limits of the insurance policy and will thus be liable for the full amount of any resulting judgment, no matter how much that judgment exceeds the limits of the policy.[27] Given the potentially very large damages at stake in a securities class action, and the small size of any individual D&O policy in relation to those damages, the duty to settle places disproportionate pressure on D&O insurers.[28]

Indeed, our plaintiffs' lawyer participants confirmed that they craft their settlement offers precisely to put this kind of pressure on insurers: "[I]t is great to [make a demand to settle within limits] because then you put the insurers in a bad faith posture potentially."[29] Defense counsel, in turn, are apt to emphasize that an insurer's failure to settle at an amount that his or her client considers fair might expose the insurer to a bad faith claim. As one defense lawyer described the situation, "[I]f you are a defendant, you want a policy limits demand because that is what puts you in a position to say [to the insurers], 'You can now settle this case without hurting me, and I demand you do it.'"[30] Another defense lawyer was still more direct on this point: "[W]hen I'm talking to coverage counsel, I always use little terms to remind them [about bad faith]."[31] An insurer confirmed this dynamic in the following colloquy:

A: [A]sserting that the failure to consent to the settlement has been made in bad faith is something which is, you know, an occurrence that people are used to in this arena.

Q: It is part of the dance?

A: Well, I wouldn't call it a dance, because at that point it is kind of a—it's more wrestling than a dance.[32]

Corporate insureds are also aware of the pressure that such a demand can place on their insurers. As described by one of our participants, "Insurance is very much a factor in settlement amounts. Companies are much more willing to pay with insurance company money than with their own money. They are very much mindful of setting up the bad faith case in their settlement strategy."[33] Mediators too are well aware of this pressure and are occasionally able to use it to bring about settlement. As described by a plaintiffs' lawyer, "really good mediators are particularly sensitive to insurance carriers and particularly sensitive and aware of putting carriers in a bad faith posture. So that's the only thing that can really create the leverage."[34]

The second constraint on the insurer's settlement authority comes from the contract law principle obligating insurers to exercise their authority to withhold consent only in good faith. This principle appears explicitly in many D&O insurance policies. For example, one commonly used policy form provides, "The Insureds agree not to settle any Claim . . . without the Company's written consent, which shall not be unreasonably withheld." Because insurance companies do not have the legal authority to withhold their consent to a reasonable settlement, they do not have an actual veto on settlement. Insurers can insist that the policyholder seek their consent. Indeed, there is legal authority to the effect that a policyholder who settles a case without first seeking the D&O insurer's consent forfeits coverage under the policy.[35] Insurers can also refuse to consent to a settlement that they do not regard as reasonable. But they may be forced in the end to pay that settlement. The policyholder can choose to settle the case despite the insurer's objection, pay for the settlement out of the corporate treasury, and then initiate a breach of contract action against the insurer, alleging that the insurer unreasonably refused to consent to the settlement.

Corporations are not eager to settle a case without their insurer's consent, and the norm clearly is to obtain consent before settling. But the policyholder's ability to limit its downside risk—by settling now and fighting with a recalcitrant insurer later—surely affects the willingness of a D&O insurer to refuse to consent, particularly when other insurers in the program do consent and, even more particularly, when an insurer that sits higher in the program has consented to the settlement. We explore this dynamic shortly.

Summing up, what these observations suggest to us is that the insurer's principal means of creating leverage at settlement—the power to refuse to consent to proffered settlements—is very significant, but it is constrained by the risks associated with refusing a reasonable settlement and by the policyholder's ability to settle now and fight with the insurer later. There is, of course, a second means by which the insurer might gain leverage vis-à-vis the insured in settlement negotiations—namely, by the threat to rescind or otherwise deny coverage. We treat the question of coverage defenses on its own in chapter 9. But, looking ahead to that chapter, we will note here that our participants do indeed report the strategic use of coverage defenses—that is, to extract greater contributions from the insured toward settlement. In combination, these levers give insurers much more direct control over settlement than they have over the defense of securities class actions.

Insurance Structure and Settlement Outcomes

In evaluating the impact of D&O insurance on the settlement of shareholder litigation, it is also important to consider certain structural features of D&O policies that may influence outcomes at settlement. Central among these are the limits and layers of the policy. We already saw how the layered nature of D&O insurance programs may increase defense costs. We will now explore how this layered structure may affect settlement.

Limits

The limits of D&O insurance policies are an obvious and widely noted structural factor affecting the value of settlements in shareholder litigation.[36] Insurance money, as we noted above, is seen as relatively easy money. As a result, plaintiffs will seek to settle within limits whenever possible. In the words of one respondent, "[M]ost plaintiffs' lawyers are very mindful of the policy limits, and they realize that if they are reaching beyond the policy, this is a different case. [If] you talk about the company coffers, people are going to resist heavily, [but] the company doesn't care about the insurance company's money."[37] Reaching for damages beyond insurance limits can be difficult, as described by a plaintiffs' lawyer:

> [I]t is just easier to get money out of an insurance company. [Paying claims] is what they do. . . . [Y]ou are going to have a bigger fight if you are trying to get the issuer itself to pay up, just as you know you are going to have an even bigger fight if you are trying to squeeze money out of individual managers.[38]

Insurance limits, in other words, drive settlements. Limits may, in some cases, pull settlement amounts up—by giving plaintiffs' lawyers a set target—the D&O policy—to shoot for, thus allowing them to recover an amount they might not have received but for the insurance. Indeed, some of our respondents went so far as to suggest that the best way to avoid shareholder litigation would be not to have any D&O insurance. Clearly, this was a facetious suggestion—a highly solvent underinsured company might be as desirable a target as an adequately insured company—but it nevertheless underscores the perceived importance of insurance in settlement.

In other cases, limits may serve to reduce settlements. To see this, consider that average investor losses at issue in a securities claim are significantly higher than average coverage limits, even for large-cap companies. NERA estimates that the median investor loss among all settled cases was $340 million, which is more than the highest amount of insurance coverage available during our research ($300 million).[39] Indeed our intuition is that the variance in investor losses is larger than the variance in settlement amounts and that insurance policy limits play a significant role in the dampening effect that this relationship suggests. Put another way, average settlements are likely to be pulled down to be in line with average limits, as much or more than they are influenced by average investor loss. The same dynamic might explain why settlement amounts do not increase proportionally with increases in investor loss—for example, for a case settled in 2006, a $100 million investor loss would result in an expected settlement of 5.1 percent of loss value, compared with only 1.1 percent for a $1 billion loss.[40] This strongly suggests that settlements have at least as much to do with insurance limits as with investor loss. These and other related propositions are testable, in theory, but the data needed—the D&O limits of companies settling shareholder litigation—are not publicly available.

We will argue in chapter 10 that the limits and other aspects of D&O insurance should be publicly available. Here we pause only to note the following implication: if indeed settlements track limits more than they track investor loss, then in a period such as the late 1990s and early 2000s, when public company market capitalizations increased, thereby raising potential investor losses in securities suits, and D&O coverage limits did not experience a similar increase, D&O insurance limits may actually have resulted in less damages being paid than legally recognizable loss would have dictated. In this way, insurance may reduce plaintiffs' recovery from claims as well as increase it.

Insurance policy limits, of course, operate as a hard boundary only for insolvent defendants. Plaintiffs' lawyers claimed to be more or less indifferent to insurance if the corporate defendant was financially strong. "If it is a large-cap company," one plaintiffs' lawyer told us, "I don't care what the policy is."[41] And indeed, there occasionally are settlements in excess of D&O policy limits. Additionally, defendants sometimes contribute to settlements that are less than the available limits of D&O insurance.

Nevertheless, given that insurance funds a large portion of settlements even for solvent corporations and that all our participants reported that insurance is at least somewhat easier to get than damages from the corporation itself, it would not be surprising to find that plaintiffs are, more often than not, willing to settle for insurance money alone. And indeed, this is what we find. All of this leads to an interesting dynamic: once a claim is moving toward settlement at or near the limits of the D&O policy, the plaintiffs and the defense have common adversaries—namely, the D&O insurers. Rather than operating as adversarial parties seeking to disprove the arguments of the other, plaintiffs and defendants have a common interest in persuading the D&O insurers to part with their reserves.

This dynamic, in which plaintiffs and defendants join in a common interest against the insurers was explicitly confirmed by our respondents. Indeed, they occasionally described it in terms of express collusion. As one plaintiffs' lawyer told us, "[I]t is great to [make a demand to settle within limits] because then you put the insurers in a bad faith posture potentially. [And that] really does strengthen the hand *of the defendants against the insurers*."[42] Notice that the plaintiffs' lawyer is aware of strengthening of the hand of his supposed adversary, the defense counsel, against the insurer. Another plaintiffs' lawyer told a similar story, involving a more direct joining of forces:

> I can think of at least three times in the last two years that I have had a defense counsel say to me, "We could settle this, but the carrier is giving me a hard time you know and this is all an off the record conversation, etc., etc., but if you want to write a letter like this or you want to do that," or "Listen, when we go to the mediation session, I am going to have these two guys from the carrier there. I suggest you say in your presentation X, Y and Z." I mean they script it for me.[43]

Although such collusion between plaintiffs' and defense attorneys may seem jarring, from the defense counsel's point of view, settling within insurance limits, even up to the maximum insurance limits, may be the best way of serving the interests of his or her client. Consider, on that point, the following anecdote related by one of our participants:

> I can remember a mediation I was once at, and the mediator was going around the room and asking everybody to introduce themselves with the plaintiffs' counsel. There was a company principal senior officer, and he said, "My name is such and such, and I'm," I can't remember, the CFO or the treasurer or whatever, "and my purpose of being here today is to get the case settled for any amount up to and including the full amount of the limit."[44]

The defense lawyers that we talked to confirmed that much of their role involves persuading the insurer to pay—often, as we described above, by warning them of the potentially severe consequences of failing to settle.

Similarly, plaintiffs-style damages models also become a tool used by defense attorneys against the insurers. As candidly described by one defense counsel, "sometimes you want to use [plaintiffs-style damages] to scare the insurance company to pony up more jack."[45] And, indeed, insurance carriers confirmed the use of such tactics, noting,

> It is almost routine now to see a plaintiffs-style damage analysis filed by Cornerstone and others and given to defense counsel. . . . They are often given to defense counsel who tend to use those, not necessarily with the plaintiffs' counsel but with the carriers saying, "Oh my god, we hired this big expensive group of economists, and they are smart people and they did all this number crunching, and look, there is a catrillion dollars in potential damages here!"[46]

The phenomenon of defense lawyers and plaintiffs' lawyers cooperating to place pressure on liability insurers is hardly unique to securities class actions. Indeed, it is a well-recognized feature of personal injury litigation. But in personal injury litigation, the insurance company chooses the defense lawyer, so the lawyer's long-term interest in getting business from the insurer moderates this phenomenon to at least some extent. By contrast, D&O insurers do not choose the defense lawyers or control the defense. Instead, D&O insurers pay the defense costs of the securities defense lawyer that the policyholder selects, subject only to the dollar limits of the policy and the difficult to enforce requirement that defense costs be reasonable.

In sum, limits serve as a frame for settlement amounts. In some cases the limits may pull settlements up, and in other cases they may pull settlements down. When the limits substantially exceed even the upper end of the range of prior settlements in comparable cases, the limits likely have no impact on the settlement amount. When the limits are in the lower end of the range of prior settlements or below that range, the limits likely reduce the settlement amount. And when the limits are in the upper range of comparable settlements, the limits likely increase the settlement. If information about corporations' D&O insurance programs and the amount of the insurers' contribution to defense and settlement were publicly disclosed, this hypothesis would be easily testable.

Cases in which the defendant pays deserve careful attention in any effort to provide a comprehensive analysis of settlements since they may be more likely to be meritorious claims. Defendants have to pay their own money for one of three possible reasons: the amount of the damages so greatly exceeds the insurance limits that the plaintiffs are unwilling to settle within those limits, one or more of the D&O insurers in the program is insolvent (an uncommon situation), or some or all of the D&O insurers in the program have strong coverage defenses. High-damages cases are widely regarded by researchers to be more meritorious than low-damages cases, and thus excess-of-limits settlements likely have a strong claim to merit. Similarly, cases in which corporate insureds contribute to within-limits settlements may also suggest considerable insurer leverage at settlement, either because the insured is pressed to settle, perhaps as a result of unrelated business exigencies, or perhaps because the insurer has been able to extract concessions from the insured owing to a coverage defense, a possibility we explore in greater detail in chapter 9. Looking ahead to that chapter, we can report here that some of the most important coverage defenses are more likely to be raised in a very meritorious case.

Layers

The question of limits fundamentally is the question of what amount of insurance is available. But, as our participants emphasized, "It's not just the amount of insurance. It's amount and structure."[47] In discussing the structural elements of insurance, our participants drew our attention to the design of the insurance tower. In describing how settlement offers are strategically crafted, one of our respondents emphasized the structure of the tower as follows:

> When they craft settlement offers that are less than the total tower, they will craft those offers mindful of the structure of the tower so as to put pressure, say, on level 3 carrier, level 4 carrier, that you know any time that you offer to settle

within limits of level 3, then you have got as your ally levels 4, 5, and 6, who are pushing level 3 to settle, and if levels 1 and 2 have already decided that it is into the third carrier level, that . . . brings a lot of pressure on that third carrier.[48]

Emphasizing these structural elements, our participants described the ability of layers within a tower of insurance to act as a "firebreak" on settlements.

DESIGN OF THE TOWER.   At the beginning of every case, the working layer of insurance is the primary insurer, which generally remains the insurer in charge of coordinating with the defense team at least through the hearing of the motion to dismiss. Many cases, in fact, will never reach the excess layers of insurance. With the exception of very large cases or cases with extensive parallel proceedings, the primary insurance policy—the bottom layer—is often large enough to cover the defense costs for a securities class action. As a result, excess layers are unlikely to be interested or involved in the early stages of a typical case. Or, more simply, as we were told, "Remember who drives the case. The case is driven by the primary carrier. It's very rare that the excess carriers are engaged."[49]

But some cases, of course, survive the motion to dismiss. Such cases may well exhaust the limits of both the primary insurer and often the initial layers of excess. In a D&O insurance policy, unlike a typical auto or general liability policy, the defense costs count against the limit of the policy. Well before their limits are actually exhausted, these carriers know that they are, in our participants' words, "toast." In this case, a conflict of interest may arise among the various layers of insurance within the tower. Layers of excess insurance will favor an early settlement at any amount that does not reach their layer, while the primary and any lower level excess carriers that are toast will prefer to delay settlement so they can maximize their own returns by holding their reserves for as long as they can.

Of course, this dynamic is subject to the risk of bad faith liability, but threatening an insurer with bad faith liability requires the ability to actually settle the case within the limits of the recalcitrant insurer. The plaintiffs are unlikely to be willing to make an offer to settle within the limits of policies that everyone agrees are toast. The settlement amount will ultimately fall within the layer of some particular carrier (or two carriers that share a single layer). The incentives thus line up as follows: all of the toast carriers—that is, those whose limits have been exceeded and who would therefore prefer simply to delay settlement so as to maximize the investment gain from their reserves—as well as the target insurer—the one within whose limits the plaintiffs and defense lawyers believe the case should settle—are united in seeking to resist settlement (at least until trial is imminent), while the plaintiffs' lawyers, the defense lawyers, and the upper-level excess carriers push for settlement. "Often what you find," one of our participants explained, "is that defense counsel is aligned with an excess layer to try to put pressure on a lower layer that won't exhaust or won't basically open up the coffers."[50]

One mediator described the push for settlement as follows:

[O]ftentimes [I] can say, "I don't know what the settlement is going to be, but it's going to be at least $50 million." And then you look at what the insurance tower is, let's say $100 million, and you look at the fact that they are spending $1 million a month. Those carriers in the higher end of the tower sort of see the hurricane coming, and they know that absent sort of a Hail Mary motion to dismiss or summary judgment ruling, it is going to be at least a $50 million settlement. If you don't settle for two years, we are going to get through $24 million, and so they see it coming, and they are urging early settlement because it is in their interests at this time since the hurricane won't get to them, and that is why those insurers at the top become much more aggressive advocates for an early settlement, whereas the ones down below know that they are toast under any circumstances, whether they get wiped out by the cost of defense or wiped out by the minimum $50 million settlement.[51]

In this dynamic, the primary carrier's deeper knowledge of the details of the case, as well as the details of settlements in other cases, gives it influence over the other insurers. The primary carrier has more information about the case in question because it has been working with the defense lawyers from the beginning of the case. If the primary carrier is one of the few insurers with a large market share, that carrier will also have more information about the details of other settlements as well. This information gives the primary carrier an edge in the settlement discussions, limiting the power of the excess carriers to push for early settlement.

The excess insurers themselves could, of course, simply become more involved in earlier stages of claims. In general, however, they do not do so. The exception to this general rule may arise when companies within the same corporate group act as a primary insurer and an excess insurer, in which case the primary carrier can protect the limits of its corporate affiliate by settling earlier at a lower total amount.[52]

It strikes us that another way for multiple insurers in a single-coverage package to align their incentives would be to underwrite coverage not, as most now do, as a tower of horizontal layers, but rather to enter into what is sometimes referred to as a "quota share" structure. Under a quota share system, each insurer sells a specified percentage of any claim, up to the total limits of coverage. So a 15 percent quota share underwriter in a $10 million total limits package would pay $150,000 toward a $1 million settlement and $1,500,000 toward a $10 million settlement. Each insurer, in other words, would participate in every claim, according to its quota share, and one insurer (or claims management consultant) would manage claims on behalf of all of the insurers in the program. This, of course, is dramatically different from the typical tower arrangement where upper-level excess carriers rarely have any liability even when claims are settled against the program. Because it aligns the interests of each insurer within the total program, and because conflicts of interest among insurers were cited by our respondents as a significant source of friction in settlement, we are surprised that the quota share structure is not more common in D&O programs in the United States, especially because it is common in D&O insurance programs in Europe. Our best explanation is that U.S. insureds do not want their D&O insurers taking a more active role in the management of defense or settlement and therefore are willing to buy D&O insurance policies with inherent conflicts among their insurers.

To reiterate, settlement dynamics are shaped not only by limits but also by the structure of coverage, and tiered towers of coverage frequently give rise to conflicts of interest among the insurers within the tower. Lawyers craft their settlement strategies mindful of the layers of coverage and the likelihood of conflict between layers. Moreover, once they have worked up through the insurance program, obtaining consent from at least some of the lower level insurers, to arrive at the target layer of insurance in which the plaintiffs' and defense lawyers conclude the case should be settled, they are mindful to give that insurer an incentive to settle rather than to press the fight. As described by a prominent mediator,

> I've done mediations where I simply looked at a plaintiff and said, look, if you really want to settle this case now, the reasonable people can disagree as to whether it is a $5, $10, $11, or $12 million case, but the truth is you are not going to settle this case now unless you give AIG or Chubb some opportunity to save some money off their $10 million policy, because if they get the choice of tapping themselves out now and paying their $10 million now or continuing to pay

this fireman becoming toast, you get a pretty easy choice, but if you offer them the opportunity to save $1 million off their policy, they are going to be highly incentivized to perhaps get this done.[53]

Meanwhile, carriers higher in the tower, eager to protect their own limits, may pressure the target carrier to accept the discount and settle. Once the targeted layer of insurance accepts a discount and agrees to the proposed settlement, any recalcitrant insurers in the lower layers will find that they are indeed toast. How can those insurers effectively argue that the settlement amount is unreasonable when the insurance company sitting above them in the program, which accepted less premium for the risk, has agreed that the settlement is reasonable? Yes, it is possible that the target layer is mistaken, but that will be hard to prove after the fact, once the plaintiffs and defendants settle the claim with the consent of the other insurers.

FIREBREAKS.   If increasing settlement demands are like wildfires, then the layers within an insurance tower may function like firebreaks. Each layer within an insurance tower represents a new level of insurance involvement, a new monitoring counsel, and a new team of claims managers that must approve the settlement. As described by our participants, "In a case that's not Enron or some massive fraud case, every time [the plaintiffs] hit another layer, it acts like a firebreak and makes it easier to negotiate a settlement."[54] Another of our participants illustrated this point by means of a numerical example: "If there's a $25 million first layer and there is a case that is going to settle around $25 million sometimes you will tell the plaintiffs, 'look, I can give you $25 million assuming the first layer is on board. I can give you $25 million, but if you want $28 million, you know, I'm not sure I can get it, and it's going to slow everything down by six months.' "[55] Thus, at the very least, the insurers' changing of the guard adds delay. But perhaps most importantly, the additional layers of process may act as a break on settlement amounts. One mediator described the process of working through layers as follows:

[As] I work my way up these layers, every time I am starting with a new fresh person. And do you have kids who play video games? And you get to go to a higher level? A new monster jumps out. And you slay that one? All you get is a bigger monster? That's what it feels like to me. . . . It's exhausting, and they want it to be exhausting.[56]

Plaintiffs' lawyers also readily acknowledged coverage layers as an additional burden, although they, in general, were more likely to downplay their influence in the ultimate outcome. In the words of one plaintiffs' lawyer, "[The tower] is a smaller factor than the damages and the risks and all that. [When] you have a case that you really think is worth $40 million, you are not going to settle for $12 million because that is the first layer."[57] Another plaintiffs' lawyer noted that a layered program "makes it very difficult, particularly if you have a recalcitrant level in the middle. . . . [But] I don't think it really saves them at the end of the day. It just makes the process less pleasant. . . . I don't know that it changes the outcome very much."[58]

The impact of multiple layers is not as simple as "more tiers, lower settlements." But consider a hypothetical involving three companies, A, B, and C, each facing a factually identical securities claim and each with identical aggregate insurance limits. The only difference is the structure of the tiers. Company A has a tower containing four tiers consisting of a $5 million primary policy, first excess of $5 million, second excess of $10 million, and third excess of $20 million. Company B has a single $40 million policy. And company C has what would probably be most typical, a larger primary layer of $20 million and two excess layers of $10 million. In this example, the multiple layers of coverage of company A could act as firebreaks contributing to a lower overall settlement than that paid by company B or C.[59] Although several of our participants acknowledged this effect of multiple layers in settlement, and some defense lawyers may recommend adoption of such a structure for strategic reasons, it is likely that most companies with multiple tiers have them serendipitously, because their underwriters made a decision to limit their exposure to any one risk, not because anyone consciously decided to put together a program with lots of firebreaks on the securities class action settlement process. Whether more, smaller insurance layers lead to lower settlement values than fewer, larger layers is, in theory, testable, but once again, the necessary data are not publicly available.

In this chapter, we have sought to examine the role of D&O insurers in, and the influence of D&O insurance on, shareholder litigation once a claim has arisen. We have described how D&O insurance policies give insurers no direct control over the conduct of the defense and how, in fact, D&O insurers have little ability to control defense costs. Their authority over settlements is significantly constrained by the threat of being found to have acted in bad faith by unreasonably withholding consent to settle. The settlement dynamic, however, may be influenced as much by the structure of coverage as it is by what insurers do or say. Thus, insurance limits and structure influence settlements, sometimes increasing settlement amounts and other times decreasing those amounts. Our motivation throughout this account has been to identify some means by which insurers, through their influence over defense and settlement of claims, may in effect reintroduce the deterrence function of shareholder litigation ex post through their claims management practices. Unfortunately, our principal finding in this chapter has been the relative weakness of insurers in influencing the defense and settlement of claims. Even the contractual obligation of policyholders to obtain their insurers' consent before settling does not provide insurers with as much power to force a case to trial as might be expected, once it is seen in light of legal rules regarding insurers' obligation to settle and limits on the discretion to withhold consent.

CHAPTER EIGHT

What Matters in Settlement?

A s we talked with our participants about the influence of insurance and insurers over shareholder litigation, gathering material for the previous chapter, the conversation often turned to the broader question of what factors influence outcomes in settlement. What factors make a claim ripe for settlement and bring the parties to the negotiating table? And what factors tend to increase or decrease settlement amounts? We were eager to hear what they might say on this subject since it promised some insight into the debate over the merits in shareholder litigation. Indeed, we hoped that our participants would illuminate the longstanding debate over the question, as it was provocatively framed by Janet Cooper Alexander, of whether the "merits matter" in the settlement of shareholder litigation.[1] That is, do the legally defined elements of a claim control settlement outcomes? Or do other, nonmeritorious, factors determine the outcomes?

In this chapter, we explore what matters in the settlement of shareholder litigation. We do so, as we have done throughout this book, through the eyes of our participants, those involved in the daily give-and-take of settlement negotiations. Here they primarily are plaintiffs' and defense lawyers, mediators, and the insurance companies' monitoring counsel and claims managers. We approached the question of what matters in settlement both directly and indirectly. First, we asked our study participants to describe the settlement process and to explain what factors bring the parties together to begin to negotiate a settlement. From there, we confronted the question of value, asking them to describe which factors, in their experience, are most important in determining the ultimate settlement amount. Finally, we approached the question of merits directly, seeking to understand it from their point of view. How do the participants in securities class actions understand the merits and how do they talk about them? How do they use ideas about merit in settlement negotiations? And how do they view the role of merits in shaping settlement outcomes?

Of course our qualitative research methods cannot settle the question once and for all of whether the merits matter in the settlement of shareholder litigation. Nevertheless, we believe they can produce significant insights into the settlement process, moving us toward a more nuanced understanding of what matters in settlement and what these things may (or may not) have in common with our ideas about legal merit. The sections that follow seek to relate the insights from our conversations.

Getting to Settlement

The first step in understanding settlement is to understand the incentives of the parties within the structure of a typical claim. As described in chapter 2, the earliest point when a typical claim is ripe for potential settlement is immediately following the briefing on the motion to dismiss. Prior to this time, the defendants' and the insurers' incentives are decidedly in favor of fighting the claim and forcing the plaintiffs to put their evidence and theories on the table. The plaintiffs' response to the defendants' motion to dismiss informs the court, and the defendants, of what the plaintiffs have been able to put together without formal discovery. With this information, the parties can consider an early settlement that handicaps the outcome of the motion to dismiss and projects forward the range of potential outcomes if the case were to survive the motion to dismiss.

Most cases do not settle at this point, however, and instead proceed to the resolution of the motion to dismiss. If the defendants win the motion, the plaintiffs generally have the option to amend their complaint, and the process begins again, until the motion to dismiss is denied with prejudice, the plaintiffs give up, or the defendants lose a later motion to dismiss. Once defendants lose a motion to dismiss, settlement is practically inevitable. The question is simply when and for how much. At this point, the incentives on the defense side of the table begin more obviously to diverge. The lower level insurers, as we noted in the prior chapter, have an incentive to delay settlement in order to maximize their investment returns, while the defense counsel, likewise, may prefer to enter discovery in order to be able to continue "billing the file." This dynamic was described by a monitoring counsel—"defense counsel will work a case until they have decided they have earned enough money and then they will tell you it's time to settle"[2]—and confirmed by a defense lawyer—"defense lawyers' compensation is a function of their billable hours, and they have an incentive to take these cases down-stream."[3] The defendant, however, is likely to favor quick settlement, recognizing that in losing the motion to dismiss, it loses its best chance to win the case, and since settlement is now likely in any event, the sooner the liability is off the corporate books the better, especially if settlement is largely funded with insurance money. Depending on the structure of the D&O insurance program and the amounts at stake, the excess insurers may also prefer an early settlement.

In addition to this dynamic, our participants emphasized that business exigencies may also lead the corporate defendant to press for quick settlement. A number of significant corporate events—such as a major corporate transaction, a change of CEO, or a change in accounting or auditing firms—may impel settlement. The merger partner or new CEO, for example, may want to eliminate contingent liabilities created by the ancien regime; a new auditing firm may want to close the books on old liabilities; or the CEO may want to package the settlement with some other piece of bad news, in the hope that the combined impact will be less than if the two take place at different times.

Our participants confirmed that a range of such motivations are often the driving force bringing the corporate defendant to the table. For example, a plaintiffs' lawyer reported,

> What drives a settlement? . . . Corporate events—a company may be interested in a merger, acquisition. They may be issuing stock. They may be interested in being taken over, going private, whatever. Those things will also cause companies to want to clean up litigation. . . . [Or] a company could be taking a significant write-off for unrelated reasons in a particular quarter and throwing litigation reserve on top of that might be a problem because they are already showing a loss. So they might as well clean up in that period.[4]

Similarly, a defense lawyer told us,

> [I]t could be that they want to sell the company and they want to get everything behind them. It could be that they . . . are going to get rid of the CEO for other

reasons or the CEO is going to retire and they want to have everything happen on the watch of the old CEO. There are a lot of situations like that where people want to clean things up.[5]

A company could be approaching a periodic disclosure deadline and would prefer to disclose a settlement rather than a potentially large contingent liability since, as described by a mediator, "If the litigation is material enough . . . the litigation itself has to be disclosed and discussed in filings."[6] Such business exigencies tend, it would seem, to lead to higher settlements, as the corporate defendant moves to settle the litigation sooner rather than later, pressing its insurers to get it over with and, in the event that the insurers resist, agreeing to fund a larger portion of the settlement itself in order to get the deal done. On the other hand, there may be other business exigencies, such as business failure and impending insolvency, that encourage quick settlement without necessarily increasing settlement amounts.

The plaintiffs' side, meanwhile, typically favors early settlement but may favor delay in some cases. As described by a defense lawyer, "Plaintiffs' lawyers would love to settle a case as soon as possible in the litigation, but often they will be aware of the fact that they need to get their settlement approved by a court. They believe that they must do some amount of work and have some sort of a paper record in order to get the settlement approved by a court."[7] A monitoring counsel similarly described this dynamic: "In jurisdictions where there is a lodestar approach to fee awards, there tend not to be early settlements, because the [lodestar approach] rewards the plaintiffs' lawyers working the file notwithstanding an agreement on all parts, an acknowledgment by all parties that there is decent liability."[8] Plaintiffs' lawyers may thus prefer to enter discovery at least to build the file enough to justify their fee. However, because plaintiffs' firms must fund such efforts themselves, their willingness to delay settlement will also depend on whether the firm has other cases in the pipeline and, if so, on the cash flow demands related to those other cases. As one plaintiffs' lawyer described the dilemma, "Do you need money to fund the engine while you're waiting for the huge pot of money?"[9]

In sum, the parties typically arrive at settlement negotiations sometime after the motion to dismiss has been filed, most typically after the motion to dismiss has been denied, and they are often brought there, on the defendant's side, by business exigencies pushing settlement to eliminate the contingent liability of shareholder litigation sooner rather than later, as long as the settlement is largely funded by the insurer. Plaintiffs' lawyers, meanwhile, may prefer early settlement, while remaining sensitive to the need to litigate at least long enough to justify their fee as well as the need to settle cases in order to bring operating capital into the law firm. These then are important factors that bring the parties to the table. What they talk about once they get there is the subject of the next section.

What Matters in Settlement?

Once the parties have reached a point where they are willing to consider settlement, negotiations begin. Our participants described settlement negotiations as evolving from extreme positions, typically through mediation. As described in the following colloquy with a monitoring counsel,

A: It's starting off on opposite extremes and working to the midpoint.
Q: And what are the tools that you use to get to the midpoint?
A: Basically, arguing to the plaintiffs that their case doesn't have sex appeal, doesn't have the players, doesn't have the damages, doesn't have any of the factors that make a case expensive, and sometimes you win, sometimes you lose.[10]

Consistent with the standard economic model of settlement, in which cases settle when the expected value of a case as assessed by the plaintiffs overlaps with the expected value of the case as assessed by the defendant, our participants explained the settlement process by reference to predictions about how liability and damages would be assessed at trial.[11] This separate consideration of liability and damages is conventional in the literature on settlement, and it also reflects the way that our participants described the settlement process to us. Because the end result of settlement is a value that takes both liability and damages into account, this separation is, to at least some degree, artificial. Nevertheless, in much of what follows we too will discuss liability and damages separately, while keeping in mind that a settlement conclusively resolves both.

Liability Elements: Sex Appeal

According to securities law "on the books," the core liability elements of a typical securities class action, as we explained in chapter 2, include the following: a material misrepresentation, recklessly or intentionally made, that caused some harm. We will refer to these elements in shorthand as misrepresentation, scienter, and causation. When our participants described securities law "in action"—the process of litigating and resolving the elements of liability—they focused, first, on those "factors in the litigation that give it what is normally referred to as sex appeal."[12] Sex appeal goes principally to scienter, sometimes to misrepresentation, and almost never to causation, which our participants most often treated as an aspect of damages not liability.

Cases with sex appeal, our respondents emphasized, are cases with scandalous or otherwise vivid facts. As one mediator put it, a "boring" case that "took place in a dimly lit corner of the accounting world" does not have the "sizzle" of "the SEC investigation," or "the executives being led out of the office with handcuffs."[13] Describing how to distinguish between cases with sex appeal and those without, a head of claims at a major D&O insurer said, "You take a look at what is alleged. Is this part of a scandal? Is this one where there is just outright cooking of the books? Or is it just old-fashioned misrepresentations of what they call projection cases?"[14] In the words of a monitoring counsel paraphrasing what he had heard from a mediator in a case without sex appeal,

> Look, there is no sizzle in this case. You don't have any of the upgrades that make this a nice case. You don't have the accounting restatement. You don't have the SEC investigation. You don't have the executives being led out of the office in handcuffs, all of which are sort of sizzle facts . . . that might lead to a nice settlement for the plaintiffs. You don't have any of that stuff. This is kind of a boring case.[15]

Summarizing this idea, another claims manager put it concisely: "[T]he sexier the case, the more interest there is."[16]

Factors giving a case sex appeal or sizzle include SEC investigations, criminal charges, suspicious stock repurchase programs, defendants pointing fingers at each other, the resignation of board members, whistle blowers, termination of the top officers, bad documents, and any case-specific facts that cast the defendants' motives or honesty in a bad light—the sorts of things we are likely to remember about the securities fraud cases reported in the newspaper.[17] A monitoring counsel offered a more concrete illustration: "Yeah, we've had situations where literally there were allegations of trucks just going in a circle and then, you know, coming back, you know, like an airplane that never lands, but they log it in as a flight. You know, the flight to nowhere."[18]

When our respondents talked about facts giving a case sex appeal, they often noted factors identified by other researchers as proxies for merit. For example, our respondents frequently cited earnings restatements, insider selling, and SEC investigations as key factors in their settlement negotiations, all of which can be seen as proxies for the underlying merits of the claim. This finding coincides with the econometric research into the role of merits in securities litigation done by Johnson, Nelson, and Pritchard. In their work, Johnson, Nelson, and Pritchard begin by identifying easily observable indicia of wrongdoing or fraud—such as earnings restatements and insider selling—and treating these items as proxies for merit.[19] They then find that claims with earnings restatements are more likely to settle than claims without them. Thus, insofar as this proxy correlates with the merits of claims (a correlation that they acknowledge is imperfect—some fraudulent conduct will not leave behind such a tangible trace, and sometimes the indicia of fraud do not point to actual fraud), their work supports the proposition that at least some meritorious claims are more likely to prevail than nonmeritorious claims.

Likewise, our respondents suggested that similar proxies for merit lie behind the sex appeal of a claim. Consider, for example, this plaintiffs' lawyer's off-the-top-of-his-head list of facts that increase settlement value: "[earnings] restatement, insider selling . . . suspicious stock repurchase programs . . . accounting violations."[20] Other respondents suggested a host of other factors that might support plaintiffs' assertions that the defendants committed fraud with recklessness or intent, factors such as earnings management and questionable revenue recognition practices that coincide with compensation schemes, giving managers an incentive to misstate results. In the words of a plaintiffs' lawyer, "We used to think that just a restatement case was great because it was an admission, but you need more than just a restatement. You need a restatement, and you need [to show] that somebody benefited by the wrong."[21] Someone benefiting from the wrong, of course, provides a basis to argue scienter.

Or, again, as illustrated in the following anecdote from a plaintiffs' lawyer,

> [I had] a one-quarter restatement case. At the end of the quarter, the company booked a sale where the customer had the right to return the goods. So, instead of it being a bona fide final sale where the risk of loss transferred to the customer, instead it was a conditional sale where the customer could take the goods and if he could sell them or wanted to return them he could. And so

that doesn't qualify for revenue recognition, because basically the transfer of risk never left the seller to go to the buyer. . . . And then the company within a quarter or two after that disclosed the fact that they improperly—they didn't use the word "improper"—but that they booked revenue they shouldn't have and . . . restated.

But the case lacks sex appeal. Why did it lack sex appeal? At the end of the quarter what I would have liked to have seen was some insider selling, so that the guy who improperly booked the thing and basically inflated the price in the marketplace benefited by selling some of their stocks and say, *ah-ha*, the reason they did this is because they wanted to sell stock . . . . So the motive for keeping the revenue and earnings up and everything else would be to keep the price of stock up. [But] nobody sold their stock. And so the argument then that's being made by the defendants is, "Oh, this was a, you know, this was negligence, it wasn't fraud, what's the dah, dah, dah, dah, dah." . . . And I don't have an answer because I don't have any juice, I don't have any sex appeal.[22]

Note from this quotation that a restatement—clear evidence of a misstatement and an obvious grounds for a 10b-5 claim—is not viewed as sufficient without something extra. Here the something extra is insider trading, which of course is not a necessary element of a 10b-5 claim but which nevertheless provides evidence of motive, which goes to scienter, a necessary element of the claim. Commenting on whether this is merit or not, a defense lawyer put the point concisely: "[I]nsider trading makes a dramatic difference in terms of the value of a case. Now you say, 'Well that's not really the merits. That's the cosmetics.' Okay, but they merge a little bit."[23] All of which is to say that sex appeal functions, in part, as a proxy for merit.

Like all proxies, the fit is not perfect. Accordingly, as used by our respondents, "sex appeal" was not a simple code word for "merits." Indeed, we suspect that much of what our participants put under the rubric of sex appeal are things that cognitive psychologists might consider part of the "availability heuristic,"[24] a decision-making shortcut where judgments are made on the basis of those factors that are most easily called to mind rather than on those factors that are strictly relevant. The availability heuristic can lead to systematic errors in judgment by overemphasizing vivid or emotionally charged bits of evidence over statistics and other, more banal pieces of data. Viewed in this way, sex appeal is not merely another way of talking about merit. Rather, it suggests that vivid and exciting facts are likely to increase the settlement value of a claim by more than would be warranted according to the law on the books.

Claims with exciting or embarrassing facts may thus settle for more than they would be worth, in an ideal world, while claims without such facts may settle for less. This seemed to be a common understanding of our respondents, especially where facts, were they to come out at trial, might embarrass executives. As described by a claims manager,

> More often than not . . . we hear there is really nothing there, but there's these documents and these e-mail messages that if taken out of context could be embarrassing and maybe would put things together so that we would have something to explain to a jury, and by the way, our president and CFO and CO, there's no way we can possibly present them to a jury.[25]

Others noted that executives are often unwilling to take the stand to explain a bad business outcome and emphasized the cost to the organization of bad publicity in a high sex appeal case. Another lawyer described a situation in which at least part of the sizzle was sharp business practices that called into question the business ethics of the defendants. But sex appeal or sizzle does more than inconvenience or shame defendants; it makes the plaintiffs' story more appealing and pulls the imaginary jury in the defense lawyers' minds closer to the plaintiffs' view of the case, increasing the plaintiffs' lawyer's bargaining power at settlement: "It's about telling the story and having somebody gasp as you are saying it and say, you know, I can't believe it."[26]

In sum, when our respondents talked about the liability elements of a claim, they spoke in terms of sex appeal. Many sex appeal factors can be understood by reference to the underlying elements of the claim, either as providing direct evidence of the particular element, as in the case of an accounting restatement, or as providing plaintiffs with a basis from which they can construct a theory that satisfies a particular liability element, as in the case, for example, of insider trading and scienter. But other sex appeal factors cannot be understood in reference to the elements of a claim and, instead, are factors that render a claim more vivid or sensational: the outrageously expensive shower curtain, the executives facing a criminal trial. Such facts are not directly related to the liability elements of the claim but rather help the plaintiffs tell a compelling story to a jury, if the case were ever to get that far, and, more importantly in most cases, help the plaintiffs tell a compelling story to the defendants' D&O insurance claims managers. Such factors, although they do not always correlate perfectly with the legally identified elements of a claim, may nevertheless point to some form of wrongdoing or mismanagement that, from a broader social policy standpoint, might be worth deterring. In the words of a monitoring counsel, "If you pay attention to what [is] really . . . meaningful at the friction points in either mediations or other settlement discussions, it is ultimately the fear of bad facts being proven, and I think that is merits."[27]

Damages Elements: Investor Loss

How then do all of these arguments about wrongdoing and intent turn into a number? How do all of the allegations and recriminations translate into an actual dollar amount at which the claim will settle? It largely depends, our respondents answered, on the potential damages.

Our respondents overwhelmingly emphasized the role of potential damages on settlement amounts. Damages, our respondents insisted, drive settlements. On this point, the following comment of a monitoring counsel is typical: "You said you wanted to talk to me about why they don't get tried, and it's real simple. The stakes are just too high."[28]

When our respondents talked in loose, general terms about damages, they often were referring to the initial damages estimate—what some called "plaintiffs-style damages." Our respondents used this phrase somewhat imprecisely, to mean different things in different contexts. Sometimes they used "plaintiffs-style damages" to refer, simply, to the total investor loss, as measured by the difference between the market capitalization at the peak price during the class period and the market capitalization once the accurate information was revealed. At other times it was simply a term of opprobrium for an inflated damages number produced using methods that, in the defense lawyers' view, failed to take loss causation adequately into account. In general, however, we observed that our participants used the term "plaintiffs-style damages" to refer to the very first cut in measuring damages, without correcting for other events in the market that may have had an impact on the relevant market capitalization. Today, the real damages demands by successful plaintiffs' lawyers are based on statistical models that attempt to make these corrections. Thus, the label "plaintiffs-style damages" is not a descriptively accurate term for investor loss, but many of our participants used that term for that purpose nevertheless.

Whatever the precise term used for the initial, rough estimate of the potential damages in a case, the resulting number can easily be astronomical, presenting an unacceptable risk to corporate defendants. As one defense counsel reported, "If your exposure is $5 million, you will handle the case one way; if it is $500 million, you are going to handle it another way."[29] Similarly, a monitoring counsel explained, "Suppose they have a defense that in a $500,000 case every single lawyer worth his salt says, "Go to a jury because you can prove this, and you will prove this. You can't go wrong with this." Take the 500 and make it 3 billion. Everybody changes their mind."[30] Our respondents repeatedly emphasized that the larger the investor loss, the less other factors actually matter. Indeed, our participants agreed, the single most significant settlement factor, the "driving force . . . is investor loss."[31]

Of course, investor loss is not the amount of damages that would be found by a court deciding the case. Indeed, as any securities law student can report, investor loss is typically much higher than the legally compensable damages.[32] Nevertheless, investor loss provides an easy, useful means of computing the outer limit of what is at stake. The head of one D&O claims department described how he used the investor loss to set his initial reserve on a case:

> When I get a securities claim in, one of the very first things I do is pull up just some core statistics and do a true back-of-the-envelope plaintiffs-style damages calculation. . . . So I will go to Yahoo. . . . I will quickly just pull up the chart as I am looking at it and take a look at the alleged stock drop . . . and the key is to go to the key statistics page and take a look at the float. How many shares were outstanding and what the float is. . . . That is, I'm giving the full benefit to the plaintiffs. So take the full float, times dollar amount of the drop. So say a hundred million shares times $7 a share is $700 million of potential damages. From that I apply what is generally understood—not written anywhere, but generally understood in the industry for whatever reason, and it is just averages I guess, that the garden variety 10b-5 claim will settle for somewhere around 5 percent give or take of plaintiffs-style damages, generally speaking. . . . So here is . . . $700 million in damages. Five percent of that is $35 million. I'm 10 × 80.[33] Right there I look at it and say I'm probably not going to be involved in this case just through that back of the envelope.[34]

In his view, the larger this rough-and-ready number, the less likely any of the parties to the litigation would be willing to take the case to trial:

> Pfizer has—I'm talking off the top of my head—3 billion shares outstanding, and the stock went down 10 bucks. That's $30 billion of damages. Five percent of that is $1.5 billion. Settlement. And you go to a judge and say, "The damages are $30 billion. We are proposing a settlement that is 5 percent. How can you

say that is unreasonable?" And we say, "It's unreasonable because it doesn't reflect the liability." And they say, "Sure it does. It's 5 percent of the total, but it could happen. So it is 5-to-95 chance to win. Yes, it's a perfect discount." But we say, the carriers, "Wait a minute. Wait a minute. They have a $250 million D&O policy. Are you telling me it is torched on a claim where they did nothing wrong?" And so sometimes the numbers will in and of themselves take over, and I have that on a number of the pharmaceutical companies or large jumbo cap companies. I have it with General Motors, General Electric. The stock ticks down $2, which isn't enormous. It's not a free fall. [It's] based on some news that might be innocuous, and it's enough because that creates a damage pool that is into the billions, which immediately gets the plaintiffs' lawyers out because there is damages, and the case has value irrespective of the merits.[35]

Of course, smaller investor loss cases also almost always settle, so we are skeptical about the claim that the size of the investor loss alone explains the aversion to trial. This insurer's focus on investor loss nevertheless reveals that this factor is of some importance in settlement.

Ultimate settlement amounts, of course, are nowhere near the total investor loss. Instead, our respondents described how they derived a percentage estimate of total investor loss, itself derived from other settlements, to guide them to the ultimate settlement. As described by a monitoring counsel,

> I think the largest and most determining factor is potential damages, and all these—the studies like Cornerstone's that we refer to—are extrapolations from what we refer to as plaintiff's style damages. And they say if the plaintiff's style damages expert says that damages are X, then the settlement value is a percentage within a fairly narrow band of X. And that's pretty much where you wind up.[36]

Settlements, in other words, are ultimately based on other settlements, with the parties using trends from other cases to guide them to an acceptable settlement range for their own. Of course, there is still plenty of room for dispute within the range, as described by a claims manager:

> You know, the plaintiffs' firm is bringing in their economists, and com[ing] up with some inflated crazy stuff. And obviously the defense tries to counter it, and actually I think it has worked out pretty well. If you look at the numbers, the settlement compared to the damages—you are talking anywhere from 2 to 6 percent of plaintiff's style damages [i.e., investor loss] if indeed truly you

think there was something done wrong, I think it is actually pretty reasonable. So I can't really dispute. You know, there may have been a few individual cases where, probably rightfully so, that the case settled higher because they had more leverage.[37]

Investor loss, in other words, sets the outer limit of settlement, while other factors determine where, beneath that limit, a particular case will settle. Where exactly the case will settle within that range may depend on sex appeal and other liability elements and also, our participants emphasized, on arguments about causation.

Perhaps the best way for defendants to fight plaintiffs-style damages is by arguing causation. One defense lawyer explained the importance of causation as follows:

> In a securities case, if a statement is made in a large-cap stock and there's a big drop you know in the stock when that statement is shown to be arguably inaccurate, OK, . . . the issues of loss causation, that's what the case is about. I mean, big stock drops don't occur for only one reason, so that this aggregation of those causative factors, particularly after the Supreme Court's decision in *Dura*, that's frequently the only thing that the case is about. I mean there's no dispute about what was said originally, because it's in a filing. And there's no dispute about what numbers they reported. The numbers they reported are the numbers they reported. But the question of, you know, whether or not people knew that they were reporting something or saying something that was misleading is a critical issue, but so are the issues that relate to loss causation.[38]

Once the initial round of motions is decided, causation may be the most important issue, as the following colloquy suggests:

A: By the time you get to mediation, damages is very much in the forefront of the discussion.

Q: Not liability so much?

A: Well, liability is there too, but, you want to know something, it's much harder to back people off on liability. It is much more complicated. It's a lot easier just to say, "OK, just suppose for argument's sake you are right. There was a terrible fraud here. How much are you using by way of an inflation assumption? What is your trading model? What is your theory of causation?" . . . In other words, "You tell me this drug was trading based on its cancer cure, and the whole thing of the cancer cure was wobbly BS. I'm telling you this company offered a metabolite for Prozac, and until the Prozac folks walked away from metabolite, that was chasing the stock price up!" OK, so you do focus on analysts' reports, stock price movements, OK. Marketplace news, baskets of comparables, and then very divergent forms of assumptions about who was trading and what and so forth and so on.[39]

Defense counsel often claim that they have the better causation and damages experts and that the law is moving their way, but the monitoring counsel and mediators stressed the uncertainty in the law and, especially, in the application of the law to facts.[40]

Indeed, one of the defense counsel who was openly scornful of plaintiffs' damages experts candidly admitted that he doesn't have a good answer to the following argument:

> You can have, you know, plaintiffs just saying, "Listen, I'll go up in front of a jury and I'm going to show $2 billion in investment loss that you are going to have to explain why it is really only $200 million. In any event, you only have $100 million [of D&O insurance] in the tower, and I will settle for $124 [million]."[41]

In other words, as long as the plaintiff is willing to settle the case within a range that is reasonable based on past settlements and either within or close to the limits of available insurance, defense counsel's claimed ability to make a technically superior legal argument may not matter. The willingness to settle then compounds the problem going forward, since neither the defendant's allegedly superior damages models nor the plaintiffs' alternative models are tested in court. One monitoring counsel put it this way: "These [plaintiffs'] damages models . . . were very often BS, but an important factor here . . . is that the damages models are never tested."[42] Causation may thus be the defendant's best argument to cut down the plaintiffs' demand, but it does not necessarily trump the other incentives to settle that are embedded in the process.

In sum, parties expect to settle for an amount that is within a range of the percentage of investor loss, adjusted by the current state of the art in modeling damages and trends in settlements. This range of numbers is arguably the most important factor driving settlement. Exactly where in the range any particular claim will settle, however, is a product of a negotiation that takes a variety of factors into account, including differing estimates on probable damages as well as arguments about causation and other liability elements. This process is somewhat analogous to the underwriting process we described in chapter 5. Just as D&O insurance underwriters make an initial assessment of the premium based on a simple financial algorithm, so too do D&O claims managers make an initial assessment of the settlement valuation based on simple investor loss. And just as D&O insurance underwriters arrive at a final price through a credit and debit process that takes into account "deep governance" of the prospective insured, so too do D&O claims managers arrive at a settlement price that they are willing to pay through a negotiation process that takes into account other variables, at least some of which relate to the strength of the evidence of fraud and the strength of the evidence linking the fraud to the harm. Finally, just as the ultimate premium that an underwriter will charge depends on the state of the insurance market, the ultimate settlement of the claim must be in line with other settlements.

Litigation Dynamics

Litigation dynamics also affect the timing and amount of settlements. One defense lawyer put it this way:

> I look at litigation as sort of a play that comes together with all these participants, and the dynamic of that mix sort of produces its own dynamic about settlements and numbers. In other words, you know, how is the judge reacting? Is he looking like he is going to be awful? You know it would be nice if you could do D&O litigation like you did bridge, where you give twenty teams the same cards, and you see, and it goes beyond just that some lawyers are better than other lawyers. There is a factor in litigation that fascinates me that has to do with the personal dynamic that develops because of the mix of the persons that it just involves in a case. You know, how stupid is the adjuster, how smart, how mean is the judge, how fast is the case moving on the track, is this judge actually going to give you a trial, you know what is the personality mix between the plaintiff's and defendant's attorneys. . . .?[43]

Within this general category, factors that matter include the jurisdiction in which the case is filed, which judge is assigned to the case, how many securities class actions the judge has handled in the past, the competence and experience of the plaintiffs' and defense lawyers, the demeanor and availability of key witnesses, and similar intangibles that affect how the parties assess the strength of their case, conceptually apart from the other factors we have considered so far. As important as these dynamics may be, we did not focus intensively on them in our interviews because, apart from the topics that we have discussed separately (for example, insurance and the use of prior settlements), our participants did not suggest that the litigation dynamics in shareholder cases differ significantly from other sorts of high-stakes litigation, at least in terms of the systematic shaping of settlement outcomes.

Settlements Based on Settlements

As noted above, our respondents often reported that they view other settlements as the best guide to assessing the reasonableness of any given settlement. Both sides use trends derived from other settlements, and these trends give rise to widely used rules of thumb. In the words of the claims manager quoted above, "[I]f you look at the numbers, the settlement compared to the damages—you are talking anywhere from 2 to 6 percent of plaintiff's style damages."[44] This basic rule of thumb, as we have said, is drawn from statistics about average settlements, regularly reported in the industry literature.[45] Settlements, in other words, are based on other settlements. Sometimes our participants talked about these settlements in terms of the expected value of the case if it goes to trial, but with so few trials to use as comparisons, expected trial value calculations are essentially fictions.

To see this point more clearly, consider the standard economic model of settlement: a $200 million settlement of a securities fraud action with a 5 percent chance of success represents the ordinary and unremarkable operation of the civil justice system, if the likely damages that would be awarded in the event that plaintiffs successfully proved fraud are approximately $10 billion. Yet without trials, no one knows how real judges or juries would assess the relative weights of the liability elements, and, even more importantly, no one knows the relative value of competing damages models. Lawyers do use mock juries in shareholder actions, but our sense is that these mock juries are most useful for evaluating themes and the strengths and weaknesses in the presentation of a case, not for evaluating the credibility of the experts who will be used to present competing damages models or to determine how, exactly, the jurors will put a damages number on a case at the end of the trial. In any given mock trial, the jury hears real witnesses from only one side of the case, and even then, the presentation of evidence is radically truncated. As a result, a statement that $30 million is an acceptable settlement because there is a 10 percent chance of being held liable for $300 million cannot be justified on the basis of experience. The number of trials is simply too small to justify any such conclusion.[46] Yet lawyers do talk that way, and these assessments may be "objective" in the sense that the assessments are shared by others in the field. But they are, in effect, "guesstimates" with little empirical basis.

Because there is so little adjudication beyond the motion to dismiss in the securities law context, practitioners' only objective basis for evaluating the value of a case is other settlements. And it is important to remember that every other settlement before their own was equally improvised. The settlements being used as points of reference faced the same lack of adjudicated guidance and were themselves settled by reference to other settlements, so that the problem becomes, in effect, one of infinite regress.

The problem of infinite regress involves an attempt to solve a problem by introducing a proposition that itself requires the support of another proposition, which requires the support of another proposition, and so on, ad infinitum. The problem is never solved because the support for each underlying proposition is never supplied since the basic problem is reintroduced into each proposed solution. A classic formulation of the problem appears in a parable in Stephen Hawking's *A Brief History of Time*, in which a scientist has just finished a lecture on the origin of the galaxy:

> At the end of the lecture, a little old lady at the back of the room got up and said: "What you have told us is rubbish. The world is really a flat plate supported on the back of a giant tortoise." The scientist gave a superior smile before replying, "What is the tortoise standing on?" "You're very clever, young man, very clever," said the old lady. "But it's turtles all the way down!"[47]

Justice Scalia recently offered another version of the story in a Supreme Court opinion:

> [A]n Eastern guru affirms that the earth is supported on the back of a tiger. When asked what supports the tiger, he says it stands upon an elephant; and when asked what supports the elephant he says it is a giant turtle. When asked, finally, what supports the giant turtle, he is briefly taken aback, but quickly replies "Ah, after that it is turtles all the way down."[48]

Such is the dilemma posed by determining settlement amounts by reference to prior settlement amounts. Ultimately, "It's settlements all the way down."

Because virtually all cases settle, there is no other objective reference point for settlement negotiations. There is no body of trial precedents. Legal theories—especially, our participants suggested, damages theories—go untested in court, and the weight of various facts is rarely litigated through to a meaningful conclusion. The securities class action field works insofar as it produces case outcomes that the parties can live with and that are predictable enough to allow D&O insurance companies to sell insurance at a price that companies are willing to pay. But we have no basis for evaluating the relationship between these outcomes and the outcomes that would result if more cases went to trial.

Is This "Merit"?

If we were to review some of the key insights gleaned from our participants about what matters in settlement, described both here and in the previous chapter, we would emphasize (1) the amount of investor loss alleged by plaintiffs; (2) insurance limits and, in some cases, the structure of coverage; (3) sex appeal, which may or may not correspond to specific elements of the underlying claim; (4) litigation dynamics; and (5) trends in shareholder settlements generally. Thinking through this list of key factors, we can easily imagine someone asking, "That's all well and good, but what do those things have to do with the merits of the claim?" Do these features of the settlement process pull settlement values closer to or push them farther away from a valuation based on the underlying merits of the claim? What, in other words, do these findings tell us about whether the merits matter?

Before we can hope to answer the question of whether merits matter, we must first determine what we mean by "merits." What are the merits? What are people talking about when they talk about merits?

The term "merits" regularly appears in both academic and popular discussions of litigation, often in opposition to the term "frivolous."[49] In this common usage, a lawsuit is understood to be meritorious if its facts fit the legally defined elements of liability in a given cause of action. That is, it is meritorious if the facts the plaintiff alleges are true and if the plaintiff's legal theory is sound. By extension, the merits matter if the resolution of the case strongly depends on the probability that the facts are true and the legal theory is sound. By contrast, a lawsuit is frivolous if the facts the plaintiff alleges are false or if the plaintiff's legal theory is unsound. By extension, the merits do not matter if the probability that the facts are false or the legal theory is unsound does not strongly affect the resolution of the case. On this view, the merits of a case consist exclusively in the liability elements of the claim.

Although they came out differently on the question of how merit affects the ultimate resolution of a claim, most of our participants seemed to embrace this understanding of merit, focusing largely on the liability elements of claims: misrepresentation, scienter, and perhaps loss causation. As one of the defense lawyers we talked to suggested, merits do matter from this point of view, but "it's like the difference between gross motor skills and fine motor skills. Merits matter, but they matter at the level of the gross motor skills."[50] Many of our respondents were still more pessimistic. Consider, for example, this quotation from a claims manager at a major D&O insurer: "I like the concept of settling the cases based on the merits. I haven't quite given up on that hope, but it just doesn't happen. The most I can hope to achieve is to get a reasonable settlement value based on what other cases, similar cases, are being resolved for."[51] Similarly, another defense lawyer bluntly observed, "My experience is that the level of settlement has nothing to do with the merits of the claim."[52]

Taking all such comments together, what are these participants telling us about merit? We suspect that those who were most pessimistic on the question of merit were focusing exclusively on the liability elements of the claim, and those on the defense side were reacting negatively to the fact that some claims with very weak liability nevertheless settled for substantial dollar amounts. Likewise, from the plaintiffs' point of view, the pessimists complained that not every case of real securities fraud survives dismissal—especially, they were eager to point out, since the adoption of the heightened pleading standard of the Private Securities Litigation Reform Act. Our respondents seemed to confirm, in other words, that the motion to dismiss is not a perfect filter for separating good liability cases from bad liability cases. Because all cases that survive a motion to dismiss are settled, and because most cases that do not survive the motion to dismiss do not settle, some bad liability claims are paid and some good liability claims are not—the same pattern, by the way, that troubles some people about the medical malpractice arena, in which trials are a regular occurrence.[53]

Nevertheless, once securities class actions are in the settlement process, other comments, such as the defense counsel's gross motor skills/fine motor skills distinction, suggest that there is some differentiation among cases, even in terms of this more narrow understanding of the merits. Weak liability claims tend to settle for a smaller percentage of the plaintiffs' best damages estimates, while strong liability cases settle for a higher percentage of the plaintiffs' damages estimates. In other words, the liability merits matter enough to affect the settlement amount, conditional on the case surviving the motion to dismiss (or settling in advance of the decision on the motion to dismiss).

We conclude that these participants' liability-centered model of merit disregards a significant legally defined element of the claim—namely, damages. Law, after all, defines not only the conduct to be proscribed but also, by establishing a measure for damages, the consequences that are to follow for transgressions. For this reason, the merits, properly understood, should include damages. Leaving damages out of a model of merit means leaving out any account of the incentives for the parties to evaluate not only whether a given activity is permitted but also what the costs of the activity are likely to be. In this more expansive view, the merits matter as long as settlements bear a reasonable relationship to the probability that the defendants committed fraud multiplied by the potential damages. Put another way, the merits matter as long as the fault and loss causation variables would be positive and significant in a well-constructed regression model of securities class action settlements in which the settlement amount is the dependent variable.

So understood, the "do the merits matter?" question is an appeal for objective evidence that the litigation and settlement process tends to hold the right people accountable in the right amount for doing what the law forbids. And indeed, if the merits in securities litigation could be objectively shown, it would be possible to resolve this question once and for all. The challenge to find a clear, objective standard is not unique to securities litigation. Researchers have long sought, in various areas of the law, an objective standard by which to judge the liability elements of a claim. In the context of medical malpractice litigation, for example, medical experts have conducted large-scale, closed-claim file reviews, making independent judgments about the merits of claims, then comparing their judgments against the settlements of the actual claims.[54]

Unfortunately, there are no comparable closed-claim studies of securities class action settlements. Worse, there is good reason to doubt there ever will be such studies in the securities class action context, considering that a key liability element, the defendants' state of mind—that is, whether they in fact acted with an intent to defraud or with reckless disregard for the truth—lies hidden in a way that the factors underlying a typical negligence determination—for example, whether a doctor's conduct was consistent with the customary standard of care—do not. As a result, the best researchers can do is to construct, as Johnson, Nelson, and Pritchard have done, a set of easily observable proxies for merit and to check for the presence or absence of these merit proxies in actual settlements. But insofar as these outwardly observable proxies for merit are not perfectly aligned with the elements of the underlying claim, one of which, scienter, is inward and subjective, such studies cannot definitively answer the challenge posed by the merits question.

Given the inscrutability of intent, the question whether the objectively true merits matter is, for us, very nearly a useless question, not because it is unimportant, but because it cannot be answered. The better question, in our view, is, How do the things that our participants tell us matter in the settlement process align with traditional notions of merit? As previously noted, our participants suggested five key features as principally responsible for determining settlement values: (1) investor loss; (2) insurance limits and, in some cases, the structure of coverage; (3) sex appeal; (4) litigation dynamics; and (5) trends in shareholder settlements generally. What is the relationship between these settlement drivers and the merits?

First, the importance of investor loss in determining outcomes at settlement could be a factor unrelated to merit, if one is focused principally on liability elements in defining what merit means. However, as we have argued, damages ought to be considered part of the merits; and from this perspective, investor loss is clearly relevant to merits. Investor loss, after all, provides a useful initial estimate of damages and thus provides an easy screen to identify potential securities frauds that are worth subjecting to the intensive investigation characteristic of a securities fraud action. Of course, investor loss is not the same thing as actual damages, which compensate for the difference between the price paid (or received) for the stock under conditions of fraud and the price the plaintiffs would have paid (or received) but for the defendants' misrepresentations. Many factors that have nothing to do with the defendants' misrepresentations can affect the price of a stock—such as fluctuations in commodity prices, interest rates, general market conditions, and developments within the firm in question, to name just a few. Thus, to the extent that investor loss alone drives settlement, and some of our participants insisted that this is the case, then investor loss is, at best, an imperfect measure of the merits. Nevertheless, our sense is that efforts to identify more accurate measures of damages receive intense focus in settlement negotiations, and thus we conclude that this part of the settlement process falls strongly on the merits side of the equation.

By contrast, the second factor—insurance limits and structure—is more difficult to square with merit. Insurance coverage obviously is not relevant to the liability elements of any claim. And while the insurance limits may bear some relationship to the damages that a company's risk manager concludes that the company might cause, that is definitely not the same thing as the amount of damages that the company actually caused in a particular case. Of course, the defendant's ability to pay is a critical consideration of every litigator, but that has no direct relationship with the merits of the underlying claim. Indeed, in the securities class action context it may well be that the merits of the claim bear an inverse relationship to the defendant's ability to pay, as companies on the edge of insolvency have less to lose from securities misrepresentation and, potentially, more to gain if the misrepresentation allows them to survive to make a real profit in a later quarter. Thus, those cases that are most obviously affected by the insurance limits—cases in which the defendant is insolvent or nearly so—may be among the stronger cases on the merits. In short, we conclude that the impact of insurance in any shareholder case, whether it pushes up or down or merely speeds up or delays the settlement of the case, reduces the impact of the merits.[55]

A counterargument can be made, but it is not a strong one. The counterargument is that companies decide how much insurance coverage to buy based on their potential exposure, and thus insurance policy limits likely reflect the amount of damage that a company is likely to inflict. Thus, over the long run and in most cases, insurance policy limits reflect, rather than interfere with, the objective merits of the claim. This could be true, although we tend to doubt it because of the "infinite regress" feature of securities class action settlements. Even if true, however, it does not contradict the argument in the preceding paragraph, and it does not account for the impact that D&O insurance program structure has on the settlement. Program structure appears to be based more on underwriters' taste for limits at the time the insurance is sold than on any explicit evaluation of the best places in the program to place the firebreaks that some of our participants discussed.

The third factor—sex appeal—moves us back in the merits direction, although perhaps not uniformly. Sex appeal can be about the underlying merits of the claim, or sex appeal can be about sensationalism and scandal. To the degree that sex appeal enables plaintiffs to establish the underlying elements of a claim or to tell a story supporting those elements, it correlates strongly with even the basic liability-centered vision of merits described above. Yet if sex appeal is used to shame defendants or to emphasize facts more than they deserve, then it likely inflates the value of claims relative to what one might view as their intrinsic worth. On the whole, however, we are inclined to regard sex appeal as closely correlated with a claim's chances of success, if only because we think that it would be impossible to prevent sex appeal from affecting any adjudicator—whether jury, judge, or insurance claims manager.

The fourth factor—litigation dynamics—is, strictly speaking, not a merits factor at all. Indeed, the unifying theme of this admittedly messy, residual category is that there are aspects of the securities class action litigation process that affect the value of a particular case. Yet all cases in all jurisdictions are shaped by the dynamics of the case resolution process. That fact, by itself, is hardly worth mentioning. Our impressionistic conclusion, informed by the views of the seasoned litigators that we interviewed, was that shareholder litigation does not differ from other high-stakes litigation in terms of the impact of litigation dynamics on the settlement process. The jurisdiction matters. The judge matters. The chemistry among the lawyers and the other representatives of the parties matters. But these kinds of things always matter in litigation, so much so that it hardly makes sense to think of them as systematically interfering with the merits of the case in any real-world sense.

Finally, the last factor—the means, medians, trends, and other statistics drawn from previous settlements—may also push away from merit, although not uniformly. On the one hand, trends and other statistics drawn from prior settlements are like the insurance policy limits discussed in the counterargument about the insurance factor above. By definition, these trends and statistics reflect the best available information about the damages payable for securities class actions, in the long run and on average. But the relationship between these trends and the merits of any particular case is much more problematic. Researchers have used settlement data to develop predictive models for settlements, but these models predict settlement ranges, not point values, and these models do not incorporate one of the most important variables—insurance policy limits—because that information is not publicly available.

It may be the case, as suggested by several of our respondents and as supported by the skew in overall settlement statistics, that the comparison with other settlements matters more for the basic, unspectacular claim that has nevertheless survived dismissal and will therefore settle for some amount well within the limits of almost any D&O insurance program than

for cases with greater evidence of defendant wrongdoing or more spec-
tacular damages. If so, statistics drawn from other settlements provide the
baseline amount at which common, undifferentiated cases will settle and
do not necessarily prevent more significant settlements from more closely
tracking the merits of the particular claim. But, to the extent that these
models are used to shape settlements more broadly, then the settlements
will, by definition, be based on the model. In that event, the question will
be, "Do the merits matter to the model?"

Predictive settlement models are likely to become reasonably good at
the damages aspect of a claim, because damages in securities class actions
are themselves based on a model. It is impossible to track who purchased
which security for which price and when. As a result, damages must be
estimated, and, therefore, a predictive settlement model could be tuned
to reflect the damages estimation models currently in use. So too with loss
causation. Loss causation involves stripping the impact of factors other
than the misrepresentation from the securities price development during
the relevant period. That too involves a model. But scienter, and even its
crude proxy, sex appeal, is a product of the human mind, not a computer
model. Scienter and sex appeal undoubtedly can be approximated by a
predictive model, but not perfectly, and thus the greater the role of predictive models in the settlement of claims, the less that fine-grained, case-
specific evidence of wrongdoing will matter.

Finally, the dynamics we have discussed with regard to settlement do
not necessary render merits completely irrelevant to outcomes. After all,
the motion to dismiss is, as we have said, very much a dispositive ruling, and
it is focused exclusively on the merits of the claim. Indeed, if one assumes
that cases surviving the motion to dismiss are more meritorious than cases
failing to survive the motion—a reasonable assumption in our view—then
the fact that virtually no cases settle prior to a decision on the motion to
dismiss suggests that merits do affect outcomes in shareholder suits. Moreover, the fact that at least 25 percent of motions to dismiss are granted
suggests that a significant screening of claims takes place at that stage.
These facts belie the conclusion that merits are irrelevant to outcomes in
securities litigation. Nevertheless, if one assumes that some nonmeritorious suits survive the motions stage—another reasonable assumption in
our view—then we must still ask the question of what mechanisms exist at settlement to align outcomes with the merits of claims.[56] Indeed,
even if the motions stage provided a perfect screen for nonmeritorious
claims—if, in other words, no meritorious claims were dismissed and only

meritorious claims survived the motion—the question of how settlement practices take into account a claim's underlying merits would still be an important one in determining whether the dollar amount at settlement reflects the severity of the defendant's fraud. In a world in which merits matter, both serious and minor frauds should survive the motion to dismiss, but serious frauds ought to cost defendants more than minor ones.

In this chapter, we have examined the question of merits in settlement outcomes, but rather than seeking to answer whether the merits matter in the settlement of shareholder litigation, we have asked simply what factors matter in the settlement process and how do they matter. This investigation led us to five key features that influence settlement values: (1) investor loss, (2) insurance limits and structure, (3) sex appeal, (4) litigation dynamics, and (5) statistical information from other settlements. Although some of these features clearly have merits-relevant aspects, notably investor loss and sex appeal, others, such as insurance limits and structure and litigation dynamics, clearly do not, and we tend to doubt that settlement statistics as used today push in the merits-relevant direction (although there may be room for improvements in this regard).

As we wrote earlier, the securities class action settlement process works in the sense of producing outcomes that parties can live with and that insurance companies can predict well enough to price the D&O insurance that pays for all of the lawyers and most of the settlements. Our criticisms of the process revolve principally around the lack of transparency of D&O insurance program structure and pricing as well as the precise contribution of D&O insurers to class action settlements. Our complaints are not directed at the litigation or settlement process. Indeed, our research has left us with a picture of professionals working diligently to achieve their clients' goals within a complicated litigation and settlement environment that does not provide them with certain key information. The situation could be improved with the stroke of the SEC commissioners' pens—by providing public access to detailed D&O insurance policy information that could be used to systematically evaluate the impact of insurance on settlements. But other, even more crucial pieces of information can only be provided by more adjudication. We address these points again in chapter 10.

CHAPTER NINE

Coverage Defenses and Disputes

So far, we have studied the relationship between the D&O insurer and the corporate policyholder at three distinct points in time. First, in chapter 5, we examined the underwriting process, when insurer and policyholder agree, with the help of a broker, on the terms of coverage and the price of the policy. Next, in chapter 6, we looked at the interaction between insurer and policyholder during the life of the policy in the absence of claim activity. Then, in chapters 7 and 8, we explored their relationship in the defense and settlement of shareholder litigation. Through our accounts of each of these stages in a typical coverage relationship, we have sought to focus attention on our underlying theme: the extent to which D&O insurance constrains the corporate actor and thereby serves to reintroduce the deterrence function of shareholder litigation.

We have, however, left an important aspect of the insurance relationship out of our account up to this point—that is, the potential dispute between defendants and their D&O insurers about any insurance coverage defenses that may apply to all or part of the securities claim. As our participants described, the filing of a shareholder suit does not lead to an immediate unity of interest between insurer and policyholder in fighting the plaintiffs' claim. Instead, once the policyholder gives notice of the lawsuit, typically through an insurance broker intermediary, the insurer responds with what is referred to in the industry as a "reservation of rights" letter, the purpose of which is to notify the policyholder that although the insurer tentatively will proceed to meet its obligations under the policy, it is reserving its rights to stop doing so should it later determine that it has no such obligations, either because the claim is not in fact covered under the policy or, even worse from the policyholder's point of view, because the policy for some reason is null and void. As described by the head of claims at a leading D&O insurer, "Typically [insurers] take a hard line. When the claim comes in, they send out a twenty-five-page reservation of rights letter that recites chapter and verse as to why something shouldn't be covered."[1] The reservation of rights letter thus puts the policyholder on notice of the possibility that the carrier may have a defense to payment on the claim and sets the stage for informal negotiation about insurance coverage during settlement and, potentially, the filing of separate insurance coverage proceeding.

There is thus a coverage dispute in the background of almost every claim. Regardless of whether coverage litigation ultimately arises between insurer and policyholder, the possibility defines their relationship once a claim has arisen. As the insurer begins requesting additional information concerning the claim from the policyholder, either in the reservation of rights letter itself or soon thereafter, the policyholder will, of course, understand that such information may be used not only to value the claim for settlement but also potentially to support the insurer's case for avoiding payment. Nevertheless, failing to respond adequately to an insurer's request for information could itself invalidate coverage because of the policyholder's duty to cooperate under the D&O insurance policy.

While reservation of rights letters are routine, flat-out denials of coverage are relatively uncommon, and as a result, many seasoned participants in shareholder litigation tend not to regard insurance coverage questions as serious. Yet the issuance of the letter means that there is yet another potentially adversarial aspect to the relationship between insurer and policyholder operating throughout the claims process without some attention to which no account of the insurance relationship would be complete.

Moreover, the coverage dispute is the last opportunity for a D&O insurer to force a corporate actor to pay for the harm it has caused. This insight is critically important to our underlying theme of deterrence. If there is some correlation between coverage defenses and corporate wrongdoing—if, for example, an insurer's coverage defenses are stronger when the defendant is most likely to have done something very wrong or, in other words, when the shareholders' claim is most meritorious—then the insurer's ability to avoid payment on such claims effectively establishes an ex post deterrent to corporate misconduct. Simply stated, corporate actors may be more likely to be good because they will understand that if they are very bad, then their liabilities may not be covered by D&O insurance.

This chapter explores coverage defenses and disputes in some detail. In it, we consider, first, the basic defenses to coverage that D&O insurers may seek to assert, largely through a review of case law and legal doctrine, focusing on policy exclusions and the more drastic response of rescission. We then explore how insurers actually make use of these various coverage defenses, here drawing upon the observations of the participants in our study, finding that coverage defenses may be used to reduce an insurer's contribution to settlement even when the claims dispute is not litigated between the insurer and the policyholder. As described by our participants, it is common for insurers to "cash in their coverage defenses" in exchange for a lower overall contribution to settlement. Throughout, we conduct this survey of coverage disputes with a view to our underlying theme—the extent to which D&O insurance enhances or impedes the deterrence function of shareholder litigation.

Coverage Defenses

As we have explained, D&O insurance protects officers and directors from almost all liability-related costs arising out of any wrongful acts alleged to have been committed in the course of their duties, with comparatively few exclusions. In addition, D&O insurance covers the corporation itself for its obligations to indemnify the officers and directors and, in connection with securities claims, its own direct liabilities. D&O insurance coverage is so broad because the risk managers who purchase the insurance care much more about the breadth of the coverage than they care about the price, as one would expect for insurance that covers the personal exposure of the most senior officials in Fortune 500 and other large, publicly traded companies.

Notwithstanding the breadth of the coverage, however, the D&O insurance policy is a contract and, like all insurance contracts, it contains definitions, exclusions, conditions, limits, and other provisions that, together with custom and practice and any judicial gloss, define the relationship between the insurer and the parties covered under the contract.[2] Frictions between the contract terms and the possibilities presented by shareholder litigation lead to insurance coverage disputes. In very broad brush terms, these disputes can arise over the application of exclusions (exceptions to coverage) to the claim, questions about whether the policyholder has complied with its obligations in the insurance relationship, and the insurers' obligation to consent to reasonable settlements of a claim. We discussed the insurer's settlement rights and obligations in the preceding chapter and will not return to that topic. Here we will focus on insurance policy exclusions and on coverage defenses based on policyholders' misrepresentations in the underwriting process.

Exclusions

Policy exclusions—that is, explicit carve outs from coverage in the insurance contract—provide insurers with the most basic defense to coverage. If an insurer can point to language in the policy itself stating that a particular liability is not covered, then it may be able to avoid payment of a claim while still receiving premiums under the policy. We discussed the exclusions very briefly in chapter 3, observing that our participants reported that the exclusions generally do not stand in the way of D&O insurance coverage for claims. But there are some important exceptions, and to understand those it will be helpful to have a general understanding of the function of exclusions in liability insurance policies.

An insurance policy exclusion is an exception from the broad grant of coverage in the insurance policy. Although exclusions can seem arbitrary to someone whose claim is denied as a result, exclusions generally serve some purpose that, properly understood, helps to guide the application of the exclusion to claims. Most insurance policy exclusions can be classified into one of the following four categories, each of which has a different purpose: market segmentation, moral hazard, adverse selection, and catastrophic risk.

Market segmentation exclusions reflect the fact that some other kind of insurance policy ordinarily provides coverage for the risks in question. For example, homeowners' insurance policies exclude coverage for injuries arising out of the use of an automobile, reflecting the fact that auto liability insurance coverage is sold as a separate insurance product. D&O insurance policies contain a number of these kinds of exclusions. The exclusion for claims arising out of the Employee Retirement Income Security Act (ERISA), environmental harm, bodily injury or emotional distress, and property damage, for example, all reflect the fact that corporations generally can obtain coverage for these risks by buying other kinds of insurance policies.[3] We will not discuss market segmentation exclusions in this chapter because our participants did not discuss them with us. Most likely, this reflects the fact that corporations generally do purchase the other kinds of insurance that mirror the market segmentation exclusions and, therefore, claims that might be excluded by virtue of a market segmentation exclusion are covered by another insurance policy. Moreover, in our interviews we focused on shareholder claims that, with the exception of claims brought by shareholders who are also ERISA beneficiaries (current or former employees), would almost never fall within a market segmentation exclusion. ERISA claims can overlap with shareholder litigation, but they are covered by another kind of insurance—fiduciary liability insurance—that corporations with D&O insurance seem generally to buy.

Moral hazard exclusions reflect insurers' ordinary reluctance to insure risks that pose a very high degree of moral hazard. The arson exclusion in property insurance policies may be the most well-known example. The fact that life insurance policies typically provide coverage for death by suicide, often after a waiting period, may be the most widely appreciated demonstration of the fact that insurers are willing to cover risks that pose a fairly high degree of moral hazard in at least some cases. For purposes of our overriding theme—the relationship between insurance and deterrence in the shareholder litigation context—the moral hazard exclusions in the D&O insurance policy are very important, and we will focus intensively on those exclusions in this chapter.

Adverse selection in insurance is a very complicated topic, the full exploration of which would take us far from the objectives of this research project. It is not for nothing that two Nobel prizes in economics were awarded to economists whose major contributions related to adverse selection—Robert Akerloff and Joseph Stiglitz. For our purposes, it is sufficient to understand the adverse selection exclusions in D&O insurance policies as addressing the problem of insuring a barn that is already burning. These exclusions generate a significant amount of insurance coverage disputing and, for that reason, we will discuss them here. But, as we will explain, this disputing does not have the same importance for our project as that relating to the moral hazard exclusions.

Catastrophic risk exclusions reflect insurers' reluctance to insure highly correlated risks that have the potential to pose a solvency risk to insurance institutions themselves. The exclusions for liability arising out of nuclear accidents is an example of a catastrophic risk exclusion that can be found in some D&O insurance policies. Some insurance specialists might classify the environmental exclusion as catastrophic risk exclusion, but the growth in environmental liability policies suggests that environmental exclusions are in the process of transformation to market segmentation exclusions as insurers have become comfortable with environmental risk.

Significantly, D&O insurers have discovered that their core coverage—that for shareholder litigation—can itself be highly correlated and, thus, pose catastrophic risk. At the time of the writing of this book—2010—the reason is obvious. The precipitating event for almost all shareholder litigation is a drop in stock prices, and recent history reminds us that movements in stock prices can be very highly correlated, particularly in bubbles. The bursting of a stock bubble leads to an increase in shareholder litigation. Some of that litigation will be unsuccessful, either because the plaintiffs are unable to demonstrate any improper activity preceding the drop in share prices or because the defendants are able to prove that nothing they did had any impact on the price drop. But others will succeed.

This catastrophic and perhaps even cyclical aspect to the underlying D&O insurance risk helps to explain the "limits management" underwriting strategy of D&O insurance carriers. D&O underwriters know that they will take a big hit whenever a bubble bursts, and, thus, they manage their overall portfolio with that possibility in mind. As important as this topic is to the D&O insurance business, however, it has the potential, like adverse selection, to take us far from our research project. Thus, we will not treat it further in this chapter.

Adverse Selection Exclusions in D&O Insurance

As discussed in chapter 3, D&O insurance covers policyholders for claims that are made during the policy period. This claims-made nature of D&O insurance has the potential to expose insurance companies to the most obvious form of adverse selection: insuring a company that waits to buy insurance until its managers know that a shareholder claim is about to be filed. Economists treat adverse selection as an information problem, and this example helps us see why. An applicant who is buying insurance for the "barn that is already burning" only presents a problem to an insurer if the insurer either cannot find out on its own whether the barn is burning or does not design the insurance policy in a manner that forces the applicant to reveal that the barn is burning. D&O insurers can do both.

An insurer could choose to sell insurance on a barn that it knew was already burning, as long as it can charge the right price. What could make this transaction the sale of insurance rather than a loan would be uncertainty about the extent of the damage that would result from the fire. Ordinary D&O insurance is not insurance for the barn that is already burning, however. Some of our participants told us that a major D&O insurance carrier had experimented with selling additional insurance to cover claims already filed, but that kind of insurance was not available on the market during our interviews, and, accordingly, we did not explore it further.[4]

D&O insurers have a wide variety of strategies to address the burning barn problem. Most importantly, they can use the underwriting process to ask questions and investigate in order to reach their own conclusions regarding the likelihood of future claims and price their policies accordingly. If they think that a particular set of circumstances is too likely to produce a claim, they can draft endorsements that exclude claims arising out of those circumstances. Such exclusions are known as "laser" exclusions, reflecting the narrow, laser-like focus.

Laser exclusions generally do not eliminate coverage for a claim, however. Rather, they shift the coverage for the affected claims back in time. This is because the announcement by an insurer that it intends to include a laser exclusion in a D&O insurance policy almost always produces an immediate claim under the policyholder's current policy, under what is known as the "notice of circumstances" provision. The notice of circumstances provision allows a policyholder to file a "notice of circumstances which could give rise to a claim" under the current policy. That notice is treated under the insurance contract as a claim and has the effect of locking in coverage under the current policy for future claims arising out of those circumstances. As a result of this notice of circumstances option, insurers in most cases are reluctant to insert laser exclusions in their new policies, because they do not want their policyholders filing claims under the expiring policies, for a variety of reasons.

Most significantly, holding off on the laser exclusion typically reduces the amount of coverage available to the policyholder while increasing the amount of premiums the insurers can collect. The reason for this counterintuitive effect is as follows. As long as the policyholder has not filed a claim under the expiring policy, that policy will end without the policyholder using up any of the limits. The potential claim that could be the subject of the laser exclusion will count against the new policy limits, making less coverage available for other claims that the insurer does not know about.

If the insurer goes ahead and issues the laser exclusion, the policyholder will issue the notice of circumstances, and the coverage for the potential claim shifts back into the expiring policy, for which the insurer cannot charge any additional premium. If the insurer tries to charge a higher premium for the new policy because of a claim that might be covered under the expiring policy, the policyholder can shop around for a different insurer. By contrast, if the insurer holds off on issuing the laser exclusion, it can charge a larger premium for the new policy. Moreover, holding off on the exclusion notwithstanding the risk tends to encourage the policyholder to value the current insurers more highly, and therefore pay the higher premium for the next policy, because they are willing to stay with the policyholder through potentially tough times. Finally, notices of circumstances create administrative costs, because insurers have to set up a claim file and conduct some investigation, and they create a drag on earnings, because insurers must post a reserve whenever they receive such a notice. For all these reasons, most insurers would in most circumstances prefer to have a policyholder wait to provide notice until there is an actual claim.

This laser exclusion and notice of circumstances dynamic illustrate an important point about all of the adverse selection provisions in D&O insurance policies. These provisions mainly function to govern the assignment of claims to policy periods and to encourage long-term relationships between policyholders and insurers. The frictions from these exclusions lead to a substantial amount of disputing behavior, not only between policyholders and insurers but also between policyholders and brokers, because it is the brokers who have the responsibility to manage these frictions so that policyholders do not face gaps in coverage.

Managing these frictions and disputes helps keep brokers and insurance coverage lawyers fully employed, but it has little systematic effect on the existence or extent of the insurance-deterrence trade-off posed by D&O insurance in the context of securities litigation. Indeed, from that perspective, these frictions and related disputes function as a randomly generated deductible or coinsurance provision that may have the overall effect of reducing the extent of D&O insurance coverage but does not provide any useful deterrence signal or effect. Consistent with that view, our participants report that, almost as soon as such disputing identifies a coverage gap that cannot be solved by careful broking, the insurance policy form evolves to eliminate the gap. (Meanwhile, the insurance companies whose policies in force still contain that gap in coverage face a choice: Do they stand firm to gain the benefit of the inadvertent gap in coverage? Or do they compromise in order to enhance their reputation in the D&O insurance market as insurers that can be counted upon in tough times? Our sense is that insurance companies differ in this regard, and they may differ over time. Knowledge of those differences is part of the stock in trade of the top D&O insurance brokers.)

Before concluding this discussion, it is worth briefly mentioning several common provisions in D&O insurance policies that protect insurers from adverse selection and that guide the process of assigning claims to the appropriate policy period. These provisions are the prior claim exclusion, the interrelated wrongful acts provision, the pending and prior litigation exclusion, the prompt notice provision, and, in some policies, the prior-acts exclusion.

The first two of these provisions—the prior claim exclusion and the interrelated wrongful acts provision—prevent policyholders from obtaining additional coverage under a new insurance policy for claims arising out of the same circumstances that produced a claim under an earlier insurance policy. These exclusions prevent policyholders from using a new D&O insurance policy to obtain additional coverage for claims brought under a prior policy or for very closely related claims. In effect, these provisions help insurers limit their exposure in any particular circumstance to the amount of coverage provided in a single year of insurance coverage.

The last three of these provisions—the prior and pending litigation exclusion, the prompt notice provision, and, in some cases, the prior-acts exclusion—force policyholders to let insurers know when the barn has caught fire or, in some cases, may be about to catch fire. The prior and pending litigation exclusion applies to claims that arise out of earlier litigation that is sufficiently closely related to a new claim that it should have put a reasonable policyholder on notice of the need to file a claim. The prompt notice provision requires policyholders to do just what it says. And the prior-acts exclusion, which typically does not appear in a D&O insurance policy, functions like an omnibus laser exclusion. The prior-acts exclusion is used in a D&O insurance policy when a policyholder with a troubled litigation history wants to "start fresh" with a set of insurers willing to give it another chance. The precise operation of these provisions is technical, and the management of the associated frictions requires expertise, but the bottom line is that well-counseled policyholders should not unknowingly lose insurance coverage for shareholder litigation on this account.[5]

The Moral Hazard Exclusions

The moral hazard exclusions are far more central to our account because, as the label suggests, they have the potential to play a significant role in managing the insurance-deterrence trade-off in the D&O insurance context. There are two main moral hazard exclusions in D&O insurance policies: the fraud exclusion and the unjust-enrichment exclusion.

The Fraud Exclusion

Most D&O policies contain an exclusion that prevents policyholders from receiving insurance benefits when they have actually committed a particularly wrongful act, sometimes further defined as a "dishonest or fraudulent act or omission or any criminal act or omission or any willful violation of any statute, rule or law."[6] Because the core allegation of a great many shareholder claims focuses on misrepresentations or fraud, robust application of the fraud exclusion would seem to enable insurers to avoid payment for a large number of claims. As the head of claims for one D&O insurer put it, "You know, the ultimate paradox of this product is that we insure securities fraud. But fraud is uninsurable under this policy or anybody else's policy."[7]

The room for coverage comes from the gap between the mental state that is required to meet the insurance law definition of fraud and the mental state that is required to meet the scienter element of a 10b-5 action. As the head of claims described,

> We may insure securities fraud but not real fraud. . . . If you are going to be out and out fraud, that is uninsurable, okay. And that's the paradox of the insurance. Everybody buys the policy for when they get hit with securities fraud allegations, and if it weren't for the fact that recklessness is a standard there, we probably wouldn't be able to insure it at all, because if you had to prove outright fraud in every case, it would be uninsurable in every case.[8]

In addition, prospective policyholders are typically well counseled on the dangers posed by an overly broad fraud exclusion and therefore seek to have the exclusion apply only in the event of final adjudication of actual fraud, as we described in chapter 3. To quote one underwriter, "it is pretty standard now for the carriers to agree to final adjudication."[9] Of course, because most shareholder litigation settles, there only very rarely is a final adjudication of actual fraud. In other words, as the head of claims told us, insurers "all hide behind the recklessness piece even though that is never ever adjudicated to allow us to essentially insure these wrongdoings."[10]

This means that, in practice, insurers use the standard fraud exclusion to avoid paying claims only very rarely, most typically when a criminal conviction is obtained. Even then, the insurers will have spent a substantial amount of money on the defense of the convicted defendant, because D&O insurance also pays for criminal defense costs. Moreover, because the final adjudication must be in the proceeding for which coverage is sought, the criminally guilty defendant receives insurance protection for the civil settlement, unless the plaintiffs insist on a personal contribution from that defendant or unless that defendant is left out of the settlement. From the insurers' perspective, the settlement machinations about the one or two criminally guilty defendants almost do not matter, because there almost always are other defendants who were not the subject of criminal prosecution and, thus, do not come within the scope of the exclusion.

Yet another reason that the fraud exclusion provides a coverage defense of surprisingly little value to insurers is that plaintiffs' lawyers plead strategically in order to avoid handing the insurer a valid coverage defense. As we have noted, plaintiffs' lawyers reported that they believe that insurance money is relatively easy money and that extracting settlement dollars from defendants, even solvent corporate defendants, can be a more difficult matter. Therefore, plaintiffs' lawyers frame their facts to involve reckless misstatements rather than intentional fraud. "We make sure that we don't use words like 'you intentionally cooked the books' or 'you did this or you did that'," as one plaintiffs' attorney described, because, he said, "we don't want to provide any sort of out for the insurance carriers."[11] Thus, even when the fraud exclusion contains language that is less favorable from the policyholder's point of view—that is, language requiring only that fraud be established in fact rather than necessarily being determined in a final adjudication in the underlying case—the shareholder complaint is typically pleaded in such a way to give insurers less traction under the fraud exclusion. This careful pleading is especially important in Section 11 cases, because there is no scienter requirement for a Section 11 claim. Accordingly, using the fraud exclusion to avoid coverage for a Section 11 claim is very difficult, even with an in-fact exclusion, and essentially impossible with a final adjudication exclusion, except when a defendant pleads guilty to a criminal charge and the parties agree to craft a settlement of the securities fraud claim that leaves out that defendant.

Finally, insurers understand that, in the long run, their D&O insurance market will dry up if they press too hard on the fraud exclusion. As the head of claims put it,

> ... People buy D&O. Companies buy D&O to insure against securities fraud. It is different—they are not buying it to insure against intentional wrongdoing, but they are. They understand fraud is not covered. They understand intentional wrongdoing is not covered. Willful violations of law are not covered. But at the end of the day, *that is exactly what they are buying the policy for.*

Like the famous distinction between honest and dishonest graft, it seems that D&O insurance carriers are willing to cover honest fraud. In the words of the head of claims, "The carriers are OK to cover the fraud, but not the *fraud*." After all, protecting against securities fraud is the core coverage D&O insurers are selling.

Unjust Enrichment

Closely related to the fraud exclusion is the standard policy exclusion for the repayment of moneys to which the policyholder was not legally entitled. The AIG and Chubb specimen policies, for example, contain almost identical language excluding from covered losses any claim "arising out of, based upon or attributable to the gaining in fact of any profit or advantage to which the Insured was not legally entitled."[12] This exclusion may be seen as an extension of the common public policy rationale against unjust enrichment, prohibiting the defendants from receiving insurance against restitutionary damages since doing so effectively allows the wrongdoer to preserve its ill-gotten gains.[13] Seen in this light, an exclusion for unjust enrichment seems unremarkable. The restitutionary damages exclusion, however, has provoked interesting outcomes in a number of recent cases, largely particularly because it seemed for a time that the exclusion might be interpreted broadly to eliminate coverage for one of the main claims previously understood to be covered by D&O insurance: Section 11 claims.

The first such case, *Level 3 Communications v. Federal Insurance Co.*, before Judge Posner in the Seventh Circuit, arose out of an acquisition transaction in which the plaintiffs alleged that they had been induced to sell their shares to the acquiring company on the basis of fraudulent representations.[14] The plaintiffs-sellers sought rescission of the sale, but because the transaction could not be undone, they measured their damages by the difference between the current share price and the value they had received in the transaction. So understood, the damages amounted to disgorgement, a way of compelling the defendants to return the value of something unjustly taken. They were, in other words, restitutionary in nature. For that reason, the acquiring company's D&O insurers refused to fund the settlement of the shareholder class action, and Judge Posner decided that the insurers were correct.

Concluding that the damages did not come within the meaning of "loss" under the D&O policy, Judge Posner held that "[a]n insured incurs no loss within the meaning of the insurance contract by being compelled to return property that it had stolen, even if a more polite word than 'stolen' is used to characterize the claim for the property's return."[15] Leaving open the possibility that similar settlements might nevertheless come within the meaning of loss if a policyholder contested the allegations of ill-gotten gains and could plausibly argue that the settlement was paid, not to make restitution but merely to eliminate a nuisance claim, Judge Posner focused the meaning of "loss" to which a D&O policy might respond on actions for which no policyholder derives any direct benefit, an analysis that suggests a new front for insurers battling over coverage defenses: if amounts paid to settle shareholder claims can be recast as disgorgement for benefits improperly received by the policyholder, then the insurer may be able to avoid payment. Better yet, if a shareholder claim can be characterized as consisting of no other complaint, then the insurer may be able to deny coverage altogether.

This reasoning from *Level 3* bore fruit for insurers in *Conseco v. National Union Fire Insurance Co.*, in which the corporate policyholder sought D&O coverage for a $120 million settlement of a claim under Section 11 of the Securities Act of 1933.[16] First, recall from our discussion in chapter 2 that the damages in Section 11 claims are rescissionary in nature. In a Section 11 claim, the plaintiffs are corporate investors who essentially make a fraudulent inducement argument against the corporation that issued new securities to them. They would not have invested, they claim, if the corporation had not misrepresented its financial condition. Any settlement from the corporation to the investor can thus be construed as disgorgement—that is, the corporation, having wrongfully taken investors' money, is being made to return it. Applying the logic of

Level 3 to such settlements, insurers would thus seem to have a strong case for avoiding payment for all Section 11 settlements paid by corporations to their investors.[17] An Illinois state trial judge accepted this reasoning in denying insurance coverage for $82 million of the total $120 million settlement in *Conseco*, stating that "insurance cannot be used to pay an insured for amounts an insured wrongfully acquires and is forced to return."[18] Although other courts have declined to follow *Level 3*, its potential breadth is clearly indicated by *Conseco*.[19] Large portions of settlements previously thought to be covered by D&O insurance may be excludable as unjust enrichment.

Interestingly, our participants reported that insurers have responded to this potential coverage gap, not by seeking to preserve it as a defense to costly claims, but rather by expressly adopting a new term of coverage and selling it to policyholders, illustrating the dynamic of inadvertent gaps in coverage that we described earlier. A claims manager described the situation as follows:

> There have been a line of cases that talk about whether . . . in effect Section 11 claims for the entity are covered or whether that is really disgorgement or restitution . . . and [therefore] is not "loss" under the policy. So that is currently kind of an issue percolating out there. Some carriers have come back and explicitly made clear that there is coverage for the Section 11 claims.
> Q: In a new version of the policy you mean?
> A: Or by endorsement.[20]

Insurers have responded to the potential exclusion of Section 11 by expressly bringing such claims back under the policy, perhaps for additional premiums. Policyholders, of course, are likely to have a different perspective, viewing the temporary exclusion of Section 11 claims, which had typically been treated as covered losses under D&O policies until the *Conseco* case, as something of a dirty trick, a kind of ex post opportunism rightly corrected by the revision to their policies. For that reason, we are skeptical that insurers have been able to obtain higher premiums in return for their redrafting efforts, since most market participants thought that Section 11 claims were covered all along.

Rescission: Misrepresentation in the Application

In addition to whatever coverage defenses may be embedded in the policy's exclusions, insurers may also seek to avoid payment by attempting to have the policy declared void in its entirety. In seeking to rescind the policy, insurers typically employ a version of the basic fraud-in-the-inducement defense to contract. In the D&O context, their argument typically will turn on false information supplied in connection with the application for insurance. The insurers seeking to void coverage will argue that any such misstatements are material and that they relied on these material misstatements in entering into the insurance contract. Insurers who can establish these elements may either terminate coverage by simply cancelling the policy and returning any premiums paid by the policyholder, or they may sue to have the policy declared void ab initio in a rescission action.

As we noted in chapter 5, the D&O insurance application calls for a wealth of information from prospective policyholders, including information on the corporate officers and directors, information on the financial condition of the company, and disclosure of any pending or threatened litigation or any circumstances likely to give rise to a claim under the policy. Additionally, most applications call for corporate financial reports to be attached as exhibits, which may operate to make all statements made within them a formal part of the application itself. Applicants are typically made to certify the veracity of all representations made in connection with the application. A Chubb D&O application, for example, provides,

> The undersigned ... declare that to the best of their knowledge and belief, after reasonable inquiry, the statements made in this Application and in any attachments or other documents submitted with this Application are true and complete. The undersigned agree that this Application and such attachments and other documents shall be the basis of the insurance policy ... ; that all such materials shall be deemed to be attached to and shall form a part of any such policy; and that the Company will have relied on all such materials in issuing any such policy.[21]

This is an advertisement, in other words, that the insurer is collecting information in the application process that might later be used to rescind coverage.

Courts have held that "an insurance policy issued in reliance on material misrepresentations is void from its inception" and that intent to deceive is not required.[22] The insurer's right to rescind on the basis of misrepresentations is buttressed by policy language that, like the Chubb policy quoted above, requires the policyholder to acknowledge that all statements made in connection with the application form the basis of the policy and that all such statements are true.[23] Similarly, the insurer's right to rescind will be strengthened by policy language that clearly indicates that the policy may be rescinded on the basis of misrepresentations to the insurer.[24]

Financial misrepresentations, in particular, are a common basis of rescission actions. Because D&O insurers base their risk assessments in large part on the financial condition of prospective policyholders, misstatements of financial information are frequently material to an insurer's underwriting decisions.[25] Material omissions can also form the basis of rescission actions if the insurer can establish that the applicant knew its financial status was materially worse than information submitted to the insurer suggested, thus giving rise to a duty to disclose greater detail concerning the prospective policyholder's financial situation. If sufficient additional information is not provided, the insurer may be entitled to rescind.[26] Furthermore, documents attached to D&O applications, if incorporated into the policy application, can create grounds for rescission.[27]

In addition to financial misrepresentations, rescission has been allowed for failure to disclose pending or potential litigation against insured persons and for failure to disclose a material change in circumstances between the application and the effective date of the policy. Failure to disclose potential litigation has been held as sufficient grounds to void a D&O policy both when the policyholder failed to disclose that it had received notice that a claim would be filed and when the policyholder was in possession of facts clearly indicating that a claim would be filed.[28] Again, because such third-party claims are likely to be based on financial misrepresentations, failure-to-disclose litigation arguments are likely to overlap substantially with financial misrepresentation arguments. In one sense, failure-to-disclose litigation arguments can be seen as having greater breadth than misrepresentation in the application arguments since the former do not require the insurer to prove that the misrepresentation became a part of the application for insurance. Rather, the insurer need only show that the policyholder knew of the misrepresentation that was likely to form the basis of a third-party claim at the time it entered into the application. Yet this level of knowledge may indeed be more difficult for the insurer to prove than the simple existence of a material misrepresentation in the application documents and, in this sense, may be seen as a narrower basis for rescission.[29] Similarly, any relevant change in circumstances between the application and the effective date of the policy is likely to involve the prospective policyholder's financial condition.[30] At any rate, what most of these potential grounds for rescission have in common are inadequacies in statements concerning the finances of the policyholder.

Because they are typically grounded in a policyholder's financial misrepresentations, an insurer's action to rescind D&O coverage will frequently involve precisely the same conduct that is the basis of the underlying shareholder complaint. For example, in *Federal Insurance v. Homestore*, the insurers' rescission action and the shareholders' class action was based on the same misrepresentations in the same 10-Q filing. Because the 10-Q had been attached to the D&O renewal application, which unambiguously allowed the contract to be voided for false statements provided to the insurers in connection with the application, the court allowed rescission, thus taking away coverage for the shareholder claims on the basis of the same conduct that led the shareholder claims to be brought.[31] This close relationship between an insurer's rescission action and a shareholder's underlying claim suggests that insurers will have a plausible rescission argument for much shareholder litigation. Indeed, the most common basis for what we have been treating as the prototypical 10b-5 class action is a financial misrepresentation in a public disclosure document that, as long as it is also provided to the insurer in connection with the policy application or a renewal application, will also provide a strong basis for a rescission claim. Because the same conduct provides the basis for both claims, it would seem that insurers often will have a plausible basis for rescission and an ability to at least threaten to deny coverage to the basic shareholder cause of action.

The effect of rescission, moreover, is to invalidate the policy as a whole, thereby denying coverage to all policyholders under the policy, not only those who in fact made the misrepresentation, which is an important difference between the rescission defense and the fraud exclusion. This difference is striking given that only one or, at most, a few of those covered under the policy are likely to have had any part in the application process, and most of those covered under the policy may be wholly unaware of the misrepresentation. Nevertheless, courts and legislatures have endorsed this seemingly harsh result, effectively imputing the misrepresentation of one officer or director to everyone covered under the policy.[32] To avoid this outcome, policyholders have increasingly sought to include severability provisions in their D&O policies—that is, terms that expressly provide that actions taken by one or more covered persons cannot be imputed to other covered persons who are not themselves involved in the same conduct.[33] Severability, in other words, becomes a subject of explicit bargaining between insurer and policyholder, upheld by courts in the spirit of effectuating the bargain reached by contracting parties with the effect, in the words of one court, that "[c]o-insureds under a policy [with a severability provision] are treated as though they are covered under separate policies except that the aggregate policy limits apply to both."[34]

Such severability provisions have prevented insurers from rescinding D&O policies in several notorious corporate frauds. For example, in the coverage litigation that followed upon the shareholder litigation against HealthSouth Corporation, insurers were prevented by a severability provision from rescinding against the company's "innocent" policyholders, notwithstanding the guilty pleas entered by Richard Scrushy and other officers, who admitted that they had conspired to misrepresent the company's finances.[35] On the basis of a clause that provided that "no statement in the application or knowledge possessed by any Insured Person shall be imputed to any other Insured Person for the purpose of determining if coverage is available," the court held that recission was precluded for the other defendants in the securities class action.[36] Similarly, the litigation involving the D&O coverage of former officers and directors of the WorldCom corporation, after the corporation was bankrupted by Bernard Ebbers's accounting fraud, settled with an agreement that operated much like a severability provision, separating innocent policyholders from those culpable in the accounting fraud and providing coverage for the innocent directors.[37]

In addition to severability, another D&O insurance policy provision that may effectively serve as a bar to rescission is a broadly worded knowledge qualifier, such as an applicant's certification that publicly filed financial information is true "to the best of [his or her] knowledge and belief." Such language would protect against rescission by forcing the insurer to establish that the challenged misrepresentations were knowingly made.[38] In the absence of such helpful policy language, a policyholder's best argument against rescission may be to argue that too much time has passed for rescission or that the insurer has otherwise taken action to effectively waive its right to rescind. An insurer that receives information potentially entitling it to rescind the policy but that nevertheless continues to treat the policy as valid—by, for example, continuing to accept premium payments—may be estopped from rescinding the policy on the basis of the misrepresentation.[39] However, insurers will typically be accorded a reasonable amount of time to investigate before being deemed to have waived their right to rescind.[40]

Regardless of whether they intend to pursue rescission, once a claim arises under the policy, insurers typically are required by courts to pay defense costs until they have won their rescission case. In the coverage dispute that followed upon the shareholder claims brought against Tyco and its former CEO Dennis Kozlowski, another infamous case of fraud, the D&O insurer was denied the right to rescind unilaterally once the shareholder claims had arisen and instead was made to advance amounts to the policyholder to defend against the civil securities class action as well as criminal actions brought against former directors and officers.[41] In *Tyco*, the insurer had responded to the policyholders' notice of a claim and request for the advancement of defense costs by returning the policy premium and providing a notice of rescission. However, the court held that the insurer was not absolved from its defense obligation on the basis of its unilateral decision to rescind a policy, a holding that was affirmed on appeal.[42] The appellate court emphasized that rescission by notice is effective only when there has been no change in the parties' respective positions from the time they entered into the contract and that the assertion of a claim against a policyholder makes rescission by notice no longer available, stating that "[i]n such circumstances, a rescission by notice cannot, without legal sanction, have retroactive effect and serve to suspend, even temporarily, obligations that—absent a basis for rescission—have accrued under the policy."[43]

Cashing in the Coverage Defense: How Insurers Make Use of Coverage Defenses

As our discussion in the prior section reveals, D&O insurers will often have a coverage defense. If they do not have an exclusion that is directly relevant to the underlying shareholder claim, they may well have a colorable basis for a rescission claim against one or more defendants, often based on the same financial misrepresentation as the shareholder suit. Because the insurer's coverage defenses and the shareholders' claim are often based on the same underlying facts, our sense, supported by our participant's observations, is that the strength of insurers' moral hazard exclusion and misrepresentation defenses will vary proportionally with the strength of the underlying shareholder claims. Roughly speaking, the bigger the fraud and the easier it is to prove, the stronger the insurers' rescission or fraud defenses will likely be. It is worth noting, in connection with this hypothesized relationship, that insurers litigated coverage defenses in each of the major frauds from the last round of corporate scandals—including Enron, WorldCom, Tyco, and Adelphia.

Nevertheless, our participants emphasized that separate rescission actions are something of a rarity. Nor, they suggested, do insurers typically try to stretch available exclusions to avoid coverage in cases in which they are marginally applicable. There are exceptions, of course, including those we noted in the prior section surrounding efforts to avoid Section 11 liability under the exclusion for unjust enrichment, but most reservation of rights letters are, as practitioners sometimes put it, dogs that don't bark. The rarity of rescission or outright denial of coverage can be explained in large part by the adverse market impact that attends a carrier with a reputation for rescinding or denying coverage. Our respondents repeatedly emphasized that, in particular, a rescission action can have immediate negative consequences for an insurance carrier. Not only does it make other policyholders worry that the carrier will seek to rescind their policies, it also substantially harms the community of insurance brokers who assured their clients when placing their coverage that the carrier would be there to cover any liabilities that might subsequently arise. When the client suddenly discovers that it has no coverage, the brokerage firm not only suffers a substantial blow to its reputation but may also face liability issues itself should the client bring an action against it. The broker thus would likely be the first to adjust to a carrier's attempts to rescind. If an insurer often seeks to rescind, the response can be dramatic, as described by one of our participants: "At some point the brokers would stop bringing business. . . . And every time you raise a rescission issue, you raise a broker [liability] issue, and you know, as long as it is an intermediary driven market, the brokers are going to help steer where the business goes."[44] Brokers, in other words, will quickly stop placing policies with carriers who develop a reputation for aggressively asserting coverage defenses.

More than one of our participants illustrated the theme of market discipline for insurers with overly aggressive claims practices through an anecdote involving the Genesis Insurance Company. When Cutter & Buck sought to contest Genesis's effort to rescind its D&O policy, the dispute went to court, where Genesis pursued the claim aggressively, asserting fraud in the application and seeking to impute the misrepresentation against all policyholders under the policy. The court ultimately sided with Genesis, and the policy was fully rescinded.[45] Nevertheless, *Cutter & Buck* is viewed by many in the industry as something of a Pyrrhic victory since, although victorious in litigation, Genesis soon failed. The reason for the insurer's failure, our respondents asserted, was that Genesis had shown itself to be overzealous in avoiding the payment of claims, a reputation that brought immediate negative consequences in the D&O insurance market. In the words of a claims manager at a different insurance carrier: "Genesis successfully rescinded *Cutter & Buck*. That was a huge nail in their coffin.... Brokers talked about that endlessly. They pulled accounts from them and wouldn't put new business with them."[46] The lesson, our respondents emphasized, was that, although rescission legally may be an option, it will often be a bad idea from a business perspective.

How then do insurers make use of their coverage defenses? If litigating coverage defenses has negative reputational consequences, what are insurers supposed to do? Simply sacrifice their interests and pay claims notwithstanding their ability to avoid them, effectively leaving money on the table?

Of course not, our respondents answered. Instead, insurers extract value from their coverage defenses by insisting on concessions in settlement from their policyholders. Most often, our respondents told us, insurers trade any applicable coverage defenses, promising not to pursue them, in exchange for greater contributions from their policyholder to settlement amounts that the insurers otherwise would be obligated to pay. Insurers, in other words, use their coverage defenses to threaten not to pay, a threat that is more or less credible depending on the strength of their argument for rescission and that is, in any event, taken seriously by both plaintiffs and defendants alike. As described by a plaintiffs' lawyer in the following colloquy:

> Q: Do you feel like [insurers] use [coverage defenses] in settlement negotiations?
> A: Oh, yes.
> Q: Because they say, "Hey, we have this good coverage defense." Is that meaningful to you?
> A: Absolutely, because I mean it's a credible threat.

Coverage defenses thus are rarely used to avoid payment altogether but are more often used to reduce the amount that insurers must ultimately pay at settlement. As one claims manager frankly described,

> So this is the dynamic. Everybody has a little bit of pressure on them, and what happens is nine times out of ten in those types of situations the larger the fraud, you are going to get a discount on your limit. You are going to cash in essentially your coverage case. . . . So I mean that's like a bar fight if you think about it. You know, in your standard general liability claim there is an intentional harm

exclusion, and there is a fight in a bar, and you know, nobody wants to go to trial in a bar fight. The damages are going to be ugly. But on the other hand, maybe the guy did it on purpose. So the settlement, the carrier saved some money off the policy limits, but on the other hand they pay a lot because the person is really damaged. They got, you know, the guy shoved a broken bottle in a person's face or whatever.[47]

Several of our respondents asserted that this trade-off or "cashing in" of the rescission claim in fact happens with some frequency and explains corporate contributions to settlements that are within the total limits of the D&O insurance program. We would very much have liked to test this assertion, to support it with statistics. Such a test, in theory at least, would be simple to run, simply by examining all cases that settled within total insurance limits and that, therefore, should have been wholly funded by insurers in excess of the policy deductible and counting what fraction of these cases nevertheless involved a substantial contribution to settlement from the corporate policyholder. Unfortunately the data necessary to run such a test are not publicly available, including firm-specific information on D&O policy limits and deductibles as well as information on how settlements are funded and to what extent funds are provided by insurers or policyholders. As we will argue in chapter 10, this information should be made publicly available.

In any event, our respondents told us that insurers make use of their coverage defenses in bargaining with the policyholder and, if the policyholder is in poor financial condition, with the plaintiffs' lawyers as well, effectively cashing in their grounds for rescission in exchange for a discount on their contribution to settlement. This finding is directly relevant to the question of deterrence. If, as our respondents suggested, the strength of a policyholder's coverage defense is proportional to the strength of the underlying shareholder claim—or, to paraphrase one of our respondents, the larger the fraud, the bigger the discount—then by forcing policyholders to make additional contributions to settlement on the basis of their coverage defenses, insurers effectively offer less coverage for worse frauds. In other words, these insurance coverage defenses are an important fulcrum around which all of the parties involved in shareholder litigation negotiate the degree of pain that will be directed against the corporation and the individual defendants. In this way, they increase the perceived cost of shareholder litigation for less well-governed firms. If worse-governed firms pay more in connection with shareholder litigation, then the deterrence function embedded within shareholder claims may indeed be operative in spite of insurance.

To summarize the discussion of this chapter, the coverage dispute is the last opportunity for a D&O insurer to force a bad corporate actor to pay for its bad acts. As such, it is the last moment when the deterrence function of shareholder litigation can be reintroduced by an insurer. In this chapter, we summarized insurers' basic coverage defenses. We also pointed out that in spite of being widely available in D&O claims, coverage defenses are in fact rarely asserted in a way that would result in litigation. Instead, we found that insurers use their coverage defenses to strengthen their hand in bargaining with insureds and sometimes get a discount from the amount of a settlement for which they would otherwise be liable as a result of their potential coverage defenses. This has important implications for deterrence since, as long as there is a loose correlation between coverage defenses and corporate wrongdoing—that is, the insurer's coverage defenses seem strongest when the plaintiffs' underlying claim is meritorious—then by imposing additional costs on the basis of their coverage defenses, insurers are effectively increasing the cost of shareholder litigation on those firms that are most likely to have done wrong, a prerequisite for the deterrence function of shareholder litigation to have any effect. We would like to test this mechanism, evaluating how frequently it is used and in which cases it appears, but the data necessary to do so in a systematic way are currently unavailable. Therefore, we cannot draw a strong conclusion about the ability of these practices to reintroduce deterrence. Indeed, on balance we conclude that in claims management, as in underwriting and during the life of the insurance contract, insurers in fact are able to do relatively little to reintroduce the deterrence function of shareholder litigation.

CHAPTER TEN

Policy Recommendations: Improving Deterrence

This book has examined shareholder litigation through the lens of D&O insurance in order to evaluate whether shareholder litigation succeeds or fails in its regulatory objective. By surveying the principal players in the industry—those directly involved in the buying and selling of D&O insurance as well as those involved in the litigation and settlement of shareholder claims, our investigations have brought forth a diverse set of observations on D&O insurance and shareholder litigation. Throughout, our exposition has been guided by a central theme—namely, the way in which D&O insurance mutes the regulatory effect of shareholder litigation. In this chapter, we return to our central theme, confronting the problems raised by the participants in our study and offering solutions.

The insurer's role, of course, is to pay liabilities on behalf of the policyholder, and in this way, D&O insurance transfers the risk of liability from the defendant to the insurer. But in transferring risk of loss from the defendant to an insurer, insurance also transforms it. By removing the risk of loss from defendants, insurance may reduce or even destroy the deterrence function of shareholder litigation, unless the insurer has some means of preserving the deterrence function.

As we have explained, there are several ways in which D&O insurance theoretically might preserve the deterrence function of shareholder litigation. First, by pricing coverage to risk, D&O insurers might preserve the deterrence signal. Requiring riskier corporations to pay more for coverage encourages them to improve their governance in order to reduce the risk of shareholder litigation and, thereby, their D&O premiums. Second, D&O insurers could monitor corporate policyholders during the life of the contract, forcing them to steer clear of risky conduct or to adopt governance practices designed to prevent the kinds of events that lead to shareholder litigation. Third, D&O insurers could exert control over defense and settlement to ensure that outcomes at settlement reflect the underlying merits of claims, so that the loss component of insurers' pricing algorithms is based on the right people being held responsible in the right amount. Fourth, insurers could deploy their moral hazard claims defenses to force defendants to pay more toward the defense and settlement in those cases in which there is greater evidence of genuine wrongdoing, leaving a greater portion of the cost of such claims on the policyholder and thus incentivizing prospective defendants ex ante to avoid conduct that may reduce their coverage ex post.

When we pursued these possibilities in our interviews, however, we found that each is decidedly problematic in practice. First, as described in chapter 5, although D&O insurers do seek to price coverage to risk, there is reason to doubt that this differential pricing of D&O premiums deters wrongdoing or provides a substantial incentive to improve corporate behavior. Second, as described in chapter 6, insurers have virtually no role in monitoring the policyholder (and thus no role in deterrence) during the life of a policy, other than through repricing the coverage for the next policy period (which leads back to the limits of pricing discussed in chapter 5). Third, although they do have some control over settlements, as described in chapter 7, insurers have almost no control over the conduct of the defense, and there are many features of the settlement process, described in chapter 8, that prevent insurers from concluding with confidence that settlements correlate to the underlying merits of claims. Finally, although our respondents reported that insurers do sometimes use the threat of a coverage defense to insist on greater contributions to settlement and defense costs from defendants in cases that have generated greater evidence of actual wrongdoing, we also reported in chapter 9 on several limitations on an insurer's ability to deploy these defenses to provide this ex post deterrent.

Each of these problems increases the likelihood that insurance substantially mutes the deterrence effect of shareholder litigation. This is a grave concern indeed, considering that, with the abandonment of the compensation justification, deterrence is the raison d'être of shareholder litigation.

If shareholder litigation fails to constrain corporate wrongdoing because insurance largely undercuts deterrence, then shareholder litigation is essentially waste—little more than pocket shifting between insurance companies and the shareholders of defendant corporations, minus significant amounts siphoned off by plaintiffs' and defense attorneys. Legal reformers would thus be right to call for its abolition or, alternately, for the abolition of D&O insurance.

Simply put, our entire system of shareholder litigation is at stake in this question. If insurance severs the deterrence function of shareholder litigation, we might as well scrap the system and start over. Before we go this far, however, we ought to pause to consider whether there are any features of the current system that can be reformed to reinvigorate the deterrence function of shareholder litigation in an environment of insurance. How, in other words, can we solve the most serious problems uncovered in our interviews without abolishing either shareholder litigation or D&O insurance? After all, public company managers manifestly would like to buy this insurance; insurance companies are willing to sell it; and, apart from us, almost no one has called the market into question, leading us to conclude that reform ought to be tried before entertaining serious proposals for abolition. In this chapter, we offer some suggestions to improve the present system. Most significantly, we propose that the SEC mandate the disclosure of D&O insurance information.

The Pricing Problem

In chapter 5, we discussed how D&O insurers seek to price coverage. Insurance pricing is critical to deterrence. If insurance is not priced to risk, the policyholder does not have an adequate incentive to take care to control insured losses resulting from the underlying risk. If, on the other hand, the insurance premium is closely tied to the risk that the prospective policyholder creates, the premium itself may serve as an inducement for the policyholder to avoid loss. The policyholder may no longer be thinking as much about the underlying risk—here, shareholder litigation—but may nevertheless be motivated to avoid litigation in order to pay a lower insurance premium.

As we reported, our respondents told us that D&O insurers do indeed seek to price coverage to risk. Nevertheless, our respondents also left us with several reasons to doubt that D&O premiums will be sufficient to induce corporations to alter their governance practices. Most basically, D&O insurance premiums may not be large enough to change corporate behavior, either because D&O premiums are an insignificant portion of a large corporation's total costs or because the marginal difference in premiums between good firms and bad firms may not be large enough to induce bad firms to change their ways. The latter point, for us, is the more serious one—that is, even if D&O premiums are nontrivial, the difference between the premiums paid by good and bad firms may not be sufficiently large to force bad firms to improve. Good firms might pay too much while bad firms pay too little because of errors and inefficiencies in underwriting or in the liability system itself. As a result, the cost of liability falls too evenly on both good and bad firms, thwarting the deterrence effect of the liability regime.

And so, although insurers seek to price according to risk, we ought not to expect the pricing mechanism alone to preserve the deterrence function of shareholder litigation, especially under the current system in which the amount that a corporation pays for its coverage and the details concerning the structure of its coverage are kept secret. The good news is that this part of the problem has a tantalizingly simple solution: spread the secret. Reinvigorate deterrence, in other words, by forcing corporate disclosure of D&O insurance information, amplifying the corporate governance signal of the D&O insurance premium by broadcasting it through the capital market.

The Disclosure Solution

Even if the cost of D&O insurance does not provide a sufficiently strong incentive to spur a corporation to optimize its governance structure, the cost and structure of a firm's D&O coverage package nevertheless encodes important information about its governance quality. Most basically, the more a corporation pays for its D&O coverage, all other things being equal, the greater the shareholder liability risk it poses. Because a significant component of the risk assessment of D&O professionals is the governance quality—including the deep governance variables of culture and character—the premium can be expected to encode this information concerning governance quality. This assessment of governance quality is uniquely credible because it is made by an insurer that will be forced to suffer the costs—in the form of payout obligations—of getting the estimate wrong. D&O insurance underwriting decisions are, in the jargon of economics, both "revealed preferences" of the insurers and "bonded" assessments of the risk. Moreover, a company's D&O insurance premium is based on information that is uniquely available to the insurer—the private underwriters' meetings with management—which therefore may not already be in the market, making it particularly valuable to investors and other market participants. A company's D&O insurance premium would thus seem to be a valuable proxy for information that is not otherwise available.

Of course, as we described in chapter 5, a company's insurance premium is not based purely on corporate governance factors but contains a number of basic financial factors as well, such as market capitalization and share price volatility. However, professionals could easily back these factors out of the premium number, thus turning a company's insurance premium into a measure of governance quality. The necessary adjustments are relatively simple. First, because insurance premiums depend in part on the coverage limits and the firm's retention, premium data must be adjusted for effective coverage amounts. This, however, would be a relatively easy adjustment to make, given data that included each company's insurance premiums, limits, and retentions under each part of the D&O coverage. Second, in addition to these features of the insurance policy itself, insurance premiums may correlate to other features of the corporation or its business. For example, firms within a particular industry may be subject to systematically higher D&O insurance rates than firms in other lines of business with less industry-wide risk of shareholder litigation. However, this distortion too could be corrected by comparing D&O insurance pricing across a set of firms within a specific industry in order to identify norms and outliers. Finally, the distortion introduced by market capitalizations and measures of volatility can be eliminated by controlling for those factors. Thus, in spite of the noise in insurance prices, with a few adjustments, a firm's premium for D&O insurance should convey important information concerning the firm's corporate governance. Most basically, the more a firm pays, all other things being equal, the worse its governance.

Beyond the premium, information may also be conveyed to market participants by the amount of insurance a company purchases. Other things being equal, a relatively high level of coverage (high limits, low retentions) may signal that the corporation's managers are uncomfortable with the firm's governance risk and therefore insist on a higher level of coverage. Meanwhile, low limits and high retentions suggest that managers do not expect their firm to generate significant liabilities from shareholder litigation. In this way, the level of coverage alone may signal the managers' own assessment of governance risk.

Understanding these proxies for governance quality, fund managers, arbitrageurs, and other professional investors can be expected to build these signals into their models of firm value. And, once incorporated into pricing models, D&O premium information and other policy details would recreate the deterrence function of shareholder litigation. If a D&O insurance policy reveals negative information—for example, unusually high premiums—traders' pricing models would likely discount the company's share price in capital markets. Facing this discount, firms would have an incentive to improve governance practices in order to avoid it.

Disclosing D&O Insurance Information

American companies do not disclose the details of their D&O policies. Annual reports and other corporate filings typically do not disclose D&O coverage limits, retentions, or premiums, and firms do not attach copies of their D&O policies as exhibits to their public filings. U.S. law, for the most part, does not require these disclosures. Neither federal securities laws nor Delaware corporate law compels corporations to disclose information concerning their D&O coverage. Interestingly, New York State does mandate disclosure of some D&O insurance information for companies incorporated there, but not enough companies are incorporated in New York to make this information useful in the way we have hypothesized. Interestingly, Canadian law mandates disclosure of this information, and research into Canadian data confirms some of the relationships we have hypothesized.

STATE LAW ON D&O DISCLOSURES. As noted in chapter 3, state corporate law places no limits on the ability of corporations to purchase D&O insurance. Regardless of whether the corporation would have the power under state law to indemnify its directors against a particular loss, it can insure them. Moreover, state corporate law typically does not require disclosure of D&O policy details. In Delaware, the primary source of American corporate law, no part of the General Corporation Law requires firms to disclose information concerning their D&O policies. Most states follow Delaware, but New York State is an exception.

Like Delaware, New York is broadly permissive of D&O insurance.[1] Unlike Delaware, however, New York requires D&O insurance contracts to include retention and coinsurance in amounts deemed acceptable by the state's superintendent of insurance before the contract can cover non-indemnifiable losses.[2] Also unlike Delaware, New York does not allow insurance payments other than defense costs to be made in the event that final adjudication establishes material "acts of active and deliberate dishonesty" or that the director or officer "personally gained . . . a financial profit or other advantage to which he was not legally entitled."[3] Although each of these provisions plainly regulates the relationship between insurer and policyholder to a much greater degree than Delaware law, it is not clear that these requirements do anything more than mimic the terms that the parties would otherwise agree to. As we discussed in detail in chapter 3, D&O insurance contracts often include retention amounts and coinsurance, and deliberate fraud and final adjudication of wrongdoing are common exclusions. The most significant difference between the New York and Delaware statutes may be in New York's disclosure requirement.

New York law requires disclosure of D&O policy information. Section 726(d) of the New York Business Corporation Law provides,

> The corporation shall . . . mail a statement in respect of any insurance it has purchased or renewed under this section, specifying the insurance carrier, date of the contract, cost of the insurance, corporate positions insured, and a statement explaining all sums, not previously reported in a statement to shareholders, paid under any indemnification insurance contract.[4]

New York corporate law, in other words, includes a mandatory disclosure rule that triggers the release of some D&O policy information in the company's proxy statement. Because several prominent firms are incorporated in New York, § 726(d) would seem to trigger the release of much interesting information.

Unfortunately, our survey of the disclosures made by New York companies, including American Express, Bank of New York, and Sears Roebuck, revealed significant limitations in the disclosures made by New York corporations. For example, the New York statute does not require disclosure of policy limits, and indeed most of the New York companies we researched did not include it in their filings. This is a severe limitation because without information about limits, the D&O premium cannot be adjusted to reflect the amount of insurance purchased. A per-dollar cost of coverage figure therefore cannot be determined to enable comparisons. This severely limits the usefulness of the New York disclosures. Other weaknesses in the New York data include the failure to require disclosure of retentions and coinsurance amounts, making it impossible to evaluate actual coverage amounts, and no requirement that firms break out different lines of coverage—that is, A, B, or C coverage. Companies typically disclose only an aggregate premium amount and no information about the lines of coverage available under the policy or the different limits, retentions, and coinsurance amounts under each.

Finally, and perhaps most basically, New York is not Delaware. Several important firms are incorporated in New York, but most are not. Because the signaling value of D&O premiums lies in comparisons between similarly situated firms, we cannot know the real significance of the D&O premiums paid by New York companies unless we know the premiums paid by comparable companies, many of which are not New York companies. The D&O disclosures compelled by the state of New York are intriguing, but ultimately unhelpful. Worse, unless every company moved to New York, the legislators in Albany cannot solve the problem.

FEDERAL LAW ON D&O DISCLOSURES. Federal securities regulators have adopted a tortured, somewhat contradictory approach to the issues raised by D&O insurance. Congress has never explicitly addressed the matter, but the SEC, following Congress's stated intent of inducing compliance with the securities laws,[5] has taken a firm position against the indemnification of officers and directors for securities law violations, requiring that all registrants under the Securities Act of 1933 include the following language in their registration statements:

> Insofar as indemnification for liabilities arising under the Securities Act of 1933 may be permitted to directors, officers and controlling persons of the registrant pursuant to the foregoing provisions, or otherwise, the registrant has been advised that in the opinion of the Securities and Exchange Commission such indemnification is against public policy as expressed in the Act and is, therefore, unenforceable.[6]

The SEC's position on indemnification is rooted in the view that transferring the cost of legal sanction renders managers less likely to comply with the law. Because insuring directors and officers against these costs would seem to implicate precisely the same policy concerns as indemnifying them, it would be reasonable to suppose that the SEC similarly opposes D&O insurance. This supposition, however, appears to be incorrect.

The SEC takes a milder position on D&O insurance than it takes on indemnification. The SEC has not declared insurance against securities law liabilities to be a violation of public policy. In fact, the SEC has arguably endorsed the corporate purchase of D&O insurance, stating that the maintenance of a D&O policy, even when paid for by the company, will not bar acceleration of a registration statement.[7] Moreover, unlike the harsh language imposed on registrants adopting indemnification provisions, the SEC requires only that the existence and "general effect" of D&O insurance policies be disclosed.[8] This disclosure is triggered by each of the major forms governing the registration of securities, including Forms S-1, S-2, S-3, S-4, and S-8. Considering that insurance and indemnification raise the same policy concerns, the maintenance of distinct positions seems inconsistent and in any event has never been explained by the SEC.

The regulation that requires registrants to disclose the existence of D&O insurance does not require the disclosure of any policy details. Item 702 of Regulation S-K merely requires that registrants "[s]tate the general effect of any statute, charter provisions, by-laws, contract or other arrangements under which any controlling persons, director or officer of the registrant is insured or indemnified in any manner against liability which he may incur in his capacity as such."[9] Although the general effect of D&O insurance may be read to require some discussion of policy details, registrants generally provide nothing more than an opaque statement that coverage will be available, subject to unstated limits, to cover liabilities arising from the directors' or officers' conduct as such. For example, Yankee Candle made the following statement of the general effect of D&O insurance in a registration statement:

> Policies of insurance are maintained by Yankee Candle under which its directors and officers are insured, within the limits and subject to the limitations of the policies, against certain expenses in connection with the defense of, and certain liabilities which might be imposed as a result of, actions, suits or proceedings to which they are parties by reason of being or having been such directors or officers.[10]

By granting effectiveness to these registration statements, the SEC effectively accepts such nondescriptive language in fulfillment of the required disclosure.

The SEC has the legal authority to require much more detail. The SEC could, for example, treat D&O insurance as a "material contract" and require that policies be filed as an exhibit to the registration statement.[11] It could also treat D&O insurance as an aspect of executive compensation, triggering full description of policy features, including the cost and value of the policy, as it does in the case of life insurance provided to corporate executives.[12] However, the SEC has made neither of these choices and instead has expressly stated that it will treat D&O insurance separately from executive compensation: "Premiums paid for liability insurance for officers and directors and benefits paid under such insurance plans are not forms of remuneration to the extent that the insurance plan is intended to relieve officers and directors of liability relating to their job performance."[13] Unfortunately, in taking this position, the SEC has kept the required disclosure of policy details to a minimal discussion of the policy's general effect.

It is puzzling, given both the SEC's strident position on indemnification and the valuable information that D&O policy details may convey, that the SEC does not require disclosure of registrants' D&O policy premiums, limits, and retentions. Indeed, this is especially strange considering the position taken by our neighbors to the north and the useful data that Canadian securities regulators have produced by requiring disclosure of precisely these items.

A CANADIAN COMPARISON.   Unlike their counterparts in the United States, Canadian securities regulators do require disclosure of D&O insurance details. Public companies in Canada must disclose basic information concerning their D&O insurance policies, including coverage limits and premiums, in their proxy filings and registration statements.[14] This provides the opportunity to conduct a natural experiment. Can the information disclosed in these Canadian filings be used to establish a link between corporate governance and D&O insurance? Research using this data has confirmed this link and yielded several interesting insights.

Professor John Core has studied Canadian data to determine whether D&O premiums can be related to corporate governance variables.[15] Hypothesizing that D&O premiums would be a function both of business-specific risk factors and governance-related risk factors, Core separated proxy variables relating to each. Grouping measures of ownership structure, board size, and management entrenchment together as indicators of governance quality, on the one hand, and firm size, financial performance, and U.S. exchange listing as proxies for business risk, on the other, Core regressed each variable against D&O premiums, finding approximately half of the governance quality variables to be statistically significant, while each of the business risk variables was statistically significant.[16] Significant governance quality variables—including insider stock ownership and voting control, director independence, and executive employment contracts—enabled Core ultimately to conclude that Canadian data support an association between D&O premiums and governance quality.[17]

One of the most significant variables in the Core study, however, underscores the inherent limitations of the Canadian experience. Core found that Canadian firms that are also listed on a U.S. exchange, thus exposing them to U.S. securities litigation, have significantly higher D&O premiums than peer firms not listed in the United States. This emphasizes the difference between U.S. and Canadian liability risks. At least with regard to shareholder litigation and perhaps representative litigation generally, the legal systems of the two countries are different enough to make cross-country comparisons somewhat tenuous. Canada retains the English "loser pays" system, increasing the risk borne by the plaintiffs' lawyers. As a result, contingent fees are used less often and, when they are used, are subject to a reasonableness standard. In addition, class actions and derivative suits are filed less often. The Canadian environment, on the whole, is thus considerably less favorable for entrepreneurial plaintiffs' lawyers. As a result, although the Canadian studies ultimately support a link between corporate governance and the pricing of D&O insurance, U.S. data are needed to confirm their results. Unfortunately, the same data are not available for U.S. companies.

Professor Martin Boyer has recently extended this research by studying whether D&O insurance prices paid by Canadian corporations contain enough meaningful information to enable investors to design a profitable trading strategy.[18] He first developed a measure called the "unit price" of D&O insurance, which is the total D&O insurance premium divided by the total limits in the D&O insurance program. Then he compared the performance of publicly traded Canadian companies over a five-year period (1993–98) according to the unit price of insurance they paid. Among other interesting conclusions, he found that large firms with a low unit price performed significantly better over the period (61 percent) than large firms with a high unit price (35 percent) and that, therefore, an investment strategy of going long in low-unit-price firms while shorting high-unit-price firms was profitable. Boyer concluded that D&O insurance prices do contain useful information about corporate governance risk and, therefore, "shareholders should value D&O insurance information."[19] Citing Griffith's 2006 article calling for the disclosure of D&O insurance information in the United States, Boyer concluded with the following observation: "Given that so much is [already] revealed about the compensation of top executives and the structure of the board, it appears to me paradoxical that information as easy to present as D&O insurance policy limits, deductible and premium, and so informative as to the governance health of a firm does not find its way into the annual reports."[20] We turn to this topic next.

EXPLAINING THE ABSENCE OF VOLUNTARY DISCLOSURE.   For all of the reasons stated above, we believe that disclosure of details concerning D&O coverage would provide useful information to capital market participants and, even more importantly, might provide the link in the chain necessary to reinvigorate the deterrence function of shareholder litigation. U.S. securities regulators ought to follow the Canadian example and mandate disclosure of this information in even greater detail. However, before arguing in favor of mandatory disclosure, it is worth pausing to consider why firms do not already voluntarily disclose this information. Indeed, if the details of a firm's D&O coverage convey such important data regarding the governance quality of the firm, why are these details not disclosed? Why do individual firms not voluntarily disclose this information?

Capital market dynamics naturally produce disclosures. All firms that seek to raise capital from investors will seek to convince investors that they are issuers of high-quality securities. Because it is difficult for investors to distinguish between high- and low-quality securities, firms will produce information to persuade investors that their securities are the former rather than the latter. This information is credible, owing largely to the presence of rules against fraud. To encourage investment, firms will be especially eager to release good news. Firms' natural incentives to disclose good news, however, will cause investors to be suspicious of and to discount the value of any firm not disclosing similar information. If a nondisclosing firm had similar good news, investors will reason, it would have disclosed it. Because it did not, it must have only bad news, an outcome that extends the childhood maxim—if you don't have something nice to say, don't say anything at all. Firms that do not say anything at all, the investor concludes, must have nothing nice to say. Aware of this logic and eager to avoid the resulting discount to the value of their securities, all firms have an incentive to make regular disclosures, good or bad, thus voluntarily creating an environment of robust corporate disclosure.

Because any piece of information that might affect the value of a firm's securities—including D&O policy details—ought therefore to be disclosed voluntarily, the absence of such disclosures may be taken to imply that the information is not sufficiently valuable to merit disclosure. If the information mattered, in other words, firms would release it. Is this true of the information embedded in the details of the firm's D&O policy? Does the absence of voluntary disclosure of D&O policy details imply that the information does not, in fact, matter?

Irrelevance of the information, of course, is not the only explanation for a lack of disclosure. In their seminal work, *The Economic Structure of Corporate Law*, Frank Easterbrook and Dan Fischel, who are not typically thought of as champions of mandatory disclosure rules, themselves identified three situations in which a regime of voluntary disclosure would predictably fail.[21] The characteristic problem in each of these three situations is the production of information that is of value to investors of other firms as well as to the investors of the firm in possession of the information. Because the firm with the information cannot charge the investors of other firms for it, the information is likely to be underproduced. The situations in which Easterbrook and Fischel found this problem included, first, the production of industry-wide, as opposed to firm-specific, information. Although all firms would prefer that this information be made available, no one firm has an incentive to produce it since doing so would allow other firms to free-ride on its efforts. Similarly, information that primarily facilitates comparisons among firms would be underproduced because the information is valuable only once several firms have made similar disclosures. No firm is willing to be the first to disclose because the information, by itself, is worthless and, if it includes competitively sensitive information or a damaging revelation, potentially harmful. Finally, because some disclosures are easier to understand than others, there may be information that would be valuable to investors if disclosed in a particular format, but because no firm has an incentive to search for and adopt the optimal format (again because the benefits would redound largely to the investors of other firms who cannot be charged), the information nevertheless goes undisclosed. In each of these three situations, then, a regime of voluntary disclosure can be expected to fail.[22]

D&O policy data have several of these features. First and foremost, the value of D&O policy information is purely comparative. The relevance of a firm's policy premium, limits, and retention amounts emerges only on comparison with similarly situated firms. Moreover, as noted above, comparing similarly situated firms means taking a broad industry-wide sample and controlling for such variables as market capitalization. D&O policy data, in other words, are only valuable once the data are available for an entire industry. Each of the firms within the industry, however, will be disinclined to produce the information because it is of value largely to investors of other firms who cannot be made to pay for it. It is, in other words, a paradigmatic example of a situation in which voluntary disclosure is likely to fail.

In addition to the free-rider effects focused on by Easterbrook and Fischel, investors in individual firms may not want to be the first to disclose D&O details for fear that disclosing the cost of their policy would harm the firm. Explicitly stating that a corporation pays millions of dollars per year to insure its executives against the cost of their own negligence may not sit well with investors. The amounts paid by a particular firm may be low when compared with peer firms, but with no disclosures from peer firms to enable these comparisons, such amounts, alone, may seem high. In this way, investors' views of D&O expenses may create a first-mover disadvantage. Even if investors would prefer that all firms make such disclosures, the investors in any one firm are likely to hesitate for fear of harming that firm.

In this way, the absence of voluntary disclosure of D&O policy details does not point to the irrelevance of the information but rather to a coordination problem among investors. All investors would prefer that the information be disclosed, but the investors of any one firm have disincentives to disclose arising from the inability of the firm to capture the value of the disclosure and the possibility that the disclosure of premium information, unless the firm's competitors also disclose, would harm the firm.

THE "MORE DISCLOSURE EQUALS MORE LITIGATION" ARGUMENT. Another argument that we can anticipate being raised to explain the absence of voluntary disclosure and indeed to lobby against mandating disclosure of D&O insurance information is the claim that revealing coverage limits will expose the disclosing firm to greater risk of shareholder litigation. The argument is simple: once plaintiffs' lawyers know which firms have large D&O policies, they have an incentive to sue those firms, and once they know the policy limits, they know what to seek in settlement. Although this argument may seem initially plausible, the disclosure of D&O policy details would have little impact on shareholder litigation because plaintiffs' lawyers—the driving force behind shareholder litigation—already know all they need to know about D&O insurance for their purposes. It is no secret that virtually all public companies carry D&O insurance and that average limits for small- and mid-cap corporations are in the tens of millions of dollars and that limits for large-cap companies can be in the hundreds of millions.[23] Plaintiffs' lawyers will be well aware of these facts and, because it is how they make their living, will be able to estimate a particular company's coverage within a fairly accurate range. Moreover, a company's D&O policy is routinely and quickly disclosed in the course of litigation, long before the case is settled.[24] As a result, it is unlikely that disclosure of such details will add anything substantial to the plaintiffs' lawyers' arsenal or significantly alter the dynamics of shareholder litigation.

Nevertheless, even if it will not constitute a boon to plaintiffs' attorneys, free-rider effects and coordination problems currently inhibit voluntary disclosure of D&O policy details. Although all investors would prefer all firms to disclose this information, any one firm's investors are likely to hesitate to provide it given the possible harm of such disclosures if a large number of other firms do not reciprocate. Investors in each firm face the same incentives, and as a result, all firms choose not to disclose D&O policy information. Given the failure of voluntary disclosure to trigger the release of this valuable information, we must consider a mandatory rule.

THE SEC SHOULD MANDATE DISCLOSURE OF D&O INSURANCE DETAILS.   The law should be changed to require disclosure of details concerning a company's D&O coverage. In addition to disclosing the existence of a policy, companies should be required to disclose the identity of the insurers, their location in the program, the total limits and retention under each type of coverage the limits and attachment points of the individual policies, and perhaps most importantly, the premium for each policy in the program along with the total aggregate amount. To facilitate investor use of this information, it should be required to be disclosed in a standard format. In addition, because D&O insurance policies are not standardized, public companies should be required to post them on their Web sites. Each of these disclosures should be required after each policy renewal, and, taken together, we believe would provide a valuable indicator of corporate governance quality that is currently unavailable to capital market participants. Most importantly, the use of this information by capital market participants, who would adjust assessments of risk and valuations of disclosing firms on the basis of this information, would have an impact in the capital market that will help to reinvigorate the deterrence function of shareholder litigation, notwithstanding the presence of insurance.

We have argued that the price a firm pays for its D&O coverage—the insurance premium—will convey an important signal concerning the quality of the firm's governance. Requiring disclosure of the firm's D&O premium would thus enhance the ability of investors to value the firm, and requiring it on a regular basis, with each policy renewal, would keep investors apprised of significant changes in governance risk. If, for example, a firm's D&O insurance premium significantly increased in a year in which similarly situated firms experienced no change in premium, investors would be put on notice that the firm's D&O insurers believe that something significant changed at the firm. Moreover, because the governance assessment implicit in the insurance premium is based in part on private information available only to the D&O insurer, the signal conveyed by a change in insurance premiums may alert investors to information that is otherwise unavailable to them.

Details on the amount and structure of D&O insurance purchased—that is, the company's policy limits and retentions—would also provide several vital pieces of information. First, without information on the amount of insurance purchased, data on premiums would be too noisy to be meaningful. Information on limits and retentions is necessary to specify precisely what the company is paying for and to enable comparisons across firms. Moreover, requiring information about the amount of coverage under each type of coverage—that is, sides A, B, and C—would provide additional signals to the market. As described above, side A coverage is the only form of coverage that benefits officers and directors individually. The amount of side A coverage purchased by a firm could thus convey an important signal about the confidence of its managers regarding the liability risks they expect to face. Sanguine managers may allow their firms to purchase less coverage. As a result, other things being equal, a firm purchasing lower amounts of side A insurance may tend to pose less risk of shareholder litigation. Unlike side A coverage, side B and side C coverages benefit the company only and, as described above, may be rooted in managerial agency costs. As a result, a company purchasing large amounts of coverage under sides B and C sends a signal not only that its managers believe the firm presents a relatively large risk of shareholder litigation but also that it has the kind of managers who would rather waste corporate assets in a negative net present-value investment than put their personal compensation packages at risk by allowing the firm to self-insure against shareholder litigation. In addition, information about the structure of the program—the number of layers, the attachments points, and the existence of any coinsurance or self-insured pieces above the initial retention—would allow investors to test whether this structural information contains any governance information, and it would also allow for better interpretation of settlements in future securities class actions.

Finally, the identity of the D&O insurers would provide valuable information about the gatekeeper itself. In addition to the obvious importance of the insurer's financial rating, different insurers may have different reputations for screening governance risk. As a result, investors may draw different conclusions if, for example, a company's primary D&O insurer is a market leader in D&O insurance or is an unknown, cut-rate insurer. The cut-rate insurer may have an incentive to lower premiums irrespective of governance risk in order to capture greater market share. Although this will be a losing strategy in the long run, upstart firms may try it in the short run to establish a set of clients, hoping to make up for the increased near-term risk with greater premiums in the future. More directly, some insurers may develop a reputation for developing better risk pools than others with the result, as with investment banks in securities offerings, that companies covet the opportunity to do business with a "prestige" player. The fact that D&O insurance programs typically involve a tower of coverage composed of a variety of insurers would complicate this analysis, but the size of the individual layers and the location of highly selective insurers in the tower could convey significant information. In general, the larger the layer provided by a selective insurer, and the lower it appears in the tower, the more that it could signal governance quality.

Given the potential value of this information to market participants, the SEC should change the relevant regulations to force corporations to provide it. This would be a technically simple matter. The commission could amend Regulation S-K item 702 to mandate, instead of a weak statement of the general effect of insurance arrangements, explicit disclosure of the registrant's D&O premium, its limits and retentions under each type of coverage, and the identity of the registrant's D&O insurance carriers. Then, in order to make this disclosure annual, the commission could add a cross-reference in Form 10-K to item 702, thereby requiring registrants to disclose detailed information on D&O insurance when they file their annual reports. In addition, Form 8-K should be amended to require registrants to update this information with each renewal or change in coverage.

Although such modifications would be technically simple, the commission may encounter political resistance to this change, from both registrants and the insurance industry. Registrants may resist the disclosure of D&O insurance data because, as described above, it threatens to reveal new information about the extent of their agency costs. This, of course, is precisely why the SEC should require these disclosures. Meanwhile, brokers and insurers may object because of their fear that the greater transparency of D&O pricing created by these disclosures would lead to a more competitive market for D&O insurance and less need for intermediaries. Although benefits would redound to corporate purchasers of insurance (and their shareholders), a more competitive market for D&O coverage is precisely what the insurance industry would like to avoid. Insurance industry objections to mandatory disclosure may thus be rooted in the fear that such disclosures will drive rates down and make it even more difficult for insurers to profit from their professional liability lines. Additionally, insurance brokers might worry that a transparent market might become a disintermediated market, threatening their livelihood. We doubt that disclosure would in fact eliminate the demand for brokers, because of the need to assemble towers of coverage, the nonstandard nature of D&O insurance policies, and the comparatively rapid evolution of D&O contract terms. But, in any event, these would be strange objections for the SEC to credit since they are rooted in inefficiencies and market power. From the perspective of securities law reformers, these are problems to be solved, not entitlements to be protected, and mandating disclosure of D&O policy information may be a step in the direction of solving them.

Some academics, however, have voiced skepticism about the usefulness of disclosing D&O policy information in a more or less efficient capital market. Starting from the observation that buy-side analysts for large investment funds are likely to have as much (or more) access to top corporate officials and as much (or greater) sophistication in processing financial variables as D&O underwriters, they argue that because these analysts profit from taking all relevant information into account, they must also take into account the kinds of information considered by D&O underwriters. As a result, this objection goes, much of the information that is encoded in the D&O premium is already taken into account by sophisticated market participants and already incorporated into market price. Thus, these objectors conclude, the disclosure of a firm's D&O

premium will have little if any effect on the firm's share price and an equally negligible deterrent effect.

While we are willing to grant, to some degree, the underlying basis of this objection—it probably is true that top fund managers have at least as much access to corporate managers as D&O underwriters—the objection as a whole strikes us as remarkably similar to the parable of the economics professor who refuses to believe he has found a twenty-dollar bill on the sidewalk since if it really were there, someone else would have taken it already. In other words, although some analysts may well have similar access to information as D&O underwriters, we do not believe that it follows that all of that information is therefore fully reflected in a firm's share price. Most basically, buy-side analysts and D&O underwriters are looking at different things. Analysts are focused on all of the things that might influence the value of a security, especially anything that would impact upon a firm's earnings, whereas D&O underwriters are focused very precisely on the possibility that a prospective policyholder will face significant shareholder litigation. While it is certainly possible that shareholder litigation could affect earnings, as long as the defendant has adequate D&O coverage, any hit to earnings is unlikely. We therefore suspect that analysts do not much focus on shareholder litigation risk when valuing firms.

Now, on the one hand, it is obviously entirely justifiable for an analyst not to be concerned with anything that does not have an immediate impact on firm value. But, on the other hand, the connection between shareholder litigation and governance quality elaborated in chapter 5 suggests that more may be amiss at a high-risk firm than simply facing a greater possibility of being made a defendant in a shareholder suit. This high risk means that such firms are more likely to suffer business reversals more generally, which harm shareholders as much or more than D&O insurers. Dramatic business reversals should, of course, be of keen interest to analysts, but we suspect that such events are regarded as too hypothetical to make it into most valuation models, leading to a greater focus within the analyst community on the short-term most likely probabilities than on underlying indicators of downside risk. This special focus of D&O underwriters thus brings more careful attention to some factors than analysts might otherwise give them. Additionally, as we emphasized above, D&O underwriters have a direct financial incentive to get their assessments of risk right, while analysts, even buy-side analysts, have somewhat more attenuated incentives. Finally, we note that Professor Boyer does seem to have built a successful trading model based on D&O premiums paid by Canadian firms, which suggests that this information was not already fully reflected in market price. This is enough, in our view, to make our disclosure solution worth a try. There is after all, relatively little cost associated with the additional disclosure and at least the possibility of a significant benefit.

Other academics have also cautioned us that if such disclosures ever were made mandatory and the disclosure of high premiums did indeed convey the negative signal that we have hypothesized, corporations would quickly develop ways of hiding the real cost of their D&O programs. For example, policyholders could engage in tying arrangements with D&O insurers where the policyholder purchases, for example, property and casualty insurance from the same insurer and, in order to keep D&O premiums down (and thus avoid the negative signaling effects), agrees, in exchange, to pay a somewhat higher premium for its property and casualty coverage (where there is no signaling effect). We agree that such tying arrangements, were they to occur, would indeed create problems for the disclosure regime we are advocating, but we have two initial responses to this possibility. First, the tower structure of D&O insurance, with a primary insurer and multiple excess-of-loss insurers, would operate as an obstacle to such arrangements. In order to reduce its D&O premiums, a policyholder would have to secure the cooperation of every insurer in the tower, many of whom may have no other relationship with the policyholder and therefore no obvious reason to accept suboptimal premiums for D&O coverage. This structural complication may inhibit tying arrangements from arising in the first place. Second, even if such arrangements did arise, the law is not powerless to combat them. An entire strain of antitrust doctrine exists to address the problem, and additional disclosure of overlapping insurance relationships could be mandated to at least render such arrangements visible. But here, in any event, we are responding to a hypothetical problem with our proposed solution that, in fact, might never arise. Tying arrangements would be a problem for the disclosure regime and, if they did indeed arise, would need to be addressed, but this does not strike us as a reason to abandon the potential benefits of the disclosure regime.

The basic benefit of disclosing D&O policy information is improvement of capital market efficiency through the signaling effects provided by D&O policy details. A possible side benefit of mandatory disclosure of this information is the improvement of product market efficiency for this line of insurance. The additional disclosure would come at almost no additional cost, and the modification to the existing regime of securities regulation would be technically simple to accomplish. Because the benefits thus appear to overwhelm the costs, the SEC should change the law to mandate disclosure of D&O policy details in the annual filings of registrants, thus setting in motion a process that can be expected to reinvigorate the deterrence function of shareholder litigation.

The Moral Hazard Problem

In chapter 6, we discussed the control exerted by the insurer over the policyholder during the life of the insurance relationship. We hypothesized that a high degree of monitoring by the insurer, as indeed exists in other insurance contexts, might offer another means of reinvigorating the deterrence function of shareholder litigation since an insurer, whose reserves are placed at risk by the policyholder's actions, has every incentive to monitor the policyholder and constrain risky conduct. Perhaps surprisingly, we found that almost no such monitoring or control in fact exists in the typical D&O insurance arrangement. Once the risk has been underwritten, insurers do virtually nothing to monitor the corporate policyholder, other than repricing the risk for the next year (which, as we explained in chapters 5 and 6, raises all the pricing problems just discussed). Nor have they much control over defense and settlement of claims. Worse, as we described in chapter 4, the vast majority of D&O coverage programs include entity-level coverage, which, except for the deductible, serves to insulate corporations from the liability consequences of their managers' actions. In insurance industry argot, corporate defendants no longer have much "skin in the game," a situation that presents what, in the jargon of economics, is referred to as "moral hazard."

As we discussed in chapter 4, moral hazard refers to the general tendency of insurance to increase total loss by reducing a policyholder's incentive to take care to avoid loss. In the D&O context, the dynamics of moral hazard suggest that, since D&O insurance insulates corporations and their directors and officers from the financial impact of liability and since D&O insurers do little else to constrain corporate managers and prevent the kinds of activities that lead to liability, insurance seems likely to increase the amount of shareholder losses due to securities law violations. The problem of moral hazard, in other words, is that not only does D&O insurance reduce deterrence, it also increases loss.

Mitigating Moral Hazard: Reducing Corporate Coverage

One way to solve the moral hazard problem would be to abolish D&O insurance altogether. But most corporate theorists accept that D&O insurance does serve a valuable function within the corporation—namely, it prevents corporate decision making from becoming excessively risk averse. Without some stable means of avoiding their own liability risk, corporate managers might become excessively conservative in their business decisions, steering clear of high-risk/high-reward transactions for fear of being held liable if the transaction does not turn out as they might have hoped. The long-term systematic effects of such risk-averse decision making—namely, lower returns—would not prove beneficial to shareholders. The individual protection aspect of D&O insurance provides an elegant solution to this problem since it guarantees that managers will not be individually liable for their business decisions, freeing them to enter into high-risk/high-reward transactions.

A second possibility then to solve the moral hazard problem would be to eliminate the corporate coverage aspect of D&O insurance. As described in chapter 3, corporate coverage reimburses the corporation for losses in connection with shareholder litigation (including indemnification of directors and officers) but does not affect the coverage of individual directors and officers, who would retain coverage under side A of most D&O policies. Indeed, if corporate coverage were eliminated, all D&O policies would revert to pure side A coverage and pay only on behalf of officers and directors when the corporation is otherwise unable to indemnify them. This is a return to the original purpose of D&O coverage since, in the words of one of our respondents, "[T]he original intent of D&O insurance was to protect directors and officers, not the corporation."[25] By retaining side A coverage, the basic rationale for insurance coverage—individual risk aversion—would be respected. However, since this rationale does not apply to corporate coverage—indeed, as we described in chapter 4, no rationale seems to apply very well to existing corporate coverage, except perhaps managerial agency costs and the preference for income smoothing, hardly the sort of rationales that policy makers are likely to treat as sufficient justifications for its continued existence—corporate coverage could be eliminated without raising the specter of risk aversion.

Even if it does not significantly increase individual risk aversion, the elimination of corporate coverage might at first seem to threaten to raise another problem familiar to D&O practitioners—the allocation of liability costs between insurer and policyholder. As we briefly noted in chapter 3, allocation disputes first arose between D&O insurers and corporate policyholders prior to the invention of side C coverage, when D&O policies covered only the directors and officers individually, under side A, and the corporation's obligations to indemnify its directors and officers, under side B. Without side C coverage, many settlements gave rise to disputes between the D&O insurer and the corporate policyholder. Insurers could argue that some portion of the settlement represented the corporation's direct liability to the plaintiffs and was therefore uncovered under sides A and B of the policy, while the corporate policyholder would argue that most or all of the settlement amount arose as a result of its obligations to individual directors and officers, therefore entitling the corporation to reimbursement from the insurer under side B of the policy. The two sides would then argue, either across a negotiating table or in court, over how much of the settlement to allocate to the corporation's direct (and therefore uncovered) liabilities.[26]

The elimination of all entity-level coverage might seem to pose a similar allocation problem, giving rise to a dispute between insurers and policyholders over what portion of a settlement ought to be allocated to the (covered) liabilities of individual directors and officers versus the (uncovered) liabilities of the corporate entity. Upon closer examination, we can see that this is not the case, because eliminating entity-level coverage would abolish not only side C coverage but also corporate indemnification coverage under side B. Thus the only covered losses would be those arising under side A, which as noted in chapter 3, are circumscribed by contract to include only those cases in which the corporation cannot itself indemnify its officers and directors—principally including only derivative suit settlements and situations in which the corporation itself is insolvent and therefore unable to make indemnification payments. The typical settlement, therefore, would not be covered by insurance at all and therefore would not give rise to an allocation dispute. Moreover, limiting D&O policies to side A coverage also quiets the disputes that have occasionally arisen over the treatment of D&O proceeds in bankruptcy since courts typically hold that proceeds arising under side A only policies do not become property of the bankruptcy estate.[27]

Nevertheless, we are not now advocating the elimination of entity-level coverage. Instead, we advocate a more traditional, less heavy-handed and, potentially, more market-oriented solution to the D&O insurance moral hazard problem: coinsurance. Coinsurance is partial insurance, so that the policyholder would keep some skin in the game all the way up the D&O insurance coverage tower. Setting the optimal level of coinsurance would be a complicated corporate finance exercise that we will not attempt here, but our research strongly suggests that, whatever the optimum level is (which may vary by firm and industry and over time), it is well above the zero level that currently obtains in the market.

We draw support for our coinsurance proposal from the fact that the D&O insurance industry leader, AIG, offered a similar proposal in its "2002 D&O Insurance White Paper," released just when the underwriting cycle turned and it appeared that the insurance industry was going to have the market power to insist on greater moral hazard control. Explaining that the "original focus" of D&O insurance was "protecting the personal assets of directors and officers," the white paper argued that "insuring the corporate entity for its own exposure" threatened the D&O insurance industry's ability "to remain a viable source of protection for the 'Prime Movers' of Corporate America."[28] The white paper advocated reinstating "allocation for securities claims against both the corporation and its directors and officers," so that there will be "significant risk sharing between insurers and the corporations served by insured directors and officers."[29]

As the white paper explained, prior to the adoption of the side C coverage in the mid-1990s, traditional D&O insurance had included a substantial, albeit implicit, form of corporate protection coinsurance. Because side B coverage indemnifies the corporation only for its obligation to indemnify the officers and directors but not for the corporation's own exposure, the traditional D&O insurance policy form left the corporation with very significant skin in the game in shareholder class actions. Although this corporate exposure was not conceptualized as coinsurance, it nevertheless functioned that way. The white paper reports that the allocation process typically had assigned to the corporation something in the range of 30–50 percent of the cost of defending and settling securities class actions.[30] That amounts to a very significant coinsurance percentage. Moreover, our sense is that, ex ante, corporate decision makers probably expected that the corporate share of any class action settlement would be larger than that, because the D&O insurance policy did not on its face provide any coverage for the corporation's direct liability. As a result, traditional D&O insurance offered only partial coverage for the corporate entity and, thus, ensured that the settlement of any securities class action would produce a loss for the corporation, thereby reducing the moral hazard of D&O insurance.

As might be expected, some of the allocation disputes under traditional D&O insurance policies ripened into litigation between corporations and their D&O insurers. In the famous 1995 *Nordstrom* decision, the U.S. Court of Appeals for the Ninth Circuit held that, in the absence of an express allocation percentage stated in the policy, 100 percent of the costs of a settlement and related defense costs paid by the corporation should be allocated to an insurer in the facts of that case.[31] In response to *Nordstrom* and similar decisions, some insurance underwriters contemplated rewriting their companies' D&O insurance policy forms to clarify the policyholder corporation's responsibility to share in the costs of securities liability and defense in all securities class actions. But other underwriters recognized a market opportunity. They redrafted their companies' D&O insurance forms to provide what came to be known as "side C" or "entity" coverage.[32] The entire D&O insurance industry quickly followed the lead of the underwriters offering side C coverage.

As the white paper reflects, in 2002 AIG attempted to roll the clock back, on the grounds that complete corporate protection created bad incentives. This is precisely our point. The white paper focused primarily on ex post moral hazard, the reduced incentive of the corporation to hold out for a favorable settlement or to control defense costs. The white paper claimed that "[w]ith settlement costs borne 100 percent by the insurer, corporations that faced protracted and costly litigation began immediately settling suits, perhaps even for unreasonable amounts, and even if they had a good chance of prevailing."[33] As we have explained, the ex ante moral hazard of complete entity-level coverage is likely to be even more important.

The white paper created a splash among the D&O insurance cognoscenti, but it had no discernable impact in the market. AIG and other D&O insurance underwriters learned, once again, that corporate officers and directors want corporate protection without coinsurance, and they are willing to use the corporation's money to pay for it. Directors and officers who might have been concerned about losing their D&O insurance coverage to competing creditors in the bankruptcy context, had a more attractive alternative to corporate coinsurance. They could arrange for the corporation to purchase additional side A protection, on top of the existing D&O insurance program. The D&O insurance market responded to the managers' preference by continuing to offer D&O insurance policies without corporate protection coinsurance, albeit at the substantially higher prices that the post-2001 hard market made possible, with additional premiums for the extra side A coverage demanded by some officers and directors. In other words, rather than redesigning D&O insurance policies to reduce moral hazard, the underwriters priced for it.

We are not foolish enough to think that a book by two law professors will succeed in persuading the D&O insurance market to change when AIG could not. But our disclosure proposal offers us the glimmer of a chance. It is one thing for corporate managers to secretly purchase 100 percent corporate protection D&O insurance. But it is another thing for them to do so in the open, when all of the details of D&O insurance purchases need to be disclosed. In that case, buying 100 percent corporate protection insurance, with no coinsurance, would send an important and, in our view, clearly negative corporate governance signal. All other things being equal, low coinsurance signals higher corporate governance risk.

In addition, as AIG argued in the white paper, corporations with D&O insurance programs containing higher self-insured retentions and coinsurance running all the way up the D&O insurance tower will be less likely to join forces with the plaintiffs' lawyers and press for an inappropriate settlement than corporations that are fully insured. As a result of bearing a greater share of the liability risk, defendant corporations can be expected to take a greater role in contesting proffered settlements, fighting meritless claims, and preventing plaintiffs and defense lawyers from colluding for mutually beneficial settlements. More systematically, once corporate defendants as a group have more to lose from shareholder litigation, corporations can be expected to institute better internal monitoring to detect and prevent the sort of conduct that may lead to shareholder litigation. Shareholder litigation, in other words, would once again deter.

Making Merits Matter in Settlement

Thus far in this final chapter we have offered disclosure as a market-oriented solution to the pricing and moral hazard problems identified in our research. As just suggested, disclosure also holds out substantial promise for the merits problem. To recapitulate, the merits problem is that, although insurers do retain a strong voice in the settlement process and do have an incentive to use that voice to promote deterrence—for example, insurers could refuse to settle meritless cases and litigate them through to dismissal or adjudication, thereby deterring plaintiffs from bringing claims for settlement value—there are a number of limitations on insurers' ability to use their voice in this way. First, as we described in chapter 7, insurers are likely unwilling to risk a finding that they have engaged in bad faith in refusing to settle, thereby obligating them to fund all damages in the resulting adjudication, regardless of limits. Second, any attempt by insurers to settle claims in accordance with their underlying value will be limited by the ability of insurers to insist upon or even know the underlying value or merits of claims. Indeed, as our investigation into what matters in settlement in chapter 8 revealed, there are four key features—investor loss, insurance structure, sex appeal, and data from other settlements—that are not always in line with what are traditionally thought of as the underlying merits of a claim.

Making the merits matter more in settlement would improve the deterrence impact of shareholder litigation. But how to do this? What changes would make the settlement process better reflect the underlying merits of a claim and create greater differentiation between strong and weak cases? In the next subsection, we analyze a possibility that remains, in our view, deeply problematic—a rule requiring more adjudication in shareholder litigation. After that, we return, once again, to disclosure.

More Adjudication

Perhaps the most significant problem facing the settlement process is that settlements are largely unguided by meaningful precedent. By meaningful precedent, we do not mean statistics concerning averages and trends in settlements generally, which our participants told us do in fact guide settlement. Rather, by meaningful precedent, we mean cases that reach adjudication on the merits. Such cases are conspicuously absent in the context of shareholder litigation for two basic reasons: cases settle and insurers pay.

First, cases settle. There is very little adjudication beyond the initial motion to dismiss because, most often, once the motion to dismiss is decided, the case is ripe for settlement. Securities class actions very rarely reach trial, and, when they do, they remain just as likely to settle before the end of trial as to proceed to verdict.[34] Dispositive summary judgment rulings are nearly as rare. As a result, neither the basic facts of the claim nor the technical details of the damages model are tested by a neutral arbiter. Instead, in most cases, the motion to dismiss is the only dispositive decision that a court will make. But the denial of a motion to dismiss indicates only that the plaintiffs have fit their allegations into a recognized legal theory. It does not render judgment on the truth of the allegations, nor does it provide any guide to the amount of damages that the defendants would be required to pay if those allegations were proven.

Second, insurers pay. With few exceptions, settlements are funded largely, most often entirely, by D&O insurance. This means that, in most cases, insurance companies are the real parties in interest. Although in such situations it is common to see the insurer as stepping into the shoes of the defendant, it may be more accurate to see the insurer as stepping into the shoes of the finder of fact, because, at some point in the litigation, all defendants come to favor any settlement that is within the limits of insurance. The insurer, after all, is the one ultimately approving the settlement in most cases, and plaintiffs' and defense lawyers are aware of this fact. As a result, each side casts its arguments with a view toward the insurer. Plaintiffs' lawyers report that they are careful not to plead facts giving rise to a coverage defense—for example, facts indicating intentional fraud—and they shape their settlement offers to create pressure on the insurance tower. They also described settlement meetings in which the defense counsel essentially scripted the plaintiffs' arguments in order to induce the insurers to settle. Likewise, insurers described how defendants change their characterization of a claim—from defensible to indefensible—in order to induce the insurer to settle. And the defense lawyers confirmed that they adjust their estimates of the value of the claim to keep insurers moving toward settlement. Settlement outcomes, in other words, are determined not by the opinions of judges or juries but by the consent of D&O insurers.

As a result of this dynamic, insurers understand that they cannot be guided solely by the representations of plaintiffs or defendants, both of whom have their own reasons strongly to favor settlement, and that they must find some objective means of quantifying the value of the claim. The absence of adjudication, however, deprives them of meaningful precedent by which to evaluate the weight of various facts and the viability of competing damages models. As a result, they reach for the only objective information that is available—namely, settlement statistics. Yet, by looking to other settlements, insurers are bargaining, not in the shadow of the law, but rather in the shadow of prior bargains, at a further remove from decisions by judges or juries on the merits. Moreover, because all settlements suffer the same lack of guidance, settling by reference to other settlements creates the problem of infinite regress, in which "it's settlements all the way down."

If the problem thus is too few adjudicated outcomes to guide settlement, an obvious solution would seem to be the creation of more adjudication. With more adjudication—particularly trials—the weight of basic facts in establishing liability would become a matter of precedent, and the likelihood of success on the merits of a variety of basic fact patterns would be known. Of equal importance, the details of competing damages models would be tested by neutral arbiters, leading to a body of precedent in which certain approaches to damages would be rejected. With greater guidance on the weight of basic facts and the credibility of various approaches to measuring damages, it would be possible to create more reliable models, both of the probability of success and of the likely cost of damages. The world of securities litigation, in other words, could begin to resemble the model of civil litigation propounded by legal academics.

And so, if those involved in the settlement process would benefit from more adjudicated outcomes, why do they not simply litigate more claims to adjudication? Why, in other words, have those who would benefit from more adjudication not simply refused to settle more cases? The answer, it would seem, is that the creation of greater certainty through more adjudication faces a collective action problem.[35] That is, in spite of the desirability of negotiating in an environment of greater certainty, for any pair of litigants, the costs of taking their own case to trial will exceed the benefits of additional adjudication. That this is so is obvious—otherwise there would be no lack of adjudication since litigants would choose to take more cases to trial. Why this is so has to do with the fact that the benefit of additional adjudication is enjoyed collectively by all firms, but this collective cannot be made to compensate those firms that produce adjudicated outcomes by taking their cases to trial. In other words, the social benefit (negotiating in an environment of more adjudication) requires great individual sacrifice (foregoing settlement in favor of adjudication). Because no one will willingly make this sacrifice—all, in other words, rationally prefer to free-ride—the social benefit of more adjudication does not arise.

One possible solution to collective action problems such as this one would be to seek to force the parties to the socially optimal outcome through a mandatory rule. So, for example, we could force more adjudication by making a rule that barred settlements of shareholder claims.[36] But this solution clearly creates more problems than it solves. Indeed, a rule barring settlement would have the paradoxical effect of destroying the beneficial effects of more adjudication since the benefit of more adjudication is enjoyed by parties in settlement. The baby, in other words, goes out with the bath water. What we would need, then, is a rule that creates some more adjudication, not one that requires every case to go to summary judgment or trial.

What rule could create more adjudication without requiring every case to go to summary judgment and, if necessary, trial? Consider, if only as a hypothetical possibility, a lottery system. The lottery system could be designed to select, at random, some percentage of all shareholder class actions surviving the motion to dismiss, say 5–10 percent. Selected class actions would then be barred from settling and could only be resolved through adjudication—that is, summary judgment or trial—or by the voluntary dismissal of a case with no payment from the defendants.

The intended benefit of such a system—more adjudication—is a public good that would be shared by all litigants. At first blush, however, the cost—being barred from settlement—might seem to be unjustly suffered by a few—namely, those unlucky enough to be chosen in the lottery. However, we think the perceived injustice suffered by the lottery's loser is illusory. Indeed, the lottery actually corrects the collective action problem noted above by changing the effective ex ante bargain among all prospective litigants. Now, when filing a claim, all litigants should do so understanding that there is a 5 or 10 percent chance (whatever their probability of selection in the lottery) that their claim will be chosen for adjudication rather than settlement. They should therefore factor the cost of adjudication, discounted by the probability of not being selected in the lottery, into the value of their claim when they file. In this way, viewed from an ex ante perspective, the lottery system distributes the cost of extra adjudication across all claims, even though it is ultimately borne by only a few.[37] It creates a benefit for all prospective litigants, more adjudication, that is paid for by all prospective litigants in facing a greater ex ante cost of claims.

Nevertheless, we can imagine a wide variety of objections to such a lottery. Some of these, we expect, would be framed as moral objections to the use of a lottery system to allocate legal rights and entitlements. Although we tend to disagree with their moral basis, especially in the context of shareholder litigation, we acknowledge that such objections are likely to be persuasive to lawmakers (or their constituencies) and that, as a practical matter, such objections may indeed carry the day.[38] Regardless of its real-world plausibility, however, we think the lottery system is worth exploring as an intellectual exercise in imagining how a system to promote efficient settlements through more adjudication might work. And working through the possibilities along these lines, perhaps the most damning objection to the lottery model is that it may not generate answers to the most pressing open questions. Once their claim is selected in the lottery, parties might choose dismissal over litigation. Indeed, we suspect that a substantial fraction of the claims selected in the lottery would be dropped immediately by plaintiffs' law firms, reasoning that pursuit of the claim all the way to final adjudication (as opposed to settlement) would turn the claim into a negative net present-value investment and that, as a result, their firms' resources would be best deployed on other claims not selected for adjudication.[39] It is well-known, after all, that settlements are much less costly than trials, and a rational plaintiffs' lawyer, when suddenly faced with the additional costs of trial without a concomitant rise in the expected value of a claim, can be expected simply to drop at least some cases. Dropped claims, of course, are not the objective of the lottery system but are likely impossible to avoid. Even were we to try to fashion a rule to correct this problem, such as for example, barring dropped claims, rational lawyers would likely respond by ceasing to invest in the claim, stopping work, and ceding defeat. Because there is no means of monitoring the amount of effort plaintiffs' lawyers invest in their claims, any such rule designed to force adjudication seems destined to fail.

Moreover, cases selected randomly for adjudication may not be those that present the issues that present the most pressing need for adjudication. At least some of the cases most likely to be abandoned may well be those that are also most likely to produce useful precedent in adjudication—for example, making use of controversial damages models. More basically, because settlement is, quite sensibly, a favored outcome of civil litigation, it is highly unlikely that policy makers would seriously consider a rule that forced the parties to litigate through to adjudication, even in a small sample of cases.[40] Thus, although we suspect that more adjudication would cure some of what ails the settlement process, we are not hopeful that a rule will soon be enacted that successfully produces that result. And so, as in the context of pricing, we fall back on the remedy of disclosure.[41]

The Disclosure Solution in the Settlement Context

We have already advocated disclosure as the missing piece of the deterrence puzzle in the context of pricing and in the absence of insurer monitoring. So too in settlement we believe there to be significant benefits from additional disclosure. Currently, although settlement amounts are matters of public record and indeed are carefully tracked by industry sources, there is no systematic information about how settlements are funded.[42] Perhaps most importantly, we cannot be sure, based on publicly available information, what percentage of any given settlement is funded by insurance versus funded by the corporation itself. Sometimes defendants issue press releases that indicate whether the settlement was covered by insurance, but, in the case of a dispute over coverage at the time of claim, the results of the insurance coverage litigation in our experience typically do not become public. Moreover, even if we are able to determine whether the corporate defendant contributed to the settlement, we cannot determine whether that was because the settlement exceeded the insurance policy limits, the corporation had a large coinsurance or self-insurance arrangement, or one or more of the insurance companies in the D&O insurance tower had a strong coverage defense. We also do not know what additional amounts, beyond the total settlement, were spent in defense of the claim. In the settlement context, useful information could be gleaned by disclosure of (1) the amount and structure of a corporation's insurance coverage and (2) information on how settlement and defense costs are funded.

Information on how settlements and defense costs are funded—that is, what percentage of the total settlement is paid for by insurance versus by the corporation itself—would prove most useful when interacted with information on the amount and structure of coverage. First, these two pieces of information together could yield valuable insight into the cashing in of coverage defenses—the bargain in which the insurer agrees to drop potential coverage defenses in exchange for a larger contribution to settlement and/or defense costs from the corporate defendant. This is particularly valuable because the practice of cashing in coverage defenses, which our participants reported takes place with some frequency in the give-and-take of settlement, may shed light on the question of merit in any given claim. Claims for which insurers are able to cash in substantial amounts seem likely, on the whole, to be more meritorious claims, for two reasons. First, some of the insurer's strongest coverage defenses—for example, the actual fraud exclusion or the fraud-in-the-application defense—are implicitly based on the underlying merits of the claim. Second, the more realistic the possibility of a plaintiffs' verdict in excess of the policy limits, the more willing defendants will be to contribute to a within-limits settlement. As a result, a claim in which an insurer is able to cash in its coverage defenses, should be, on average, a claim of greater underlying merit.

This dynamic would be exposed if insurance limits and structure could be compared with how settlements and defense costs are funded. A strong inference of merit could thus be drawn concerning those cases in which a corporation has contributed substantial amounts to a settlement and/or defense costs when the total settlement is nevertheless within the limits of the corporation's D&O coverage. The more a corporation contributes in such cases—after taking into account, of course, deductibles and coinsurance and other possible reasons for an insurance shortfall—the more likely there is to be actual fraud underlying the plaintiffs' claim. To see this, compare, for example, two hypothetical settlements for the same amount, $10 million. Each defendant has, let us say, $20 million in total limits of D&O coverage, so both settlements are well within the limits of each defendant's D&O program. However, if one settlement is funded entirely by the D&O insurer, while the other settlement is funded $7 million by insurance and $3 million by the defendant, we would have a strong indication that the insurer and the defendant had come to some sort of bargain in the second case. The difference is likely a result of the insurer having cashed in its coverage defenses, and, given the size of the defendant's contribution, the coverage defenses must have been substantial. Because coverage defenses are stronger when the plaintiffs' underlying claim is of greater merit, we can conclude that the plaintiffs' claim seems likely to have some basis in merit. By exposing such bargains in the settlement process, we would thus uncover another proxy for merit.

A number of other useful pieces of information would also be uncovered by these disclosures. We would know, for example, where cases tended to settle relative to coverage limits. This too would provide useful information about the underlying merits of claims since, for example, above-limits settlements on the whole are more likely to be meritorious than within-limits settlements since they involve contributions by the corporate defendant who, as we described in chapter 9, can be expected to contest settlements more effectively than the insurer. Thus claims that exceed insurance limits and require contribution from the corporate defendant are likely to be more meritorious than those that do not. Additionally, the effect of limits on settlement amounts could be better understood if limits were disclosed along with every settlement. Large-scale quantitative studies could then be run to evaluate whether limits do in fact serve, as our participants suggested, to frame settlement amounts, pulling some settlement values down and others up.

In sum, we have advocated disclosure of D&O policy limits and structure as well as details concerning how D&O settlements are funded in hopes of providing information of use to capital market participants. Such information ought, in our view, to enable outsiders to interpret the meaning of shareholder settlements and draw better conclusions about whether defendants have, in fact, engaged in bad acts. Once capital market participants put this information to use in their trading decisions, firms whose managers have engaged in bad acts may find share prices facing deep discounts and, with these, discover yet another incentive to monitor and prevent such acts.

Throughout this chapter and throughout this book as a whole we have examined shareholder litigation through the lens of liability insurance in order to explore whether shareholder litigation accomplishes its regulatory objective of constraining managers from defrauding shareholders. D&O insurance threatens this regulatory objective because it mutes the deterrence function of shareholder litigation. Nevertheless, we have identified several means by which the D&O insurer might preserve the deterrence function of shareholder litigation and thus protect its regulatory effect—namely, underwriting, monitoring, and settlement. The body of the book reports on extensive interviews with professionals in the field in which we analyzed how each of these methods works in practice and found each to come up short as a means of reinvigorating deterrence.

Having seen the shortcomings, this chapter offers solutions. We have suggested three narrowly tailored solutions to the problems introduced by D&O insurance. First, because the pricing of D&O insurance may not sufficiently distinguish between good governance risks and bad governance risks to induce poorly governed companies to change their ways, we advocated the mandatory disclosure of D&O policy details in order to signal information to the capital markets that, once incorporated into pricing, may provide additional incentives for corporations to improve their governance. Second, because significant risk of moral hazard is created by the lack of insurer monitoring and the availability of entity-level coverage, we argued in favor of coinsurance for the corporate protection aspect of D&O insurance coverage in order to give the corporate policyholder more skin in the game and therefore greater incentive to monitor managerial conduct and insist that settlements in securities class actions reflect the merits of the claim. Third and finally, we recommended additional disclosure of information at settlement—including insurance structure and limits and the extent to which settlement and defense costs are funded by insurance—in order to provide capital market participants a window into the merits of claims, which they could then incorporate into their valuation of the defendant's shares, thereby inducing prospective defendants to improve their governance quality in order to avoid meritorious claims.

Taken together, we believe that these proposals may serve to reinvigorate the deterrence function of shareholder litigation. This is a critically important goal since, as we have argued, deterrence is the raison d'être of shareholder litigation. If shareholder litigation does not deter, then it is, as its critics contend, nothing more than waste. But if we can improve the capacity of shareholder litigation to deter while still protecting individual directors and officers from liability, then we will have accomplished our goal without the dislocating effects of more radical solutions, such as the abolition of shareholder litigation or prohibitions on the purchase of some or all of the parts of D&O liability insurance. We strongly urge the commissioners of the SEC, corporate law scholars, and D&O insurance market participants to consider these proposals to enhance the regulatory effect of shareholder litigation.

Notes

Chapter One

1. Cornerstone 2009; Plancich and Starykh 2008.

2. Plancich and Starykh 2008, 6.

3. Ibid., 7.

4. In the field of tort law, there is a competing, nonconsequentialist justification referred to as "corrective justice" or "civil redress." In the context of shareholder litigation, however, where all liabilities are ultimately funded by shareholders, such a justification seems self-defeating since shareholders would thus be forced to correct injustices perpetrated against themselves. As a result, such justifications have not found acceptance in corporate law and finance, and, accordingly, we will not address them here.

5. The consensus position is concisely summarized in Rose 2008. Prominent academic lawyers writing from the consensus perspective include Alexander 1996; Coffee 2006; Easterbrook and Fischel 1985; Langevoort 1996; Pritchard 1999.

6. Easterbrook and Fischel 1985.

7. Plancich and Starykh 2008, 14.

8. On the problem of setting sanctions to promote optimal deterrence, see Shavell 2004, 483.

9. The problem of the plaintiffs' attorneys' incentives or "litigation agency costs" has been studied by Bebchuk 1988; Coffee 1985; Katz 1990; Romano 1991; and Rosenberg and Shavell 1985. Litigation agency costs can be understood as interfering primarily with the effectiveness of specific deterrence—that is, whether a claim, once brought, will succeed in reforming the governance practices of the corporate defendant. It is on this point that, for example, Romano expresses doubt when she charges that "shareholder litigation is a weak, if not ineffective, instrument of corporate governance." Romano 1991, 84. Nevertheless, shareholder litigation is often viewed as a more or less effective instrument of general deterrence—that is, the tendency of prospective defendants to adjust their practices on the basis of

their perceived liability risk. From the perspective of general deterrence, the question is whether shareholder litigation overdeters or underdeters. For an excellent discussion of overdeterrence and underdeterrence in the context of 10b-5 litigation that thoroughly reviews the current literature, see Rose 2008.

10. *Blue Chip Stamps v. Manor Drug Stores*, 421 U.S. 723, 737 (1975); *Tellabs, Inc. v. Makor Issues & Rights, Ltd.* 551 U.S. 308, 319 (2007).

11. Towers Perrin 2008. This annual survey of D&O purchasing trends in the United States, although based upon a nonrandom sample, provides the only currently available aggregate data on coverage. It is therefore an invaluable source in understanding broader patterns in D&O coverage.

12. Defendant payment cases constitute 8 percent of the cases for which a final payment is reported. We computed this number by using the description of the class actions on the Stanford Class Action Clearinghouse Web site to identify payments by defendants, and, where it was not possible to determine whether the payment reported was within the deductible or self-insured retention, we used a cutoff of $5 million, which is a conservative (i.e., low) proxy for the deductible amount in a corporate D&O insurance policy. These calculations were based on the cases reported on the Clearinghouse Web site in the fall of 2008, with an update for the latest settlement information conducted in June 2009. These estimates are biased in a variety of ways. First, our sense is that the Stanford Class Action Clearinghouse has more complete information on the larger cases and more visible cases. For reasons explained in chapters 8 and 9, we believe that more visible cases are more likely to be more meritorious cases, and more meritorious cases are more likely to include defendant payments. This problem would tend to bias our estimate of the percentage of defendant payment cases upward. Second, the Clearinghouse collected information on defendant payments by examining the defendants' financial reports during the litigation. These reports may not include defendant payments that are nonmaterial to the financial health of the corporation but that would nevertheless be worth counting for this purpose. This problem would tend to bias our estimate of the percentage of defendant payments downward. Third, the Clearinghouse does not report whether the payment that was made fell within the self-insured retention or was within a layer (or layers) of insurance with coinsurance or an insolvent insurer. This problem would tend to bias our estimate of the percentage of defendant payments upward. Without the public disclosure that we call for in this book, more accurate estimates would be very difficult to make.

13. Klausner & Hegland 2010a.

14. Shavell 1979, 1982. This literature is collected and analyzed in Baker 1996.

15. For a very recent exception see Cheyne and Nini 2010.

16. But see Black, Cheffins, and Klausner 2006. Cf. Romano 1989 and 1991.

17. Ericson, Doyle, and Barry 2003 (offering an institutionally informed account of the governance role of a variety of forms of first-party insurance). See

also Ericson and Doyle 2004, 5 (describing the underappreciated prominence of uncertainty, as opposed to risk, in the insurance business) and Heimer 1985 (investigating how insurers use contract provisions to manage moral hazard.

18. Our research protocols are approved by the institutional review boards of the University of Connecticut and Fordham University. Interviewees participated under a promise of anonymity. The interviews were recorded and transcribed, with participant-identifying information removed from the transcripts.

19. Monitoring Counsel no. 3, 73.

20. Monitoring Counsel no. 8, 25.

21. These figures were computed from Savett 2007 using the "SCAS 50—Total Settlements" table. Of note, we treat Milberg, Weiss and Lerach Coughlin as two separate firms even in 2003, and we treat firms that have retained the same key name partner(s) over the years as the same firm. See also Choi and Thompson 2006, table 3 (reporting that four firms handled cases that represent 50 percent of the total settlement value since 1995).

22. AIG and Chubb account for approximately 60 sixty of the market by premium volume. Towers Perrin 2007, exhibit 54. By policy count, they rank third and first (ACE ranks second). Towers Perrin 2007, exhibit 54.

23. Only about twenty-six brokerage firms are active in the public D&O insurance market at any time. Towers Perrin 2007, exhibit 54.

24. See Baker forthcoming (summarizing research using insurance statistics and insurance field research to understand liability law in action).

25. See Abraham 2008 (exploring the relationship in a variety of fields throughout the "liability century"); Baker 2005b (exploring the relationship in the medical malpractice field).

26. See, e.g., Shavell 1982.

27. See, e.g., Zeiler et al. 2007 (examining the impact of insurance policy limits on the settlement of medical malpractice litigation; Baker 2002 (exploring the role of insurance in settling personal injury litigation); Pryor 1997 (explaining how liability insurance exclusions lead parties to "underlitigate," forgoing intentional injury claims in favor of negligence claims); Baker 1998 (describing how the lack of insurance for punitive damages in some jurisdictions leads parties to "transform punishment into compensation").

Chapter Two

1. Eisenberg and Miller 2004, 54 (finding that 77 percent of shareholder actions from 1993 to 2002 were securities class actions); see also Towers Perrin 2007, exhibit 83 (reporting that more than 80 percent of claims made against public companies dealt with securities issues).

2. "The big exposure to D&O, as I am sure you know, that is number one,

head and shoulders above everything else, is securities class actions. . . ." Defense Counsel no. 1 at 11.

3. Defense Counsel no. 3, 5.

4. Cornerstone 2006 (estimating susceptibility to a federal securities class action for "companies listed on the NYSE, Nasdaq, and Amex" at the start of 2005 at 2.4 percent). See also Miller, Foster, and Buckberg 2006, 3 (estimating susceptibility of all publicly traded corporations in 2005 at 1.9 percent).

5. Towers Perrin 2008, 52.

6. In 2008, the three industrial sectors receiving the most securities class action filings were Finance, Consumer Non-Cyclical, and Industry. Cornerstone 2009, 18. In 2004, by contrast, the top three industries in terms of filings were Consumer Non-Cyclical, Technology, and Communications. Cornerstone 2006, 14.

7. Cornerstone 2009, 19.

8. Plancich and Starykh 2008, 10.

9. Ibid.

10. Ibid.

11. Ibid., 12–13.

12. For statistics on Delaware corporations, see State of Delaware, Division of Corporations, http://www.corp.delaware.gov/default.shtml.

13. Delaware General Corporation Law § 141(a).

14. See *Cede & Co. v. Technicolor*, 634 A.2d 345, 367 (Del. 1993) ("Duty of care and duty of loyalty are the traditional hallmarks of a fiduciary who endeavors to act in the service of a corporation and its stockholders. Each of these duties is of equal and independent significance.") (citation omitted); Brudney 1997 at 599, n. 9 ("Legal conventions divide fiduciary obligations into obligations of loyalty and obligations of care.").

15. *Graham v. Allis-Chalmers Mfg. Co.*, 188 A.2d 125, 130 (Del. 1963). See also *Briggs v. Spaulding*, 141 U.S. 132, 152 (1891) (requiring that directors act as would "ordinarily prudent and diligent men . . . under similar circumstances"); *Norlin Corp. v. Rooney, Pace, Inc.*, 744 F.2d 255, 264 (2d Cir. 1984) (stating that "[i]n simplest terms, the duty of care requires that directors exercise the care that an ordinary prudent person would exercise under similar circumstances").

16. *Guth v. Loft, Inc.*, 5 A.2d 503, 510 (Del. 1939) (emphasis added).

17. Clark 1986, § 3.4.

18. See *Aronson v. Lewis*, 473 A.2d 805, 812 (Del. 1984) ("While the Delaware cases use a variety of terms to describe the applicable standard of care, our analysis satisfies us that under the business judgment rule director liability is predicated upon concepts of gross negligence."); *Smith v. Van Gorkom*, 488 A.2d 858, 873 (Del. 1985) ("We think the concept of gross negligence is also the proper standard for determining whether a business judgment reached by a board of directors was an informed one.").

19. *Brehm v. Eisner*, 746 A.2d 244 (Del. 2000).

20. *Gagliardi v. TriFoods Int'l, Inc.*, 683 A.2d 1049, 1052 (Del. Ch. 1996) (Allen, C.).

21. See Del. Code Ann. tit. 8, § 144(a) (2008) (providing that conflict of interests transactions are not void or voidable if they are either approved, ratified, or fair); *Weinberger v. UOP, Inc.*, 457 A.2d 701, 710 (Del. 1983) (establishing standard of entire fairness: "[w]hen directors of a Delaware corporation are on both sides of a transaction, they are required to demonstrate their utmost good faith and the most scrupulous inherent fairness of the bargain.").

22. *In re Walt Disney Co. Derivative Litigation*, 825 A.2d 275 (Del. Ch. 2003).

23. As one of us has written elsewhere, it is not surprising that courts' analyses of fiduciary duty sometimes involve overlapping questions of loyalty and care since the common concern is simply shareholder welfare and care and loyalty are merely ways of opening an inquiry into that question. For an extended discussion of how such analyses tend to operate in corporate law, see Griffith 2005.

24. *Stone v. Ritter*, 911 A.2d 362, 370 (Del. 2006); *In re Walt Disney Co. Derivative Litigation*, 906 A.2d 27, 67 (Del. 2006).

25. See *Grimes v. Donald*, 673 A.2d 1207, 1213 (Del. 1996) (discussing distinction between derivative and direct claims).

26. *Cohen v. Beneficial Indus. Loan Corp.*, 337 U.S. 541, 548 (1949).

27. See Thompson and Thomas 2004, 137.

28. The remaining 6 percent, while also direct, did not challenge the board's conduct in an acquisition but rather sought relief for an individual shareholder's grievances. Erickson 2010 finds derivative actions more common in federal court.

29. See 15 U.S.C.A. §§ 77a-77aa (West 1997 & Supp. 2006).

30. See 15 U.S.C.A. §§ 78a-78mm (West 1997 & Supp. 2006).

31. See generally Loss and Seligman 2004 at 4114–54 (discussing typical patterns in securities litigation).

32. 15 U.S.C. § 77l (2000); 17 C.F.R. § 240.10b-5 (2006).

33. Choi and Pritchard 2005 at 252.

34. See *Blue Chip*, 421 U.S. at 749–55 (holding that plaintiffs must be those who purchased or sold securities, not those who merely held them, between the time of the misstatement and the corrective disclosure).

35. *Ernst & Ernst v. Hochfelder*, 425 U.S. 185, 196 (1976). The first federal court to recognize the private right of action under Rule 10b-5, five years after the rule was enacted, was the Eastern District of Pennsylvania in *Kardon v. National Gypsum Co.*, 69 F. Supp. 512 (E.D. Pa. 1946).

36. *Blue Chip*, 421 U.S. at 737.

37. All statistics in this paragraph are taken from Cornerstone 2009 at 25.

38. E.g., Coffee 2006, 1545 ("[A]lthough it would be an overstatement to say that the securities class action exclusively polices fraud in financial reporting, this seems to be its primary role.").

39. See *Ernst & Ernst*, 425 U.S. at 193, n. 12 (holding that private plaintiffs must

show scienter and rejecting a negligence standard but reserving the question of whether recklessness satisfies the standard).

40. E.g., *AUSA Life Insurance Co. v. Ernst & Young*, 206 F.3d 202, 234 (2d Cir. 2000) ("In securities law, however, the critical issue is what a reasonable investor would have considered significant, and foreseeability is generally from the plaintiffs' point of view . . . "); *SEC v. Falstaff Brewing Co.*, 629 F.2d 62, 76 (D.C. Cir. 1980) (holding that information is material if a reasonable shareholder would consider it important in deciding how to vote).

41. Exchange Act §21D(b)(2).

42. Exchange Act §21D(b)(3)(B).

43. *Tellabs*, 551 U.S. at 314.

44. Plaintiffs' Counsel no. 3, 8–10. Defense lawyers agreed. Defense Lawyer no. 0307, 13–15. See also Claims Head no. 051607, 26–27: "Sometimes you get into discovery, and the discovery shows that what these plaintiffs thought was a real meritorious case really is nothing."

45. *TSC Industries v. Northway*, 426 U.S. 438, 449 (1976) (deeming information to be material if there is "a substantial likelihood that the disclosure . . . would have been viewed by the reasonable investor as having significantly altered the 'total mix' of information made available").

46. See *Basic v. Levinson*, 485 U.S. 224, 246 (1988) ("Recent empirical studies have tended to confirm Congress' premise that the market price of shares traded on well-developed markets reflects all publicly available information, and, hence, any material misrepresentations."). Of course, if defendants can show that the relevant market does not efficiently impound information into share price, the fraud-on-the-market presumption of reliance will not apply. See, e.g., *In re Polymedica Corp. Sec. Litig.*, 453 F. Supp. 2d 260, 272 (D. Mass. 2006) (an increase in the body of scholarship doubting the existence of perfect information efficiency sets a significant hurdle for plaintiffs).

47. *Dura Pharmaceuticals, Inc. v. Broudo*, 544 U.S. 336, 347 (2005) (holding that "allowing a plaintiff to forgo giving any indication of the economic loss and proximate cause would bring about harm of the very sort the [PLSRA] seeks to avoid.").

48. Ibid.

49. See Fox 2006 (identifying issues that remain open, including situations in which the plaintiff sells the security at a price higher than the purchase price, situations in which the price does not drop immediately after the corrective disclosure, and situations in which the plaintiffs sell shares prior to the corrective disclosure).

50. E.g., Eisenhofer, Jarvis, and Banko 2004, 1443–4 (describing a test for loss causation that determines whether disclosures revealing the effect of fraud actually affect share price).

51. Plaintiffs' Counsel no. 7, 1. See also Plaintiffs' Counsel no. 6, 2–3 (noting that his firm monitors market developments for institutional developments and

that "one way or another we will either hear from the client or we will be reporting to the client on what we are seeing").

52. See Plaintiffs' Counsel no. 1, 11 (describing how his firm obtains clients through referrals from the brokers that his firm represents in other capacities and through other lawyers.); Plaintiffs' Counsel no. 3, 4–6 (describing how his firm relies on referrals from lawyers whose specific business is developing clients to pass on to litigation firms).

53. See Plaintiffs' Counsel no. 6, 3 ("We have private investigators and use them."); Plaintiffs' Counsel no. 7, 1 ("We employ a team of people that includes three lawyers, a former Wall Street research analyst . . . three or four private investigators that are led by a former FBI agent . . . and we employ forensic accounting consultants. . . . ")

54. Private Securities Litigation Reform Act, § 101(a)(3)(B)(i).

55. See also Cox and Thomas 2006, 1595 (describing the "rebuttable presumption that the member of the class with the largest financial stake in the relief sought is the 'most adequate plaintiff.'")

56. See also Choi and Thompson 2006, 1530 (reporting that institutional investors "tended to develop repeat relationships with select top tier law firms").

57. Plaintiffs' Counsel no. 8, 13.

58. Politan 2005.

59. See Cox and Thomas 2006, Table 3. See also Cox and Thomas 2002 at 877 (reporting similar data as above).

60. See Cox and Thomas 2006, Table 4 and text (reasoning that because institutional investors choose to appear in bigger, high-quality cases, settlement amounts will be higher when an institutional investor is present).

61. E.g., *In re Polymedica*, 453 F. Supp. 2d at 271. See also Defense Counsel no. 4, 13–14 (explaining how he challenges class certification and citing Polymedica as an example of what can work.).

62. E.g., *Oscar Private Equity Investments v. Allegiance Telecom, Inc.* 487 F.3d 261 (5th Cir. 2007) (vacating class certification order in securities action because plaintiffs had not shown loss causation).

63. Compare *Eisen v. Carlisle & Jacquelin*, 417 U.S. 156, 177 (1974) ("Nothing in either the language or the history of Rule 23 . . . gives a court any authority to conduct a preliminary inquiry into the merits of a suit in order to determine whether it may be maintained as a class action.") with *General Telephone Co. v. Falcon*, 457 U.S. 147, 160–1 (1982) (holding that courts must "conduct a rigorous analysis" of Rule 23 requirements) and *Coopers & Lybrand v. Livesay*, 437 U.S. 463, 469 n.12 (1978) (stating that the analysis of Rule 23 requirements will be "intimately involved with the merits of the claims").

64. E.g., *Szabo v. Bridgeport Machines*, Inc., 249 F.2d 672 (7th Cir. 2001) (permitting courts to "look[] beneath the surface of the complaint to conduct the inquiries identified in [Rule 23] and exercise the discretion it confers," which

inquiries, if they "overlap the merits," force the judge to "make a preliminary inquiry into the merits"). A similar rule is followed in the First, Third, Fourth, Fifth, Sixth, and Eleventh Circuits. E.g., *Waste Management Holdings v. Mowbray*, 208 F.3d 288, 298 (1st Cir. 2000) (fashioning a similar rule for the first circuit). The Second Circuit has recently moved closer to this rule as well. *Heerwagen v. Clear Channel Communications*, 435 F.3d 219, 232 (2d Cir. 2006) ("Some overlap with the ultimate review on the merits is an acceptable collateral consequence of the 'rigorous analysis' that courts must perform when determining whether Rule 23's requirements have been met.").

65. Defense Counsel no. 5, 16.

66. Choi, Nelson, and Pritchard 2007 (reporting 25%); Klausner and Hegland 2010b (reporting 34%).

67. Claims Manager no. 2, 23. See also Plaintiffs' Counsel no. 7, 19 ("The first [natural breaking point for settlement discussions] is generally after the motion to dismiss is decided. . . . "); Plaintiffs' Counsel no. 8 at 27–30 ("[T]he biggest issue is surviving the motion to dismiss. I mean, if you survive a motion to dismiss you're going to be okay until you get to summary judgment, and usually those cases settle.").

68. See Fed. R. Civ. P. 8(a). See also *Bell Atlantic v. Twombly*, 550 U.S. 544 (2007) (holding that to survive a motion to dismiss, a complaint must allege sufficient facts to support a "plausible"—and not merely "conceivable"—claim for relief); *Cool v. International Shoe Co.*, 142 F.2d 318, 320 (8th Cir. 1944) (holding that "on a motion to dismiss for insufficiency of statement, the complaint should be construed in the light most favorable to the plaintiff and with all doubts resolved in his favor").

69. Monitoring Counsel no. 8, 10.

70. Black, Cheffins, and Klausner 2006, 1064 (the statistic includes only securities law cases seeking damages from public companies, their officers and directors, or both).

71. Savett 2008, 2. National Economic Research Associates (NERA) reports somewhat larger numbers, with 21 shareholder class actions going to trial since PSLRA, and 15 of those resulting in a judgment. Plancich 2008, 8.

72. Financial Times 2007, 14. See also Levine 2007, 9.

73. Plaintiffs' Counsel no. 8, 16.

74. Plaintiffs' Counsel no. 5, 12.

75. Plaintiffs' Counsel no. 7, 19.

76. Defense Counsel no. 0307, 13–15.

77. See generally Jensen and Meckling 1976 (identifying the divergence in interests between shareholder principals and manager agents as a central feature of the corporate form).

78. See Thompson and Sale 2003 (arguing that the basic corporate governance concern—"that management has misused its position with respect to corporate assets"—has become a common underlying basis in securities fraud claims).

79. See generally Schwarcz 2005 (discussing the potential for conflict between present and future shareholders' interests).

80. E.g., *Pommer v Medtest Corp.*, 961 F2d 620, 623 (7th Cir 1992) ("The securities laws approach matters from an ex ante perspective: just as a statement true when made does not become fraudulent because things unexpectedly go wrong, so a statement materially false when made does not become acceptable because it happens to come true.").

81. Knepper and Bailey 2003, § 17.02, 17-3 to -10.

Chapter Three

1. Bishop 1966, 103.

2. Del. Code Ann. tit. 8, § 145(a) (2008). The section that follows allows corporations to indemnify against expenses in derivative actions but continues the prohibition against indemnification for judgments, fines, and settlements. Del. Code Ann. tit. 8, § 145(b) (2008).

3. Bishop 1966, 107. See also Bishop 1967, 1087 (arguing that "an insurance policy paid for by the corporation whose effect was to free corporate managers from the fear of civil liability for breach of their duty to show good faith in their dealings with the corporation" would violate public policy).

4. "Indemnification of directors" 1963, 1428 (arguing that "insurance in its present form should be voided as contrary to public policy wherever it would free the director from a burden from which he could not be freed by indemnification"); "Public policy and directors' liability insurance" 1967, 719 (arguing that insurance against breach of the duty of loyalty is contrary to public policy even if paid for by the director himself).

5. Del. Code Ann. tit. 8, 145(g) (2008). See also Bishop 1998, § 8.01 ("All states authorize the corporation to purchase and maintain insurance on behalf of directors and officers against liabilities incurred in such capacities, whether or not the corporation would have the power to indemnify against such liabilities.").

6. See Black et al. 2006. Recent settlements involving WorldCom and Enron compel the "almost" qualification. See Morgenson 2005 (describing agreement according to which former WorldCom directors will personally contribute to settlement amount). On the difficulties of reaching personal assets rather than insurance assets in the ordinary tort context, see Baker 2001, 277.

7. See Black, Cheffins, and Klausner 2006.

8. *AIG Specimen Policy* 2000, § 2(z). See also *Chubb Specimen Policy* 2002, § 5 ("Wrongful act means . . . any other matter claimed against an Insured Person solely by reason of his or her serving in an Insured Capacity."); *Hartford Specimen Policy* 1996, § IV(O)(2) (defining coverage to include "any matter claimed against the Directors and Officers solely by reason of their serving in such capacity . . .").

9. The original Lloyd's form contained two policies, "ALS(D4)" and "ALS(D5)," one for individual coverage and one for corporate coverage. See Hinsey et al. 1972, 150 ("In a documentary sense there are indeed two policies, designated . . . as ALS(D4) and ALS(D5) and bearing different policy numbers as issued.").

10. The types of coverage are named in reference to the insurance documents listing the respective rights and obligations. Side A coverage relates to "Insuring Agreement A," side B coverage to "Insuring Agreement B," and so on.

11. *Hartford Specimen Policy* 1996 § I.A. The effect of the carve out for losses paid pursuant to Insuring Agreement B is to prevent the managers from being paid twice for the same loss.

12. Ibid., § IV.J. (including compensatory damages, settlement amounts, and legal fees). Other important definitions in the policy include "claims," defined as the receipt of a written demand for relief, the filing of a civil proceeding, or the commencement of a formal administrative or regulatory proceeding. Ibid., § IV.A. Wrongful acts are defined by the policy to include errors, misstatements, omissions, and breaches of duty committed by directors and officers in their official capacities as well as any other claim against the directors and officers solely by reason of their position. Ibid., § IV.O.

13. Ibid., § I.B.

14. Ibid., § VI.F (providing that if a corporation is legally permitted to indemnify its officers and directors, its organizational documents will be deemed to require it to do so). When a corporation that is legally able to indemnify its directors and officers refuses to do so, the insurer would remain obligated under the policy's side A coverage, but the obligation would be subject to the (higher) side B retention as well as a coinsurance percentage). Ibid.

15. Betterley 2006, 4. On differences in deductibles between the different sides of coverage, see also Towers Perrin 2005, 46 (reporting that 98 percent of U.S. respondents who purchased D&O insurance had no deductible associated with their side A coverage).

16. E.g., *Nordstrom, Inc. v. Chubb & Son, Inc.*, 54 F.3d 1424 (9th Cir. 1995) (recognizing the insurer's right to allocation unless insurer has improperly refused to defend the insured or has made no claim to separate the portion of the settlement for which it was liable); *Safeway Stores, Inc. v. Nat'l Union Fire Ins. Co. of Pittsburgh*, 64 F.3d 1282 (9th Cir. 1995) (applying "larger settlement rule," entitling corporation to reimbursement of all settlement costs where corporation's liability is purely derivative of liability of insured officers and directors); *First Fidelity Bancorp v. Nat'l Union*, 1994 U.S. Dist. LEXIS 3977 at *12 (E.D. Pa. 1994) ("[B]oth the directors and officers as well as the corporate entity faced liability in the underlying litigation. The mere fact that liability arises exclusively from the conduct of the insured . . . does not provide a basis for the insurer to be responsible for the liability of those who are uninsured."); *PepsiCo, Inc. v. Cont'l Cas. Co.*, 640 F. Supp. 656, 662 (S.D.N.Y. 1986) (addressing the issue of allocation between covered and

noncovered parties and holding that the insurer bore the burden of proving that the ultimate allocation was reasonable in light of the "relative exposures" of the parties). See also Monteleone et al. 1991.

17. *Hartford Specimen Policy* 1996, § I.C. A securities claim is defined in the policy to include claims by securities holders alleging a violation of the Securities Act of 1933 or the Securities Exchange Act of 1934 or rules and regulations promulgated pursuant to either act as well as similar state laws and includes claims "arising from the purchase or sale of, or offer to purchase or sell, any Security issued by the company" regardless of whether the transaction is with the company or over the open market. Ibid., § IV.M. If the company purchases side C coverage, the definitions of "claim," "loss," and "wrongful act" expand to include the company and not just the directors and officers.

18. *See Hartford Specimen Policy* 1996, Declarations Page, Items D (providing for separate retention amount for A, B, and C coverage) and E (providing for coinsurance percentages for securities claims).

19. See *AIG Specimen Policy* 2000, §§ 4(b)–(c); *Chubb Specimen Policy* 2002, §§ 7–8; *Hartford Specimen Policy* 1996, § IV (i)–(j).

20. See *AIG Specimen Policy* 2000, §§ 4 (e)–(f); *Chubb Specimen Policy* 2002, §§ 6(a)–(b); *Hartford Specimen Policy* 1996, § V(C).

21. See *AIG Specimen Policy* 2000, §§ 4(i)–(j); *Chubb Specimen Policy* 2002, § 6(c); *Hartford Specimen Policy* 1996, § V(D).

22. See Monitoring Counsel no. 1, 13 ("[It] tends to be only in extremely unusual cases [that] the corporation has to kick in its own money because of the application of some exclusion.").

23. Executive Risk Indemnity, Inc., *Executive Liability Policy*, III.A.3. Similar language appears in the AIG, Chubb, and Hartford policies. See also note 19. A related exclusion prevents insurers from making payments to indemnify an insured person against unjust-enrichment claims, thus preventing the insured from retaining any such gains. See *AIG Specimen Policy* 2000, § 4(a); *Chubb Specimen Policy* 2002, §§ 7–8; *Hartford Specimen Policy* 1996, § V(I).

24. See Counsel no. 3, 2–3.

25. See Mathias et al. 2003, § 8.04 (collecting cases holding that "[i]f the exclusion requires a final adjudication, that adjudication must take place in the underlying action for which coverage is sought").

26. See Underwriter no. 4, e-mail to Tom Baker, (stating that "it is pretty standard now for the carriers to agree to final adjudication").

27. Plaintiffs' Counsel no. 6, 23.

28. Plaintiffs' Counsel no. 5, 24.

29. E.g., *Fidelity & Deposit Co. of Maryland v Zandstra*, 756 F. Supp. 429, 431–32 (N.D. Cal. 1990) (construing an insured versus insured exclusion clause).

30. See Jerry 2002, 1030 (explaining the purpose of insurance clauses excluding family members from liability coverage).

31. See *AIG Specimen Policy* 2000, § 4(k); *Chubb Specimen Policy* 2002, § 6(d); *Hartford Specimen Policy* 1996, § V(E).

32. See *AIG Specimen Policy* 2000, § 4(m); *Chubb Specimen Policy* 2002, § 6(f); *Hartford Specimen Policy* 1996, § V(G).

33. See *AIG Specimen Policy* 2000, § 4(h); *Chubb Specimen Policy* 2002, § 6(e); *Hartford Specimen Policy* 1996, § V(A).

34. See *AIG Specimen Policy* 2000, § 4(g); *Chubb Specimen Policy* 2002, § 6(g)–(h); *Hartford Specimen Policy* 1996, § V(F).

35. All of these peripheral claims are covered by other forms of liability insurance. Why the insurance market addresses all these risks in separate insurance products is an interesting question that is beyond the scope of this project.

36. Towers Perrin 2008, 15.

37. Towers Perrin reports mid-cap limits in three categories. The first, companies with market capitalizations between $1 billion and $2 billion, purchased mean limits of $37.18 million and median limits of $32 million. The second, companies with market capitalizations between $2 billion and $5 billion, purchased mean limits of $48.78 million and median limits of $40 million. Finally, the third, companies with market capitalizations between $5 billion and $10 billion, purchased mean limits of $96.25 million and median limits of $75 million. The number reported in the text is an average of these three categories, weighted for the number of observations in the sample.

38. See Risk Manager no. 3, 6 (discussing maximum amount of insurance available). See also Underwriter no. 13, 37–38 (mentioning $300 million in discussion of premiums over a given time span equaling limits).

39. E.g., Actuary no. 3, 10 (explaining management of coverage limits).

40. According to Towers Perrin, in 2005 AIG and Chubb together controlled 53 percent of the total U.S. market measured by premium volume and 36 percent of the total U.S. market by policy count. Towers Perrin 2006, 86, figures 36 and 37.

41. But see Bault 2009 (arguing that AIG is underreserved relative to its competitors).

42. For a detailed examination of the underwriting cycle that reviews the literature, see Baker 2005, 396–422 (describing the underwriting cycle as applied to medical malpractice). See generally, Doherty and Garven 1995 (exploring relationship between interest rate and capacity constraint explanations for the insurance cycle).

43. See Fitzpatrick 2003–2004, 256 (analyzing the role that underwriters, claims analysts, and actuaries play in creating the underwriting cycle). One of our participants reported, "It is funny how you find some[times] that questions either go away or they are not as substantial as they were maybe in a harder insurance market where the premiums were higher and there is less capacity." See also Underwriter no. 14, 17 (describing how the market "hardens and softens" in a cyclical manner).

44. See Underwriter no. 4, 4 (asserting that pricing is now "pretty much inadequate across the sectors"). See also Towers Perrin 2006, 3 ("[T]he market for D&O coverage has continued to soften.").

45. See Broker no. 22 ("In a soft market, you are more likely to be able to find an insurance company that will take the chance and write the policy—you know, write coverage with prior acts, maybe even off the continuity and not require a warranty application. You know, in the soft market right now one of the things that we are finding is that companies are willing to offer nonrescindable side A coverage. That is really something that has just sort of happened within the last, you know, maybe two, three, four months").

Chapter Four

1. Borch 1990, 13–15, 163.

2. Siegel 2006, slides 3, 4 (assuming an average expense ratio of 23 percent for all D&O insurance).

3. See generally Elton and Gruber 2002.

4. See Heimer 1985, 199.

5. See Baker 1996, 276. See also Heimer 1985 (studying the use of insurance contract provisions to control moral hazard); Shavell 1979 (modeling the impact of moral hazard on insurance offerings).

6. Towers Perrin 2008, 29.

7. *Hartford Specimen Policy* 1996, § V.J. Similar language appears in the AIG, and Chubb policies. A related exclusion prevents insurers from making payments to indemnify an insured against unjust enrichment claims, thus preventing the insured from retaining any such gains. See *AIG Specimen Policy* 2000, § 4(a); *Chubb Specimen Policy* 2002, §§ 7–8; *Hartford Specimen Policy* 1996 § V.I.

8. Mayers and Smith addressed this puzzle in a series of articles. E.g., Mayers and Smith 1982, 1987, 1990; see also MacMinn and Garven 2000 (summarizing prior literature).

9. See Revenue Ruling 80-211 1980-2 C.B. 57 (concluding that even "[a]mounts paid as punitive damages incurred by the taxpayer in the ordinary conduct of its business operations are deductible as an ordinary and necessary business expense under section 162 of the Code").

10. See MacMinn and Garven 2000, 559–60.

11. See Core 1997, 68, n.10 (arguing that "any tax effects are at most second-order in magnitude").

12. See MacMinn and Garven 2000, 548–50.

13. Risk Manager no. 3, 6.

14. Mayers and Smith 1987, 51–2.

15. Froot, Scharfstein, and Stein 1993, 1631.

16. Froot and colleagues also observed that hedging can provide private benefits to managers, and thus managers may act as if the cost of external capital is more costly than it is. Ibid., 1634. We regard this as an example of an agency cost, an explanation that we address more fully later in this chapter.

17. Park 2009 at 330 (citing Karpoff, Lee, and Martin 2009 as estimating that the credibility decline is "7.5 times the legal penalties imposed on the company").

18. See Mayers and Smith 1982, 285.

19. Cf. Baker 2006 (evaluating a proposal for first-party insurance against misinformation losses and rejecting the compensation justification even for nondiversified investors); Griffith 2006 (critiquing proposals for an investor insurance scheme).

20. Goshen and Parchamovsky 2006, 714.

21. Fisch, 2009 at 347.

22. Ibid.

23. See *La. World Exposition v. Federal Ins. Co.*, 832 F.2d 1391, 1401 (5th Cir. 1987) (holding that the proceeds of side A coverage are not the property of the corporation, but not deciding the allocation issues raised by the existence of side B coverage); see also *In re First Cent. Fin. Corp.*, 238 B.R. 9, 17 (Bankr. E.D.N.Y. 1999) (reviewing case law and noting that side B and side C coverage raise allocation issues).

24. Bailey 2004a, 4 ("Since the vast majority of Claims covered under a D&O policy are indemnified by the Company, a Side-A only D&O Policy allows Insurers to afford much broader coverage terms than reasonably possible under a Side-B policy.").

25. Towers Perrin 2008, 19.

26. Risk Manager no. 3, 3.

27. Ibid., 4.

28. Ibid., 5.

29. Ibid., 7–8.

30. Ibid., 9.

31. See Risk Manager no. 1, 33–34.

32. Ibid., 34 (concluding that "the knock I have heard in panel discussions, things like that, is that the credit that you get for dropping [side B and C coverage] is not worth what you are actually getting if you are losing coverage"). Complicating this analysis is the fact that side A only policies may offer broader protection for the directors and officers.

33. Risk Manager no. 2, 33.

34. Risk Manager no. 4, 15.

35. See Fitzpatrick 2003–2004 (providing a behavioral explanation for cyclical mispricing).

36. See generally Jensen and Meckling 1976, 305 (identifying the divergence in interests between shareholder principals and manager agents as a central feature of the corporate form).

37. Chalmers et al. 2002, 609–10.

38. Ibid., 611.

39. Core 1997, 81.

40. Ibid.

41. Risk Manager no. 2, 34–35.

42. Claims Manager no. 1, 27.

Chapter Five

1. Underwriter no. 9, 9–11.

2. Actuary no. 3, 13 ("[W]hat we try to stress in our portfolio is diversification by industry, diversification by size, and . . . laying a good limits management strategy on top of all that."); Underwriter no. 1 at 8–9 (reporting a strategy of risk pool diversification by industry); Underwriter no. 9, 24 ("[Portfolio underwriting in D&O], which is stepping away from an individual risk and looking at a portfolio risk[,] is also merging into yet other corporate finance concepts.").

3. Underwriter no. 15, 31.

4. Underwriter no. 8, 35.

5. Underwriter no. 2, 8.

6. Underwriter no. 4, 3.

7. Underwriter no. 6, 24–5.

8. *Chubb Application* 2003 § 5.

9. Underwriter no. 9, 29–30.

10. Broker no. 2, 16–17.

11. Risk Manager no. 2, 11.

12. Risk Manager no. 4, 3.

13. Risk Manager no. 3, 13.

14. Underwriter no. 2, 3–6.

15. E.g., Underwriter no. 1, 8.

16. Broker no. 6, 15–16.

17. Broker no. 5, 26.

18. Underwriter no. 4, 3.

19. Underwriter no. 7, 6.

20. Underwriter no. 9, 8.

21. Broker no. 1, 14.

22. Broker no. 2, 17.

23. Seminar Tape no. 1, 26.

24. Broker no. 4, 5.

25. Underwriter no. 15, 12.

26. Underwriter no. 7, 29–30 (emphasis added).

27. Underwriter no. 7, 16.

28. Risk Manager no. 4, 5 (discussing additional information underwriters seek today as opposed to fifteen years ago).

29. Underwriter no. 5, 10.

30. Broker no. 6, 34–35 (describing this as a "scenario that has occurred quite a bit in corporate America").

31. Underwriter no. 4, 32. A manufacturer that engages in channel stuffing intentionally sends its retailers more products than they are able to sell in order to inflate (temporarily) its sales figures. Unless sales suddenly increase or, in the case of channel stuffing after a downturn, recover, the manufacturer will ultimately have to adjust its accounts receivable, resulting in a loss.

32. Underwriter no. 7, 14–5.

33. Underwriter no. 8, 21 ("We look at the equity of the company very closely. It is obviously a key driver on the rating model that we use. We look at who owns the stock and why.").

34. *Examples of Questions*, n.d.

35. To an underwriter, good governance involves centralized control and multiple levels of review. As a leading broker described a good D&O risk, "They review everything. Everything is done early. . . . The CFO knows about a sale that is going on in Europe in real time and has to approve it. . . . Everything is centralize[d] control." Broker no. 6, 33.

36. Risk Manager no. 4, 5–6.

37. Underwriter no. 9, 1010–16.

38. On the history of character-based underwriting and the contrast between character-based underwriting and the economic understanding of insurance, see generally Baker 2000.

39. Broker no. 2, 17. See also Actuary no. 1, 9 ("[W]hat you're really underwriting when you underwrite D&O is, you're underwriting the people, you're underwriting the senior management, the quality of the management team.").

40. Underwriter no. 2, 18–9.

41. Underwriter no. 7, 17 (emphasizing perquisites such as "country club memberships, airplane travel, [and corporate] homes" as indicia of arrogance or lack of accountability).

42. Underwriter no. 2, 23.

43. Underwriter no. 8, 27 (discussing the importance of meeting personally with company executives).

44. Underwriter no. 15, 12–3.

45. Actuary no. 2, 23–24 (emphasis added).

46. Underwriter no. 15, 13–4 (emphasis added).

47. Underwriter no. 7, 33. See also Underwriter no. 8, 24–5 (explaining that underwriting involves "getting a sense of . . . trust. [C]an you have confidence in what they filed in their Q's and K's[?]").

48. Underwriter no. 2, 6 (emphasis added).

49. Underwriter no. 5, 18.

50. Underwriter no. 9, 21–2.

51. Chubb Group of Insurance Companies, n.d., 1–3, exhibit 23.

52. Actuary no. 3, 7 ("[T]here is very wide latitude given to underwriters in terms of what is filed with the state regulators . . . .").

53. Underwriter no. 8, 33.

54. Broker no. 2, 18–9.

55. Underwriter no. 8, 20 ("We have a clear set of guidelines around pricing plus or minus on certain items."). Note that the "board score" refers to the score on the company report prepared by the Corporate Library.

56. Underwriter no. 9, 19.

57. Actuary no. 3, 8–9 ("[W]e have concluded that the best thing is to let a very small group of experienced underwriters manage [the pricing process] without giving them a lot of constraints. . . . We have less than five underwriters who have the authority to quote [large public company] accounts."); Actuary no. 2, 10 ("We have a centralized, one location shop here" with "250 years of D&O experience on this 11,000 square feet.").

58. Risk Manager no. 2, 20.

59. Actuary no. 1, 28 (discussing the process of underwriting); Actuary no. 3, 3–4 (describing aspects of underwriting as a "pure crap shoot").

60. Broker no. 2, 21.

61. Broker no. 2, 24.

62. Phone conversation, June 22, 2006.

63. See Baker 2005a (synthesizing economic literature on the insurance underwriting cycle); Fitzpatrick 2003–2004 (providing a participant observation account of a behavioral explanation for the underwriting cycle) (note that this author was at the time the chief underwriter for Chubb's specialty lines insurance business, one of the leading providers of D&O insurance); Dolan 2003 (providing a participant observation account of the underwriting cycle) (note that this author was a former Chubb underwriter and, at the time, the CEO of a specialty lines insurer active in the D&O business).

64. See Romano 1989, 1–2 (describing hard market conditions in the mid-1980s).

65. Underwriter no. 4, 4.

66. Towers Perrin 2008, 8.

67. Actuary no. 1, 27. See also Actuary no. 3, 7 (placing the date on the new focus on corporate governance at 2001).

68. Underwriter no. 5, 13.

69. Underwriter no. 5, 30.

Chapter Six

1. Shavell 1982, 121–2.

2. Cohen 1997–98, 343.

3. Andersen and Collett 1989.

4. Ericson and Doyle 2004, 94–211 (reporting research from a variety of contexts including building construction and disability management); O'Malley 1991 (reporting research on theft prevention in private homes).

5. Hubbart 1996–97, 272–4, 276–9 (reporting research on motion picture production); Van der Veer 2005–2006, 194–204 (reporting that EPLI insurance was a by-product of D&O insurance and describing the loss-prevention aspects of EPLI underwriting and the risk management services offered to insureds).

6. See Simon 1994, 29–31 (describing the role of liability insurers in governing fraternities). Whether the insureds comply is, of course, another matter.

7. Baker 2002, 42.

8. Ericson, Doyle, and Barry 2003.

9. Holderness 1990, 116.

10. O'Sullivan 1997.

11. Abraham 2008.

12. Underwriter no. 5, 30.

13. Underwriter no. 8, 50–51.

14. Bailey 2004b.

15. Underwriter no. 5, 29.

16. Underwriter no. 7, 11. The product manager is the individual with overall responsibility for the profitability of a particular line of business in a company with multiple business areas.

17. Underwriter no. 4, 15.

18. Ibid., 16.

19. Ibid.

20. Ibid.

21. Underwriter no. 4, e-mail.

22. Underwriter no. 4, 16.

23. Broker no. 1, 7–8. The D&O product manager of yet another leading D&O insurer explained his understanding of this situation as follows:

> [Y]ou're dealing with, generally, a lot of times the CEO, the general counsel, and these guys have egos to fill this room. You're a thirty- or forty-year-old underwriter in the insurance business, and although your policy is very important to them and has been the last couple of years, since they've all been kind of crucified, you're going to have a hard time saying, you know, "You need one more outside director."

Actuary no. 2, 27 (joint interview with chief actuary and D&O product manager).

24. See D&O Company Facts.

25. Underwriter no. 7, 11–2.

26. Cowen 1992.

27. See Coase 1974.

28. As noted in chapter 3, no single D&O insurer is willing to sell very high

limits to any single corporation—$50 million is the largest limit typically available from a single underwriter—with the result that D&O insurers hold a large portfolio of D&O risks. Corporate governance rating firms, by contrast, may have conflicts of interest because they provide consulting services to corporations. See Rose 2008 (noting this conflict of interest with reference to Institutional Shareholder Services).

29. See Romano 2005, 1528–9 (describing how corporate governance entrepreneurs have advocated governance innovations that make little or no difference in a corporation's susceptibility to risk). Because the insurer ultimately bears corporate governance risk, it is unlikely to be fooled by merely cosmetic governance features.

30. See Cunningham 2004 (elaborating the FSI concept first suggested by Ronen); Ronen 2002 (describing the FSI concept); see also Cunningham 2006, 1738 (arguing that FSI should be mandatory).

31. On the increased frequency of dismissal after the PSLRA, see generally Choi 2004, 1498 (collecting research and concluding that "the existing literature on filings and settlements in the post-PSLRA time period provide[s] evidence that frivolous suits existed prior to the PSLRA and that a shift occurred in the post-PSLRA period toward more meritorious claims."). However, Choi notes that just as more nonmeritorious suits are dismissed after the PSLRA, there may be more dismissal of meritorious suits as well, making it impossible to draw a strong conclusion, on the basis of dismissals alone, about the role of merits in securities claims. On the tendency of surviving claims to take longer to settle, see Martin et al. 1999, 123, 157 (acknowledging that "the timing of settlements may indeed be reflective of a case's merits" and that "only a portion of low-valued settlements are likely to be nuisance suit settlements").

32. See Johnson, Nelson, and Pritchard 2007, 630 (finding "a significantly greater correlation between litigation and both earnings restatements and insider trading after the PSLRA").

33. See Cunningham 2004; Ronen 2002.

34. See Grundfest 2002, 7 (describing FSI with approval but noting "that the current structure of D&O insurance and auditor liability has failed to give rise to incentives comparable to those [Ronen] predicts would arise under his FSI proposal," even though "D&O insurers could today easily make the retention of insurer-approved auditors a condition of coverage"); Kahn and Lawson 2004, 424–25 (noting that "Professor Ronen is on the right track" but arguing that insurers would not be willing to serve the role that Ronen envisions); McCoy 2003, 1010–12 (discussing the various advantages and disadvantages of FSI); Ribstein 2002, 55 (same); Shapiro 2005, 1085–86 (endorsing FSI).

35. Because the accounting firm would simply be providing a warranty of the audit, we do not believe that this warranty would violate the Sarbanes-Oxley prohibition on the provision of nonaudit services. 15 U.S.C. § 78(j)–(l)(g) (2000 &

Supp. 2004). The warranty would not contravene the three principles that the SEC has stated that it will use in defining nonaudit services: "an auditor cannot (1) audit his or her own work, (2) perform management functions, or (3) act as an advocate for the client." Strengthening the Commission's Requirements Regarding Auditor Independence, 67 Fed. Reg. 76,780, 76,783 (Dec. 13, 2002) (to be codified at 17 C.F.R. pts. 210, 240, 249, 274).

36. Underwriter no. 4, e-mail.

37. We are not suggesting that side A coverage be tightly linked to monitoring services. Individual loss aversion provides sufficient justification for side A coverage; obligating individual directors and officers to follow the insurance company's loss-prevention advice on pain of losing their insurance coverage could well lead to behavior that is too cautious from the shareholders' perspective.

38. Underwriter no. 15, from notes.

Chapter Seven

1. See Abraham 2008 (describing the history of defense coverage in liability policies).

2. Baker 2008.

3. See Baker 1998, 107–8 (explaining why "[a] rational prospective insured would prefer a liability insurance contract giving the company [control over the defense] . . . [o]therwise the insured would demand at the point of claim a level of defense that he would not be willing to pay for at the time of purchasing the policy").

4. Associate General Counsel no. 1.

5. See generally Abraham 2001 (describing the "era of the big claim exclusion" that began in the 1980s).

6. Cohen 1997–98, 325.

7. See Richmond 1997.

8. Claims Manager no. 2, 20.

9. Monitoring Counsel no. 1, 11.

10. Towers Perrin 2007, 57, table 72.

11. New York Seminar no. 1 (name withheld for confidentiality), 7 ("We are seeing some abuses but, even where you don't have abuses, we are seeing defense costs not just 25–35 percent of the settlement, . . . but sometimes 50 or 100 percent of the settlement").

12. Claims Manager no. 1, 10.

13. Conn. D&O Insurance Seminar no. 1 (name withheld for confidentiality), 8–9.

14. Ibid.

15. Claims Head no. 051607, 23–25:

[D]epending upon the size of the primary layer, some carriers take the attitude of, "Well, my money is gone. If I'm a primary carrier and I have a little retention below me, and I've only got $5 million worth of coverage, then I've got big expensive Law Firm X and I've got co-counsel from big expensive Law Firm Y. You know, my $5 million is gone as soon as I lose the motion to dismiss." . . . So you sometimes observe those carriers as kind of going to sleep, not doing anything, just kind of rubber-stamping. "Yeah, do whatever you want."

16. Defense Counsel no. 3, 34

17. Monitoring Counsel no. 6, 25

18. Claims Manager no. 1, 39–40.

19. Monitoring Counsel no. 6, 26. The same participant described defense counsel as interested only in keeping the settlement within insurance limits. Ibid., 48

20. Claims Head no. 9, 12.

21. Defense Counsel no. 2, 1.

22. Plaintiffs' Counsel no. 5, 21.

23. *Best's Aggregates* 2008, 412. It is worth noting that the "other liability" category includes some occurrence-based forms of coverage that are likely to lead to a higher ratio of investment income to net premium. Investment income is likely to be smaller in relation to net premiums for claims made for forms of coverage such as D&O insurance.

24. See Ross 1970 (on insurance adjusters' desire to close files).

25. *AIG Executive and Organization Policy* 2000, § 8.

26. Monitoring Counsel no. 4 and nos. 5, 6.

27. See Syverud 1990, 1116–7.

28. See Black, Cheffins, and Klausner 2006, 1100–101 (arguing that several countervailing pressures motivate insurers with low risk exposure to settle rather than take a chance at trial).

29. Plaintiffs' Counsel no. 6, 10–11.

30. Defense Counsel no. 3, 35

31. Defense Counsel no. 0307, 36

32. Claims Manager no. 2, 32–34

33. Plaintiffs' Counsel no. 4, 13–14.

34. Plaintiffs' Counsel no. 5, 24.

35. See *Vigilant Ins. Co. v. Bear Stearns Cos., Inc.*, 884 N.E.2d 1044 (N.Y. 2008).

36. See Black, Cheffins, and Klausner 2006, 1104–5 (enumerating the factors that motivate plaintiffs' attorneys to settle within policy limits even if they believe the value of the suit to be higher than the policy limit); Romano 1991, 57 ("The plaintiffs attorney's calculus . . . [points to settlement]. . . . With a settlement, attorneys' fees will be recovered, as defendants routinely agree not to oppose petitions for fees, and, in any event, the benefit the plaintiff has conferred on the firm will

be recognized in the settlement. If a claim is litigated, however, there is some probability that the plaintiff will lose.").

37. Defense Counsel no. 3, 34.

38. Plaintiffs' Counsel no. 7, 15.

39. Plancich and Starykh 2008, 14.

40. Ibid.

41. Plaintiffs' Counsel no. 7, 14.

42. Plaintiffs' Counsel no. 6, 10–11 (emphasis added).

43. Plaintiffs' Counsel no. 7, 22.

44. Monitoring Counsel no. 8, 29–30.

45. Defense Counsel no. 4, 19.

46. Claims Head no. 051607, 37–38.

47. Defense Counsel no. 2, 1.

48. Plaintiffs' Counsel no. 4, 13–14.

49. Defense Counsel no. 2, 1.

50. D&O Roundtable, 52 (defense counsel speaking).

51. Mediator no. 2, 15–16.

52. Claims Head no. 9, 28–29.

53. Mediator no. 2, 14.

54. Defense Counsel no. 2, 2.

55. Defense Counsel no. 5, 7.

56. Mediator no. 1, 32–33.

57. Plaintiffs' Counsel no. 7, 16

58. Plaintiffs' Counsel no. 6, 10–11.

59. See Feldman, n.d. (offering a similar example and noting that company A's structure of layers "would provide strong, natural firebreaks at $5 million and $10 million" and concluding "it's a safe bet that the identical claim against [Company A] would settle for less" than the structure of company B or C).

Chapter Eight

1. Alexander 1991.

2. Monitoring Counsel no. 7, 30–31.

3. Defense Counsel no. 7, 18–19, 26.

4. Plaintiffs' Counsel no. 5, 12.

5. Defense Counsel no. 5, 15.

6. Mediator no. 1, 56.

7. Defense Counsel no. 8, 4.

8. Monitoring Counsel no. 1, 5–6.

9. D&O Roundtable, 45.

10. Monitoring Counsel no. 7, 35:

11. For a standard economic model of settlement, see Priest and Klein 1984, 6–30.

12. Monitoring Counsel no. 7, 7–8.

13. Mediator no. 2, 8.

14. Claims Head no. 021207, 35–6.

15. Monitoring Counsel no. 2, 8

16. Claims Manager no. 1, 20.

17. Plaintiffs' Counsel no. 5, 7–8 (board member resignations); Plaintiffs' Counsel no. 6, 19–20 ("suspicious stock repurchase programs"); Defense Counsel no. 3, 19 ("if people have been convicted of crimes and stuff like that, then the plaintiffs are going to hang tougher for a bigger number to get a better case"); Claims Head no. 021207, 35–36 (distinguishing between weaker "old-fashioned misrepresentation of projection cases" and "accounting manipulations" that involve "outright cooking of the books"); Monitoring Counsel no. 8, 31–2, 41–4 (describing the importance of "hot docs," termination of CEO or CFO, whistleblower); Claims Head no. 031407, 59–64 (bad documents, whistleblower); Claims Head no. 7, 34–5 (conflicts among parties on the defense side, e.g. outsiders vs. insiders).

18. Monitoring Counsel no. 8, 44–5.

19. See Johnson, Nelson, and Pritchard 2007, 630. (finding "a significantly greater correlation between litigation and both earnings restatements and insider trading after the PSLRA").

20. Plaintiffs' Counsel no. 6, 19–20.

21. Plaintiffs' Counsel no. 8, 31.

22. Plaintiffs' Counsel no. 8, 29–30.

23. Defense Counsel no. 4, 50–51.

24. E.g., Schwarz and Vaughn 2002.

25. Claims Head no. 051607, 26–7.

26. Monitoring Counsel no. 6, 31.

27. Monitoring Counsel no. 6, 29–31.

28. Monitoring Counsel no. 8, 13. Accord. Monitoring Counsel no. 7, 18 ("Because the potential exposure is overwhelming"); Monitoring Counsel nos. 4 and 5, 3 ("look, there's a very simple reason that there is too great of a risk for the insured."); Defense Counsel no. 3 at 46 ("The numbers are too big"); Mediator no. 1, 3 ("The stakes are huge, and oftentimes it requires massive document and discovery investigation, and lots of unsettled questions as to actually how to finish the case").

29. Defense Counsel no. 5, 15.

30. Monitoring Counsel no. 6, 25.

31. Defense Counsel no. 0307, 29 ("the driving force . . . is investor loss"). See also Mediator no. 2 at 4–6 ("potential damages is the number-one thing"); Policyholder no. 2, 6; Plaintiffs' Counsel no. 8, 22 ("the most important factor is the amount of the damage"); Defense Counsel no. 4, 11 ("By the time you get to

mediation, damages is very much in the forefront of the discussion."); Monitoring Counsel no. 7, 8–9 ("I think the largest and most determining factor is potential damages").

32. Damages are limited to the losses actually caused by material misstatements or omissions or what can be legally proven. See HAZEN 2002, §§ 12.12, 12.15[1][J].

33. As described in greater detail in chapter 5, 10 × 80 means that his company sold a $10 million layer of insurance that does not come into play until $80 million has been paid by some combination of the insured and the underlying layers of insurance.

34. Claims Head no. 021207, 34–6.

35. Claims Head no. 021207, 95–7. The participant, however, conceded in the next breath that "a better fraud case would settle faster." Ibid.

36. Monitoring Counsel no. 7, 8–9.

37. Claims Head no. 031407, 59–64.

38. Defense Counsel no. 5, 16.

39. Defense Counsel no. 4, 11.

40. E.g., Monitoring Counsel no. 7, 11–12 (noting that *Dura* offered "a great windfall that the defense lawyer thought was coming their way [that] just hasn't materialized because the plaintiffs have said, no you can't have periodic disclosures which have a cumulative effect of bringing the price down, so you look at the drop at the occasion of each what they call partial disclosure, and that's what creates the damages").

41. Defense Counsel no. 4, 44.

42. Monitoring Counsel nos. 4 and 5, 3.

43. Defense Counsel 3, 38.

44. Claims Head no. 031407, 59–64.

45. Laura E. Simmons and Ellen M. Ryan (2008), *Securities class action settlements: 2007 review and analysis.* Cornerstone Research. http://securities.stanford .edu/Settlements/REVIEW_1995-2007/Settlements_Through_12_2007.pdf.

46. Cf., Galanter 1990 (questioning ability of trial lawyers to predict jury verdicts).

47. Hawking 1988, 1.

48. *Rapanos v. United States*, 547 U.S. 715, n. 14 (2006).

49. E.g., Bone and Evans 2002 (critiquing the class certification rules for "avoid[ing] inquiring into the merits of substantive issues" thus "inviting frivolous and weak class action suits"); Choi 2007 (noting that "the PSLRA requires courts to review a class action on the merits . . . and impose sanctions . . . on frivolous litigation").

50. Defense Counsel no. 2, 3.

51. Claims Head no. 051607, 61–3.

52. Defense Counsel no. 6, 10.

53. See, e.g., Baker 2005b, 68–87.

54. See Baker 2005b, 68–87 (collecting and analyzing the closed-claim file litera-ture published through March 2004); Studdert et al. 2006 (reporting the results of the most recent and most definitive medical malpractice closed-claim file review). See also Peters 2007 (the latest effort to collect the research).

55. It is worth noting that liability insurance may promote merits-based resolu-tion in cases in which the defendants would not otherwise be sued at all or in cases in which the defendants would not otherwise have access to good counsel.

56. We note that it is also reasonable to suppose that some claims that would ultimately prove meritorious are disposed of at the motion to dismiss because, without discovery, not enough facts could be found to support the strong-inference standard for scienter. The motion to dismiss, in other words, is probably both over- and underinclusive as a filter for merit.

Chapter Nine

1. Claims Head no. 8, at 9.

2. See generally Baker 1994.

3. Cases upholding an insurer's denial of coverage based on a market segmenta-tion exclusion include *High Voltage Engineering Corp. v. Fed. Ins. Co.*, 981 F. 2d 596 (1st Cir. 1992) (denying coverage for a D&O claim arising out of a pollution exclu-sion); *Employers Ins. of Wausau v. The Duplan Corp.*, 899 F.Supp. 1112 (S.D.N.Y. 1995) (same). For a contrary determination of whether an underlying claim arises out of an exclusion, see *Owens Corning v. Nat'l Union Fire Ins. Co. of Pittsburgh*, 1998 WL 774109 (6th Cir. 1998) (finding D&O claim not arising out of asbestos claim). The *Owens Corning* holding, however, was criticized in *Nat'l Union Fire Ins. Co. of Pittsburgh, PA v. U.S. Liquids, Inc.*, 271 F.Supp.2d 926 (S.D. Tex. 2003).

4. See Molot 2009, 427–28 (discussing the Brightpoint litigation).

5. E.g., Bernstein 2005; Monteleone 1993.

6. Executive Risk Indemnity, n.d., III.A.3. Similar language appears in the AIG, Chubb, and Hartford policies.

7. Claims Head no. 021207, 36–38.

8. Ibid.

9. Underwriter no. 4, e-mail.

10. Ibid.

11. Plaintiffs' Counsel no. 5, 24.

12. The quoted language is from the *AIG Specimen Policy* 2000, § 4(a). The Chubb specimen policy similarly excludes from covered losses "any Claim made against any Insured Person based upon, arising from, or in consequence of such Insured Person having gained in fact any profit, remuneration or advantage to which such Insured Person was not legally entitled." *Chubb Specimen Policy* 2002, §§ 7, 8 (extending the exclusion to side C coverage). See also *Hartford Specimen Policy*, n.d., § V(I)

(excluding from covered losses claims arising from or based on "any personal profit, remuneration or advantage to which [the insured] was not legally entitled").

13. For an opinion expressly applying the logic of unjust enrichment to disallow restitutionary damages under a D&O policy, see *Exec. Risk Indem., Inc. v. Pacific Ed. Servs., Inc.*, 451 F. Supp. 2d 1147 (D. Haw. 2006). See also *Cincinnati Ins. Co. v. Irwin Co.*, 2000 WL 18672997 (Ohio Ct. App. 2000) (denying coverage for claims against directors that would have forced them to pay back their personal profit in a transaction with shareholders).

14. 272 F.3d 908 (7th Cir. 2001).

15. Ibid., 911.

16. 2002 WL 31961447 (Ind. Cir. Ct. 2002).

17. Recall that Section 11 also allows claims to be brought against a variety of other defendants, including the directors personally, who arguably do not benefit from the investment in the same way as the corporation and who therefore may be able to assert that any portion of the settlement for which they are responsible does not constitute disgorgement. In such cases, there will thus be an allocation issue between restitution and covered losses. On this point, see, for example, *Unified Western Grocers, Inc. v. Twin City Fire Ins. Co.*, 457 F.3d 1106 (9th Cir. 2006) (requiring allocation between damages representing restitution of money and assets that were funneled to the insureds and those representing other losses).

18. 2002 WL 31961447 at *6.

19. Cases distinguishing or declining to follow *Level 3* include *Nutmeg Ins. Co. v. East Lake Mgmt. & Dev. Corp.*, 2006 WL 3409156 (N.D. Ill. 2006), and *Liss v. Fed. Ins. Co.*, 2006 WL 2844468 (N.J. Super. A.D. 2006).

20. Claims Head no. 021307, 6–7.

21. *Chubb D&O Elite Application*, n.d., § 5.

22. The quoted language is from *Republic Ins. Co. v. Masters, Mates & Pilots Pension Plan*, 77 F3d 48, 52 (2nd Cir. 1996). See also *In re Liquidation of Union Indem. Ins. Co.*, 611 N.Y.S.2d 506, 511 (N.Y. App. Div. 1994). On the meaning of "misrepresentation" in this context, see N.Y. Ins. Law § 3105(a) ("a representation is a statement as to past or present fact, made to the insurer by, or by the authority of, the applicant for insurance or the prospective insured, at or before the making of the insurance contract as an inducement to the making thereof. A misrepresentation is a false representation, and the facts misrepresented are those facts which make the representation false."). Cases not requiring intentional fraud to allow rescission are too numerous to cite. However, a few courts have adopted the view that although an intent to deceive is not required, the misrepresentation must have been knowingly made. See, e.g., *Transit Cas. Ins. Co. v. Nationwide Mut. Ins. Co.*, 537 F. Supp. 65, 68 (E.D. Pa. 1982); *Jacobs v. Prudential Ins. Co. of America*, 582 P.2d 697, 698 (1978); *Hollinger v. Mutual Ben. Life Ins. Co.*, 560 P. 2d 824, 827 (1977); *Essex Refining Corp. v. Home Ins. Co.*, 394 N.Y.S.2d 507, 508 (Sup. 1975).

23. E.g., *National Union Fire Ins. Co. of Pittsburgh, Pa. v. Xerox Corp.*, 25 A.D. 3d 309 (N.Y.A.D. 2006) (denying a rescission action on the grounds that the binder containing the alleged misrepresentation was never incorporated into the policy application); *National Union Fire Ins. Co. of Pittsburgh, Pa. v. Continental Ill. Corp.*, 643 F.Supp. 1434 (N.D. Ill. 1986) (holding that misrepresentation could not be raised by an insurer whose application did not expressly include the alleged misrepresentation and did not require the policyholder to certify the truth of the alleged misstatements).

24. E.g., *Federal Ins. Co. v. Homestore, Inc.*, 144 Fed. Appx. 641 (9th Cir. 2005); *TIG Ins. Co. of Michigan v. Homestore, Inc.*, 137 Cal. App. 4th 749 (2d Dist. 2006).

25. Under New York law, for example, the test for materiality of a misrepresentation is not whether the company might have issued the policy even if the information had been furnished but rather whether the company had been induced to accept an application that it might otherwise have refused. See *Am. Int'l Spec. Lines Ins. Co. v. Towers Fin. Corp.*, 1997 WL 906427 (S.D.N.Y. 1997).

26. E.g., *Jaunich v. National Union Fire Ins. Co. of Pittsburgh, Pa.*, 647 F. Supp. 209 (N.D. Cal. 1986). In *Jaunich*, although the applicants had submitted the latest financial data to the insurer and were under no obligation to issue interim financial reports, because the business situation of the prospective insured rendered these reports materially misleading, the court held that the applicant was under a duty to disclose additional detail.

27. *National Union Fire Ins. Co. of Pittsburgh, Pa. v. Sahlen*, 999 F. 2d 1532 (11th Cir. 1993). See also *Cutter & Buck, Inc. v. Genesis Ins. Co.*, 306 F. Supp. 2d 988 (W.D. Wash. 2004), aff'd on other grounds, 144 Fed. Appx. 600 (9th Cir. 2005).

28. See *Travelers Indem. Co. v. Bally Total Fitness Holding Corp.*, 448 F. Supp. 2d 976 (N.D. Ill. 2006) (holding that the policyholder's failure to disclose that it had recently reported accounting irregularities with the SEC that were likely to form the basis of a subsequent claim was sufficient to void a policy); *McCuen v. International Ins. Co.*, 1988 WL 242680 (S.D. Iowa 1988) (holding that the policyholder's failure to disclose receipt of notice of a pending claim by the Federal Savings and Loan Insurance Corporation was sufficient to void a policy).

29. For examples of cases finding the failure to disclose pending or potential litigation as insufficient grounds for rescission, see *In re Bank of Louisiana/Kenwin Shops, Inc.*, 1999 WL 1072542 (E.D. La. 1999) (failure to establish knowledge); *Walbrook Ins. Co. Ltd. v. Spiegel*, 1993 WL 580759 (C.D. Cal. 1993) (ambiguity in the insurer's query); *Mt. Hawley Ins. Co. v. Fed. Sav. & Loan Ins. Corp.*, 695 F. Supp. 469 (C.D. Cal. 1987) (failure to inquire with sufficient specificity); and *Fed. Ins. Co. v. Oak Indus., Inc.*, 1986 WL 2699 (S.D. Cal. 1986) (known fact not material).

30. For a case allowing rescission on the basis of changed circumstances, see *In re Jasmine, Ltd.*, 258 B.R. 119 (D.N.J. 2000) (bankruptcy court applying New Jersey law allows rescission on basis of insured's failure to disclose lawsuits filed against it prior to the inception of the policy).

31. *Federal Ins. Co. v. Homestore, Inc.*, 144 Fed. Appx. 641 (9th Cir. 2005).

32. Cases allowing rescission against all insureds include, for example, *Nat'l Union Fire Ins. Co. of Pittsburgh v. Sahlen*, 807 F. Supp. 743 (S.D. Fla. 1992) (allowing rescission against all directors because the underlying policy contained no express severability clause); *Shapiro v. American Home Assurance Co.*, 584 F. Supp. 1245 (D. Mass. 1984) (holding that although the innocent directors had never seen the insurance application because it called for facts known by any director that might lead to a claim, coverage was voided for all directors as a result of the president's misrepresentations). California expressly incorporates this outcome in their insurance statute, which provides that rescission "shall apply to all insureds under the contract, including additional insureds, unless the contract provides otherwise." California Insurance Code § 650.

33. Severability provisions may apply either to prevent the imputation of one insured's misrepresentation or other wrongful conduct to other insureds or to preclude those insureds who were not actually aware of a misrepresentation made in connection with the application from losing coverage as a result. The former is sometimes referred to as a "severability of conduct" provision, and the latter as a "severability of application" provision.

34. *5801 Assocs. Ltd. v. Continental Ins. Co.*, 983 F. 2d 662, 666 (5th Cir. 1993).

35. *In re HealthSouth Corp. Insurance Litigation*, 308 F. Supp. 2d 1253 (N.D. Ala. 2004).

36. Ibid., 1259.

37. *In re WorldCom, Inc., et al.*, No. 02-13533 (S.D.N.Y. Bankr. 2002) (approving the settlement agreement between WorldCom and National Union Fire Insurance of Pittsburgh, Pa.).

38. E.g., *Executive Risk Indem., Inc. v. AFC Enterprises, Inc.*, 510 F. Supp. 2d 1308 (N.D. Ga. 2007).

39. E.g., *Jaunich v. National Union Fire Ins. Co. of Pittsburgh, Pa.*, 647 F. Supp. 209 (N.D. Cal. 1986) (finding potential grounds for waiver on the basis of insurer's failure to act on receipt of information concerning insured's changed financial circumstances).

40. E.g., *Admiral Ins. Co. v. Debber*, 442 F. Supp. 2d 958, 970 (E.D. Cal. 2006) (accepting nine months as reasonably prompt); *Monumental Life Ins. Co. v. U.S. Fidelity and Guar. Co.*, 94 Md. App. 505 (1993) (allowing rescission four years after receipt of underlying facts where a lengthy investigation was necessary to determine the insurer's right to rescind).

41. 784 N.Y.S. 2d 920 (Table) (N.Y.Sup. 2004).

42. *Federal Insurance Co. v. Kozlowski*, 792 N.Y.S. 2d 397, 401 (N.Y. App. Div. 2005).

43. Ibid., 402.

44. Monitoring Counsel no. 2, 11–12.

45. E.g., *Cutter & Buck, Inc. v. Genesis Ins. Co.*, 144 Fed. Appx. 600, 601, 602 (9th Cir. 2005).

46. Claims Head no. 031407, 68–9.

47. Claims Head no. 021207, 42–3.

Chapter Ten

1. See NYBCL § 726(a).

2. NYBCL § 726(a)(3) (allowing insurance payments "[t]o indemnify directors and officers in instances in which they may not otherwise be indemnified by the corporation . . . provided the contract of insurance covering such directors and officers provides, in a manner acceptable to the superintendent of insurance, for a retention amount and for co-insurance").

3. NYBCL § 726(b)(1).

4. NYBCL § 726(d).

5. H.R. Rep. 1933, 3, 5, 9; S. Rep. 1933, 5 (stating an intent "to impose a duty of competence as well as innocence" in the Securities Act of 1933). See generally Landis 1959 (providing a personal and anecdotal account of the passage of the Securities Act).

6. Regulation S-K, item 510, 17 C.F.R. § 229.510 (requiring that this statement be included in the registration statements of registrants not requesting acceleration of effectiveness). For registrants requesting acceleration of the effective date, the same statement is required as well as the following additional language:

> In the event that a claim for indemnification against such liabilities (other than the payment by the registrant of expenses incurred or paid by a director, officer or controlling person of the registrant in the successful defense of any action, suit or proceeding) is asserted by such director, officer or controlling person in connection with the securities being registered, the registrant will, unless in the opinion of its counsel the matter has been settled by controlling precedent, submit to a court of appropriate jurisdiction the question whether such indemnification by it is against public policy as expressed in the Act and will be governed by the final adjudication of such issue.

Regulation S-K, item 512(h), 17 C.F.R. § 229.512(h). These line-item disclosures are triggered in each of the major forms governing the registration of securities. See, e.g., Forms S-1, S-2, S-3, S-4, S-8, and S-11.

7. 17 C.F.R. § 230.461(c) ("Insurance against liabilities arising under the Act, whether the cost of insurance is borne by the registrant, the insured or some other person, will not be considered a bar to acceleration. . . . "). The commission does, however, consider registered investment companies a special case, requiring greater scrutiny of insurance arrangements. Ibid. See also Investment Companies and Advisers Act, 15 U.S.C. § 80a-17(h) (prohibiting "any provision which protects . . . any director or officers of [a registered investment company] against . . . willful misfeasance, bad faith, gross negligence or reckless disregard of . . . duties").

8. See Regulation S-K, item 702, 17 CFR § 229.702.

9. 17 CFR § 229.702.

10. Yankee Candle 2002, II-1.

11. See Regulation S-K item 601(b)(10), 17 C.F.R. § 229.601 (requiring that certain "Material Contracts" be filed as exhibits to the registrants public filings).

12. See, e.g., Regulation S-K item 402(b)(2)(iv)(E), 17 C.F.R. § 402 (requiring disclosure of dollar value of life insurance provided by the corporation to its executives and the premiums paid by the corporation).

13. 1978 SEC LEXIS 2277 (1978) (release regarding "Disclosure of Management Remuneration"). In taking this position, the SEC essentially follows the Internal Revenue Service, which also does not treat D&O insurance as executive compensation.

14. See Ontario Securities Commission, Form 30. This information is publicly available on the Ontario Securities Commission's online database of public filings. See System for Electronic Document Analysis and Retrieval (SEDAR), available online at http://www.sedar.com. Canadian corporations are given express permission to purchase D&O insurance under the Canadian Business Corporations Act. R.S.C., ch. C-44, § 124(6) (2004) ("A corporation may purchase and maintain insurance for the benefit of an [officer or director] against any liability incurred by the individual . . . in the individual's capacity as a director or officer of the corporation . . .").

15. See Core 2000.

16. These proxies included management experience (the longer the manager has been on the board, the lower the firm's litigation risk), financial performance (the worse the firm's return on equity, the worse its litigation risk), size (greater total assets, greater risk), prior litigation (firms with a history of litigation are worse litigation risks), and U.S. operations or U.S. listing (both of which increased litigation risk).

17. See ibid., 451 ("The results indicate that D&O premiums are significantly higher when inside control of share votes is greater, when inside ownership is lower, when the board is comprised of fewer outside directors, when the CEO has appointed more of the outside directors, and when insider officers have employment contracts.").

18. See Boyer 2007–2008.

19. Ibid., 104.

20. Ibid.

21. Easterbrook and Fischel 1991.

22. Easterbrook and Fischel do not argue that these failures of voluntary disclosure are necessarily fatal since there are information intermediaries with incentives to seek out valuable information regardless of whether it is voluntarily produced by firms. Their argument, instead, is that a regime of mandatory disclosure may be less costly overall than a regime in which information intermediaries are charged with resolving these deficiencies. See ibid., 300–314.

23. See our discussion of limits in chapter 3.

24. A defendant corporation's D&O policy is an initial disclosure item under Federal Rule of Civil Procedure 26(a)(1)(D), which compels disclosure around the time of the parties' scheduling conference—that is, prior to actual discovery.

25. Risk Manager no. 3, 7–8.

26. Major judicial decisions involving allocation disputes included *Nordstrom, Inc. v. Chubb & Son, Inc.*, 54 F.3d 1424 (9th Cir. 1995) (recognizing the insurer's right to allocation unless insurer has improperly refused to defend the insured or has made no claim to separate the portion of the settlement for which it was liable); *Safeway Stores, Inc. v. Nat'l Union Fire Ins. Co. of Pittsburgh*, 64 F.3d 1282 (9th Cir. 1995) (applying "larger settlement rule," entitling corporation to reimbursement of all settlement costs where corporation's liability is purely derivative of liability of insured officers and directors); *First Fidelity Bancorp v. Nat'l Union*, 1994 U.S. Dist. LEXIS 3977 at *12 (E.D. Pa. 1994) ("[B]oth the directors and officers as well as the corporate entity faced liability in the underlying litigation. The mere fact that liability arises exclusively from the conduct of the insured . . . does not provide a basis for the insurer to be responsible for the liability of those who are uninsured."); *PepsiCo, Inc. v. Cont'l Cas. Co.*, 640 F. Supp. 656, 662 (S.D.N.Y. 1986) (addressing the issue of allocation between covered and noncovered parties and holding that the insurer bore the burden of proving that the ultimate allocation was reasonable in light of the "relative exposures" of the parties).

27. See *In re Allied Digital Technologies Corp.*, 306 B.R. 505, 512 (D. Del. 2004) ("when the liability insurance policy only provides direct coverage to the directors and officers the proceeds are not property of the estate"); *In re Laminate Kingdom LLC*, 2008 WL 1766637 (Bankr. S.D. Fla. 2008) ("Typically, the proceeds of a directors and officers liability insurance policy are not considered property of a bankruptcy estate").

28. National Union 2002 at 1 and 3. Yes, the white paper cited Ayn Rand.

29. Ibid., at 1, 3, 13, and 18.

30. Ibid. at 10.

31. *See, Nordstrom, Inc. v. Chubb & Sons*, 54 F.3d 1424 (9th Cir. 1995) (affirming trial court decision on the grounds that the corporation's liability was concurrent with that of the directors and officers). See also *Safeway Stores, Inc. v. Nat'l Union Fire Ins. Co. of Pittsburgh, Pa.*, 64 F.3d 1282, 1288 (9th Cir. 1995) (holding that "the settlement costs were fully recoverable under the policy, unless the insurer could show that the corporation's liability had increased the amount of the settlement").

32. *See* John F. McCarrick and Joseph P. Monteleone, "Developments in Directors and Officers Liability Insurance," Practising Law Institute Corporate Law and Practice Course Handbook Series PLI Order No. B4-7199, September 1997, at 874–8 (describing different approaches to D&O insurers' response to allocation problem in the aftermath of *Nordstrom* and *Safeway* decisions).

33. National Union 2002 at 8.

34. Savett 2009 (listing seven cases in which trial opened but did not conclude and seven cases tried to verdict).

35. On collective action problems generally, see Olson 1977 (describing the free-rider problem).

36. For a proposal to bar settlement before summary judgment in order to weed out nuisance claims, see Kozel and Rosenberg 2004.

37. Duxbury 1999, 145 ("the use of randomizing techniques in legal contexts may have positive effects on people's incentives and might, also, on occasions, turn out to be cost-efficient and (more controversially) just.").

38. For some of our answers to similar objections, see Baker, Harel, and Kugler 2004, 482–3 (identifying and responding to moral objections to using uncertainty to promote deterrence in criminal and civil law).

39. Rosenberg and Shavell have proposed a new rule giving defendants the option to "have courts declare that settlement agreements will not be enforced" as a way of preventing nuisance suits in class actions. See Rosenberg and Shavell 2006, 42. While innovative and promising, this new rule is not intended to promote additional adjudication but rather to reduce the number of nuisance claims.

40. On the value of settlement from the perspective of public policy, consider Fiss 1984, 1073–4 (describing how settlement has become an explicit pretrial process); McThenia and Shaffer 1985, 1660–68 (responding to Fiss's article and arguing the benefits of alternative dispute resolution); Fournier and Zuehlke 1989, 189 (demonstrating that choices of litigants to settle arise from characteristics of our legal system).

41. It is worth noting that we considered the possibility of high/low agreements as a way to obtain trial data points without exposing the parties to unacceptable risk. In a high/low agreement, the parties agree that, no matter what happens at trial, the plaintiffs will receive at least the low amount of the settlement and the defendants will have to pay no more than the high amount of the settlement. This narrows the risk of trial to an acceptable range and is a common settlement technique in high-stakes personal injury litigation. We concluded that such agreements would not work well in the securities class action context because of the (sensible) requirement that class action settlements must be publicized so that class members have a realistic ability to object to the settlement or to opt out. Given this publicity, the risk of tainting the trier of facts' judgment seem too great for the result of the trial to produce a meaningful data point to guide future settlements.

42. On industry tracking of settlement data, the *PLUS Journal*, a trade publication for the Professional Liability Underwriting Society, publishes statistics on recent settlements, including date of settlement and total settlement amount, in each monthly issue. See, e.g., *PLUS Journal*, vol. 11, no. 10 (October 2007). The Stanford University Securities Class Action Clearinghouse also tracks settlements and provides some information about the source of the settlement payment by examining the reports that the defendant filed with the SEC referring to the settlement, but that source information is not systematic. See http://securities.stanford .edu /index.html.

References

Abraham, Kenneth S. 2001. The rise and fall of commercial liability insurance. *Virginia Law Review* 87:85–109.

———. 2008. *The liability century: Insurance and tort law from the progressive era to 9/11.* Cambridge: Harvard University Press.

AIG executive and organization liability insurance policy. 2000.

AIG specimen policy 75011. 2000. http://www.aignationalunion.com/nationalunion/public/natfiledownload/0,2138,2634,00.pdf (accessed February 9, 2007).

Alexander, Janet Cooper. 1991. Do the merits matter? A study of settlements of securities class actions. *Stanford Law Review* 43:497–598.

———. 1996. Rethinking damages in securities class actions. *Stanford Law Review* 48:1487–537.

Andersen, Hakon With, and John Peter Collett. 1989. *Anchor and balance: Det norske veritas, 1864–1989.* Oslo: Cappelens.

Bailey, Dan A. 2004a. Side-A only insurance. http://www.baileycavalieri.com/CM/Articles.

———. 2004b Directors and Officers Liability Loss Prevention (Chubb).

Baker, Tom 1994. Constructing the insurance relationship: Sales stories, claims stories and insurance contract damages. *Texas Law Review* 72:1395–433.

———. 1996. On the genealogy of moral hazard. *Texas Law Review* 75:237–92.

———. 1998. Liability insurance conflicts and defense lawyers: From triangles to tetrahedrons. *Connecticut Insurance Law Journal* 4:101–51.

———. 2000. Insuring morality. *Economy and Society* 29:559–77.

———. 2001. Blood money, new money and the moral economy of tort law in action. *Law and Society Review* 35:275–319.

———. 2002. Risk, insurance, and the social construction of responsibility. In *Embracing risk: The changing culture of insurance and responsibility*, ed. Tom Baker and Jonathan Simon, 33–51. Chicago: University of Chicago Press.

———. 2005a. Medical malpractice and the insurance underwriting cycle. *DePaul Law Review* 54:393–438.

———. 2005b. *The medical malpractice myth.* Chicago: University of Chicago Press.

————. 2006. *Insurance against misinformation in the securities market.* Task Force to Modernize Securities Legislation in Canada. http://www.tfmsl.ca/docs/V2(4)%20Baker.pdf.

————. 2008. *Insurance law and policy.* 2d ed. New York: Aspen Publishers.

————. forthcoming. Insurance in sociolegal research. *Annual Review of Law and Social Science* 5.

Baker, Tom, Alon Harel, and Tamar Kugler. 2004. The virtues of uncertainty in law: An experimental approach. *Iowa Law Review* 89:443–94.

Bault, Todd R. 2009. Non-life insurance: AIG reserves deficient, but industry flush? Won't turn market, but AIG may yet lose share. Bernstein Research.

Bebchuk, Lucian A. 1988. Suing solely to extract a settlement offer. *Journal of Legal Studies* 17:437–50.

Bernstein, Wayne E. 2005. Ensuring continuity of coverage in D&O and EPLI policies. *American Agent and Broker* (August) 108–11.

Best's aggregates and averages: Property-casualty. 2008. New York: Alfred M. Best Co., Inc.

Betterley, Richard S. 2006. Side A D&O liability insurance market survey 2006: A larger market than expected. *The Betterley report.* October. http://www.betterley.com/adobe/SADO_06_NT.pdf.

Bishop, Joseph W., Jr. 1966. New cure for an old ailment: Insurance against directors' and officers' liability. *Business Lawyer* 22:92–114.

————. 1967. Sitting ducks and decoy ducks: New trends in the indemnification of corporate directors and officers. *Yale Law Journal* 77:1078–103.

————. 1998. *The law of corporate officers and directors: Indemnification and insurance.* Rev. ed. St. Paul: West.

Black, Bernard S., Brian R. Cheffins, and Michael Klausner. 2006. Outside director liability. *Stanford Law Review* 58:1055–159.

Bone, Robert G., and David S. Evans. 2002. Class certification and the substantive merits. *Duke Law Journal* 51:1251–332.

Borch, Karl H. 1990. *Economics of insurance.* Ed. Knut K. Aase and Agnar Sandmo. New York: Elsevier Science Publishing Company.

Boyer, M. Martin. 2007–2008. Three insights from the Canadian D&O insurance market: Inertia, information and insiders. *Connecticut Insurance Law Journal* 14:75–106.

Brudney, Victor. 1997. Contract and fiduciary duty in corporate law. *Boston College Law Review* 38:595–665.

Chalmers, John M., Larry Y. Dann, and Jarrad Harford. 2002. Management opportunism? Evidence from directors and officers insurance policies. *Journal of Finance* 57:609–36.

Cheyne, Brian, and Greg Nini. 2010. Creditor Mandated Purchases of Corporate Insurance. Working paper.

Choi, Stephen J. 2004. The evidence on securities class actions. *Vanderbilt Law Review* 57:1465–525.

————. 2007. Do the merits matter less after the Private Securities Litigation Reform Act? *Journal of Law, Economics, and Organization* 23:598–626.

Choi, Stephen J., Karen K. Nelson, and Adam C. Pritchard. 2007. The screening effect of the Private Securities Litigation Reform Act. University of Michigan Law and Economics, Olin Working Paper No. 07-008. http://ssrn.com/abstract=975301.

Choi, Stephen J., and A.C. Pritchard. 2005. *Securities regulation: Cases and analysis.* New York: Foundation Press.

Choi, Stephen J., and Robert B. Thompson. 2006. Securities litigation and its lawyers: Changes during the first decade after the PSLRA. *Columbia Law Review* 106:1489–533.

Chubb D&O Elite Application. n.d.

Chubb Group of Insurance Companies. n.d. D&O elite directors and officers liability insurance actuarial memorandum. In *Application for approval of insurance rates.* California Department of Insurance file number EO CA0019310C01.

Chubb Specimen Policy 14-02-7303. 2002. http://www.chubb.com/businesses/csi/chubb2373.pdf (accessed February 9, 2007).

Clark, Robert C. 1986. *Corporate law.* Boston: Little, Brown.

Coase, R.H. 1974. The lighthouse in economics. *Journal of Law and Economics* 17:357–76.

Coffee, John C. 1985. The unfaithful champion: The plaintiff as monitor in shareholder litigation. *Law and Contemporary Problems* 48 (3): 5–82.

———. 2006. Reforming the securities class action: An essay on deterrence and its implementation. *Columbia Law Review* 106:1534–86.

Cohen, George M. 1997–98. Legal malpractice insurance and loss prevention: A comparative analysis of economic institutions. *Connecticut Insurance Law Journal* 4:305–51.

Core, John. 1997. On the corporate demand for directors' and officers' insurance. *Journal of Risk and Insurance* 64:63–87.

———. 2000. The directors' and officers' insurance premium: An outside assessment of the quality of corporate governance. *Journal of Law, Economics, and Organization* 16:449–77.

Cornerstone Research. 2006. *Securities class action filings 2005: A year in review.* http://securities.stanford.edu/clearinghouse_research/2005_YIR/2006012302.pdf. (accessed February 9, 2007).

———. 2009. *Securities class action filings 2008: A year in review.* http://securities.stanford.edu/clearinghouse_research/2008_YIR/20090106_YIR08_Full_Report.pdf. (accessed May 4, 2010).

Cowen, Tyler, ed. 1992. *Public goods and market failures.* New Brunswick, N.J.: Transaction Publishers.

Cox, James D., and Randall S. Thomas. 2002. Leaving money on the table: Do institutional investors fail to file claims in securities class actions? *Washington University Law Quarterly* 80:855–81.

———. 2006. Does the plaintiff matter? An empirical analysis of lead plaintiffs in securities class actions. *Columbia Law Review* 106:1587–640.

Cunningham, Lawrence A. 2004. Choosing gatekeepers: The financial statement insurance alternative to auditor liability. *UCLA Law Review* 52:413–74.

———. 2006. Too big to fail: Moral hazard in auditing and the need to restructure the industry before it unravels. *Columbia Law Review* 106:1698–748.

Doherty, Neil A., and James R. Garven. 1995. Insurance cycles: Interest rates and the capacity constraint model. *Journal of Business* 68:383–404.

Dolan, Matthew. 2003. Repeating the sins of market cycles. *Insights* (October). http://www.onebeaconpro.com/insights/insights_vol2_sp.pdf.

Duxbury, Neil. 1999. *Random justice: On lotteries and legal decision-making*. Oxford: Oxford University Press.

Easterbrook, Frank H., and Daniel R. Fischel. 1985. Optimal damages in securities cases. *University of Chicago Law Review* 52:611–52.

———. 1991. *The economic structure of corporate law*. Cambridge: Harvard University Press.

Eisenberg, Theodore, and Geoffrey P. Miller. 2004. Attorney fees in class action settlements. *Journal of Empirical Legal Studies* 1:27–78.

Eisenhofer, Jay W., Geoffrey C. Jarvis, and James R. Banko. 2004. *Securities fraud, stock price valuation, and loss causation: Toward a corporate-finance based theory of loss causation. Business Lawyer* 59:1419–45.

Elton Edwin J., and Martin J. Gruber. 2002. *Modern portfolio theory and investment analysis*. 6th ed. New York: J. Wiley & Sons.

Erickson, Jessica. 2010. Corporate governance in the courtroom: an empirical analysis. *William & Mary Law Review* 51:1749–1831.

Ericson, Richard V., and Aaron Doyle. 2004. *Uncertain business: risk, insurance, and the limits of knowledge*. Toronto: University of Toronto Press.

Ericson, Richard V., Aaron Doyle, and Dean Barry. 2003. *Insurance as governance*. Toronto: University of Toronto Press.

Examples of Questions Being Asked by D&O Underwriters. n.d. (unpublished broker's document designed to prepare clients for underwriters' meeting).

Executive Risk Indemnity, Inc. n.d. *Executive liability policy*.

Feldman, Boris. n.d. The veil of tiers: Shareholder lawsuits and strategic insurance layers. http://www.borisfeldman.com/Veil_of_Tiers.htm.

Financial Times (U.S.). 2007. Fighting class actions. November 29.

Fisch, Jill E. 2009. Confronting the circularity problem in private securities litigation. *Wisconsin Law Review* 2009:333–350.

Fiss, Owen M. 1984. Against settlement. *Yale Law Journal* 93:1073–90.

Fitzpatrick, Sean M. 2003–2004. Fear is the key: A behavioral guide to underwriting cycles. *Connecticut Insurance Law Journal* 10:255–75.

Foster, Todd, Ronald I. Miller, Stephanie Plancich, Brian Saxton, and Svetlana Starykh. 2007. *Recent trends in shareholder class actions: Filings return to 2005 levels as subprime cases take off; average settlements hit new high*. NERA Economic Consulting.

Fournier, Gary M., and Thomas W. Zuehlke. 1989. Litigation and settlement: An empirical approach. *Review of Economics and Statistics* 71:189–95.

Fox, Merritt B. 2006. After *Dura*: Causation in fraud-on-the-market actions. *Journal of Corporation Law* 31:829–75.

Froot, Kenneth A., David S. Scharfstein, and Jeremy C, Stein. 1993. Risk management: Coordinating corporate investment and financing policies. *Journal of Finance* 48:1629–58.

Galanter, Marc. 1990. The civil jury as a regulator of the litigation process. *University of Chicago Legal Forum* 1990:201–72.

Goshen, Zohar, and Gideon Parchamovsky. 2006. The essential role of securities regulation. *Duke Law Journal* 55:711–82.

Griffith, Sean J. 2005. Good faith business judgment: A theory of rhetoric in corporate law jurisprudence. *Duke Law Journal* 55:1.

———. 2006. Daedalean tinkering. *Michigan Law Review* 104:1247–67.

Grundfest, Joseph A. 2002. Punctuated equilibria in the evolution of United States securities regulation. *Stanford Journal of Law, Business and Finance* 8:1–8.

The Hartford, Directors, Officers and Company Liability Policy, Specimen DO 00 R292 00 0696. 1996. http://www.hfpinsurance.com/forms/nj85.pdf (accessed February 9, 2007).

Hawking, Stephen. 1988. *A brief history of time*. New York: Bantam Books.

Hazen, Thomas Lee. 2002. Law of securities regulation. 4th ed. St. Paul: West Group.

Heimer, Carol A. 1985. *Reactive risk and rational action: Managing moral hazard in insurance contracts*. Berkeley: University of California Press.

Hinsey, Joseph, William J. Delancey, Vincent Stahl, and Allen Kramer. 1972. What existing D&O policies cover. *Business Lawyer* 27:147–64.

Holderness, Clifford G. 1990. Liability insurers as corporate monitors. *International Review of Law and Economics* 10:115–29.

Hubbart, Elizabeth O. 1996–97. When worlds collide: The intersection of insurance and motion pictures. *Connecticut Insurance Law Journal* 3:267–304.

Indemnification of directors: The problems posed by federal securities and antitrust legislation. 1963. *Harvard Law Review*. 76:1403–30.

Jensen, Michael C., and William H. Meckling. 1976. Theory of the firm: Managerial behavior, agency costs and ownership structure. *Journal of Financial Economics* 3:305–60.

Jerry, Robert H., II. 2002. *Understanding insurance law*. 3d ed. New York: Matthew Bender.

Johnson, Marilyn F., Karen K. Nelson, and A.C. Pritchard. 2007. Do the merits matter more? The impact of the Private Securities Litigation Reform Act. *Journal of Law, Econonmics, and Organization* 23:627–52.

Kahn, David B., and Gary S. Lawson. 2004. Who's the boss?: Controlling auditor incentives through random selection. *Emory Law Journal* 53:391–431.

Karpoff, Jonathan, G. Scott Lee, and Gerald S. Martin 2009. The cost to firms of cooking the books. *Journal Financial and Quantitative Analysis* (available at ssrn.com/abstract=652121).

Katz, Avery. 1990. The effect of frivolous lawsuits on the settlement of litigation. *International Review of Law and Economics* 10:3–27.

Klausner, Michael, and Jason Hegland. 2010a. How protective is D&O insurance in securities class actions? Part I. *PLUS Journal* 23 (February).

———. 2010b. When are securities class actions dismissed, when do they settle, and for how much? Part II. *PLUS Journal* 23 (March).

Knepper, William E., and Dan A. Bailey. 2003. *Liability of corporate officers and directors*. 7th ed. Newark: Matthew Bender.

Kozel, Randy, and David Rosenberg. 2004. Solving the nuisance-value settlement problem: Mandatory summary judgment. *Virginia Law Review* 90:1849–907.

Landis, James M. 1959. The legislative history of the Securities Act of 1933. *George Washington Law Review* 28:29–49.

Langevoort, Donald C. 1996. Capping damages for open-market securities fraud. *Arizona Law Review* 38:639–64.

Levine, Dan. 2007. Defense verdict in a securities case: JDS Uniphase wins in class action; jury shoots down bid for $18M. *National Law Journal*. December 3, p. 9.

Loss, Louis, and Joel Seligman. 2004. *Securities regulation*. Vol. 9, 3d ed. Austin: Aspen Publishers.

MacMinn, Richard, and James Garven. 2000. On corporate insurance. In *Handbook of insurance*, ed. Georges Dionne, 541–64. Boston: Kluwer Academic Publishers.

Martin, Denise N., Vinita M. Juneja, Todd S. Foster, and Frederick C. Dunbar. 1999. Recent trends IV: What explains filings and settlements in shareholder class actions. *Stanford Journal of Law, Business and Finance* 5:121–74.

Mathias, John H., Jr., Matthew M. Neumeier, Timothy W. Burns, and Jerry J. Burgdoerfer. 2003. *Directors and officers liability: Prevention, insurance and indemnification*. 4th ed. New York: Law Journal Press.

Mayers, David, and Clifford W. Smith, Jr. 1982. On the corporate demand for insurance. *Journal of Business* 55:281–96.

———. 1987. Corporate insurance and the underinvestment problem. *Journal of Risk and Insurance* 54:45–54.

———. 1990. On the corporate demand for insurance: Evidence from the reinsurance market. *Journal of Business* 63:19–40.

McCoy, Patricia A. 2003. Realigning auditors' incentives. *Connecticut Law Review* 35:989–1012.

McGee, Robert T. 1986. The cycle in property/casualty reinsurance. *Federal Reserve Bank New York Quarterly Review* 11:22–30.

McThenia, Andrew W., and Thomas L. Shaffer. 1985. For reconciliation. *Yale Law Journal* 94:1660–8.

Mehr, Robert I., and Emerson Cammack. 1976. Principles of Insurance. 6th ed. Homewood, IL: R.D. Irwin.

Miller, Ronald I., Todd Foster, and Elaine Buckberg. 2006. *Recent trends in shareholder class action litigation: Beyond the mega-settlements, is stabilization ahead?* 3 (NERA Economic Consulting 2006). http://www.nera.com/image/BRO_RecentTrends2006_SEC979_PPB-FINAL.pdf. (accessed February 9, 2007).

Molot, Jonathan. 2009. A market in litigation risk. *University of Chicago Law Review* 76:367–439.

Monteleone, Joseph P. 1993. Directors and officers' liability insurance: A procedural and substantive primer. *Directors' and officers' liability insurance*. PLI Order No. A4-4416.

Monteleone, Joseph P., Dan A. Bailey, and John F. McCarrick. 1992. Allocation of defense costs and settlements under D&O policies. *Commercial Law and Practice Course Handbook Series*. PLI Order No. A4-4379.

Morgenson, Gretchen. 2005. Ex-directors at WorldCom settle anew. *New York Times*, March 19.

Olson, Mancur. 1977. *The logic of collective action: Public goods and the theory of groups*. Cambridge: Harvard University Press.

O'Malley, Pat. 1991. Legal networks and domestic security. In *Studies in Law Poli-*

tics, and Society, eds. Austin Sarat and Susan S. Silbey, 11:171–90. Greenwich, CT: JAI Press.

Ontario Securities Commission. n.d. *Form 30*. [This information is publicly available on the Ontario Securities Commission's online database of public filings.]

O'Sullivan, Noel. 1997. Insuring the agents: The role of directors' and officers' insurance in corporate governance. *Journal of Risk and Insurance* 64:545–6.

Park, James J. 2009. Shareholder Compensation as Dividend. *Michigan Law Review* 108:323–72.

Parr, Randy. 2004. Directors and officers insurance. *D&O Liability Insurance 2004: Directors & Officers Under Fire*. PLI.

Peters, Philip G. 2007. What we know about medical malpractice settlements. *Iowa Law Review* 92:1783–1833.

Plancich, Stephanie, and Svetlana Starykh. 2008. *2008 trends in securities class actions*. NERA Economic Consulting.

PLUS Journal. 2007 (October).

Politan, Nicholas. 2005. Mediating securities class actions: A view from the captain's quarters. *BLB&G Institutional Investor Advocate* (Fourth Quarter): 1–3.

Priest, George L., and Benjamin Klein. 1984. The selection of disputes for litigation. *Journal of Legal Studies* 13:1–56.

Pritchard, A.C. 1999. Markets as monitors: A proposal to replace securities class actions with exchanges as securities fraud enforcers. *Virginia Law Review* 85: 925–1020.

Pryor, Ellen S. The Stories We Tell: Intentional Harm and the Quest for Insurance Funding, Texas Law Review 75:1721-64 (1997).

Public policy and directors' liability insurance. 1967. *Columbia Law Review* 67: 716–30.

Ribstein, Larry E. 2002. Market vs. regulatory responses to corporate fraud: a critique of the Sarbanes-Oxley Act of 2002. *Journal of Corporation Law* 28: 1–67.

Richmond, Douglas R. 1997. The business and ethics of liability insurers' efforts to manage legal care. *University of Memphis Law Review* 28:57–115.

Romano, Roberta. 1989. What went wrong with directors and officers liability insurance? *Delaware Journal of Corporate Law* 14:1–33.

———. 1991. The shareholder suit: Litigation without foundation? *Journal of Law, Economics and Organization* 7:55–87.

———. 2005. The Sarbanes-Oxley Act and the making of quack corporate governance. *Yale Law Journal* 114:1521–611.

Ronen, Joshua. 2002. Post-Enron reform: Financial statement insurance and GAAP re-visited. *Stanford Journal of Law, Business and Finance* 8:39–68.

Rose, Amanda. 2008. Reforming securities litigation reform: A proposal for restructuring the relationship between public and private enforcement of rule 10b-5. *Columbia Law Review* 108:1301–64.

Rosenberg, David and Steven Shavell. 1985. A model in which suits are brought for their nuisance value. *International Review of Law and Economics* 5:3–13.

———. 2006. A solution to the problem of nuisance suits: The option to have the court bar settlement. *International Review of Law and Economics* 26:42–51.

Ross, H. Laurence. 1970. *Settled out of court*. Chicago: Aldine Publishing Co.

Savett, Adam. 2007. *SCAS 50 power rankings*. RiskMetrics Group.

———. 2008. *Securities class action trials in the post-PSLRA era*. RiskMetrics Group.

Schwarcz, Steven L. 2005. Temporal perspectives: Resolving the conflict between current and future investors. *Minnesota Law Review* 89:1044–90.

Schwarz, Norbert, and Leigh Ann Vaughn. 2002. The availability heuristic revisited: Ease of recall and content of recall as distinct sources of information. In *Heuristics and biases: The psychology of intuitive judgment*, eds. Thomas Gilovich, Dale Griffin, and Daniel Kahneman, 103–19. Cambridge: Cambridge University Press.

Shapiro, Amy. 2005. Who pays the auditor calls the tune? Auditing regulation and clients' incentives. *Seton Hall Law Review* 35:1029–95.

Shavell, Steven. 1979. On moral hazard and insurance. *Quarterly Journal of Economics* 93:541–62.

———. 1982. On liability and insurance. *Bell Journal of Economics* 13:120–32.

———. 2004. *Foundations of economic analysis of law*. Cambridge: Belknap Press of Harvard University Press.

Siegel, Marc. 2006. The dilemmas in the D&O market: Where do we go from here? Presentation at the D&O Symposium of the Professional Liability Underwriting Society. http://www.plusweb.org/Downloads/Events/Dilemmas_in_The_DO_Market.ppt.

Simmons, Laura E., and Ellen M. Ryan. 2008. *Securities class action settlements: 2007 review and analysis*. Cornerstone Research. http://securities.stanford.edu/Settlements/REVIEW_1995-2007/Settlements_Through_12_2007.pdf.

Simon, Jonathan. 1994. In the place of the parent: Risk management and the government of campus life. *Social and Legal Studies* 3:15–45.

Stanford University Securities Class Action Clearinghouse. n.d. http://securities.stanford.edu/index.html.

State of Delaware. Division of Corporations. http://www.corp.delaware.gov/default.shtml.

Studdert, David M. Michelle M. Mello, Atul A. Gawande, Tejal K. Gandhi, Allen Kachalia, Catherine Yoon, Ann Louise Puopolo, and Troyen A. Brennan. 2006. Claims, errors, and compensation payments in medical malpractice litigation. *New England Journal of Medicine* 354:2024–33.

System for Electronic Document Analysis and Retrieval ("SEDAR"). n.d. http://www.sedar.com.

Syverud, Kent D. 1990. The duty to settle. *Virginia Law Review* 76:1113–209.

Thompson, Robert B., and Hillary A. Sale. 2003. Securities fraud as corporate governance: Reflections upon federalism. *Vanderbilt Law Review* 56:859–910.

Thompson, Robert B., and Randall S. Thomas. 2004. The new look of shareholder litigation: Acquisition-oriented class actions. *Vanderbilt Law Review* 57:133–209.

Towers Perrin. 2005. *Directors and officers liability: 2004 survey of insurance purchasing and claim trends*.

———. 2006. *Directors and officers liability: 2005 Survey of insurance purchasing and claim trends*.

———. 2007. *Directors and officers liability: 2006 survey of insurance purchasing and claim trends.*

———. 2008. *Directors and officers liability: 2007 survey of insurance purchasing and claim trends.*

Van der Veer, Nancy H. 2005–2006. Employment practices liability insurance: Are EPLI policies a license to discriminate? Or are they a necessary reality check for employers? *Connecticut Insurance Law Journal* 12:173–206.

Wallace, Stanley L. 1966. More on sitting ducks: (Officers and directors, that is). *Insurance* (April 16) 32, 34, 36, 92, 93.

Yankee Candle Co., Inc. 2002. *Amended registration statement on Form S-3.*

Zeiler, Kathryn, Charles Silver, Bernard Black, David A. Hyman, and William M. Sage. 2007. Physicians' insurance limits and malpractice payments: Evidence from Texas closed claims, 1990–2003. *Journal of Legal Studies* 36:s9–s45.

Index